MW01253392

*International Political Economy Series*

Series Editor: **Timothy M. Shaw**, Visiting Professor, University of Massachusetts Boston, USA and Emeritus Professor, University of London, UK

*Titles include*:

Dick Beason and Jason James
THE POLITICAL ECONOMY OF JAPANESE FINANCIAL MARKETS
Myths versus Reality

Mark Beeson
COMPETING CAPITALISMS
Australia, Japan and Economic Competition in Asia-Pacific

Shaun Breslin
CHINA AND THE GLOBAL POLITICAL ECONOMY

Kenneth D. Bush
THE INTRA-GROUP DIMENSIONS OF ETHNIC CONFLICT IN SRI LANKA
Learning to Read between the Lines

Kevin G. Cai
THE POLITICAL ECONOMY OF EAST ASIA
Regional and National Dimensions

THE POLITICS OF ECONOMIC REGIONALISM
Explaining Regional Economic Integration in East Asia

Gregory T. Chin
CHINA'S AUTOMOTIVE MODERNIZATION
The Party-State and Multinational Corporations

Xu Yi-chong (*editor*)
THE POLITICAL ECONOMY OF STATE-OWNED ENTERPRISES
IN CHINA AND INDIA

Yin-wah Chu (*editor*)
CHINESE CAPITALISMS
Historical Emergence and Political Implications

Abdul Rahman Embong
STATE-LED MODERNIZATION AND THE NEW MIDDLE CLASS IN MALAYSIA

Takashi Inoguchi
GLOBAL CHANGE
A Japanese Perspective

Dominic Kelly
JAPAN AND THE RECONSTRUCTION OF EAST ASIA

L. H. M. Ling
POSTCOLONIAL INTERNATIONAL RELATIONS
Conquest and Desire between Asia and the West

Pierre P. Lizée
PEACE, POWER AND RESISTANCE IN CAMBODIA
Global Governance and the Failure of International Conflict Resolution

S. Javed Maswood
JAPAN IN CRISIS

Ananya Mukherjee Reed
PERSPECTIVES ON THE INDIAN CORPORATE ECONOMY
Exploring the Paradox of Profits

CORPORATE CAPITALISM IN CONTEMPORARY SOUTH ASIA (*editor*)
Conventional Wisdoms and South Asian Realities

Cecilia Ng
POSITIONING WOMEN IN MALAYSIA
Class and Gender in an Industrializing State

Fahimul Quadir and Jayant Lele (*editors*)
DEMOCRACY AND CIVIL SOCIETY IN ASIA: VOLUME 1
Globalization, Democracy and Civil Society in Asia
DEMOCRACY AND CIVIL SOCIETY IN ASIA: VOLUME 2
Democratic Transitions and Social Movements in Asia

Miriam Schröder
LOCAL CLIMATE GOVERNANCE IN CHINA
Hybrid Actors and Market Mechanisms

Ian Scott (*editor*)
INSTITUTIONAL CHANGE AND THE POLITICAL TRANSITION
IN HONG KONG

Mark Turner (*editor*)
CENTRAL–LOCAL RELATIONS IN ASIA–PACIFIC
Convergence or Divergence?

Ritu Vij
JAPANESE MODERNITY AND WELFARE
State, Civil Society and Self in Contemporary Japan

Fei-Ling Wang
INSTITUTIONS AND INSTITUTIONAL CHANGE IN CHINA
Premodernity and Modernization

Fulong Wu and Chris Webster (*editors*)
MARGINALIZATION IN URBAN CHINA
Comparative Perspectives

Keming Yang
CAPITALISTS IN COMMUNIST CHINA

Xiaoke Zhang
THE POLITICAL ECONOMY OF CAPITAL MARKET REFORMS IN SOUTH EAST ASIA

**International Political Economy Series**
**Series Standing Order ISBN 978–0–333–71708–0**   **hardcover**
**Series Standing Order ISBN 978–0–333–71110–1**   **paperback**
(*outside North America only*)

You can receive future titles in this series as they are published by placing a standing order. Please contact your bookseller or, in case of difficulty, write to us at the address below with your name and address, the title of the series and one of the ISBNs quoted above.

Customer Services Department, Macmillan Distribution Ltd, Houndmills, Basingstoke, Hampshire RG21 6XS, England

# Capitalists in Communist China

Keming Yang
*Senior Lecturer in Sociology, School of Applied Social Sciences, Durham University, UK*

First published 2013 by
PALGRAVE MACMILLAN

Palgrave Macmillan in the UK is an imprint of Macmillan Publishers Limited, registered in England, company number 785998, of Houndmills, Basingstoke, Hampshire RG21 6XS.

Palgrave Macmillan in the US is a division of St Martin's Press LLC, 175 Fifth Avenue, New York, NY 10010.

Palgrave Macmillan is the global academic imprint of the above companies and has companies and representatives throughout the world.

Palgrave® and Macmillan® are registered trademarks in the United States, the United Kingdom, Europe and other countries.

ISBN 978–0–230–28458–6

This book is printed on paper suitable for recycling and made from fully managed and sustained forest sources. Logging, pulping and manufacturing processes are expected to conform to the environmental regulations of the country of origin.

A catalogue record for this book is available from the British Library.

A catalog record for this book is available from the Library of Congress.

10  9  8  7  6  5  4  3  2  1
22  21  20  19  18  17  16  15  14  13

Printed and bound in the United States of America

*To my teachers*

# Contents

# List of Figures

# List of Tables

# Preface

The economic reforms in China since the end of the 1970s have produced not simply an economic miracle but some profound changes to the nation's social structure as well, which in turn have some ramifications for the nation's political development. While finishing my previous book, *Entrepreneurship in China*, I began to realize the increasing political significance of private entrepreneurs. This group of daring and hardworking people not only have overturned the dominance of state-owned enterprises in the former socialist economy but also have begun to leave their mark on the nation's political landscape, even though what they can and will do politically remains an unsettled question. I believe that it goes too far to say that they have already become a formidable (or strategic) political force, but the political significance of their existence is, on the other hand, undeniable. It is my attempt to make, as sensibly and accurately as I can, an assessment of such significance in this book.

But who are these people, politically speaking, or what is their political identity? How are they different from the older generation of capitalists? How do they relate themselves to the Chinese states (national and local)? What do they do in dealing with the regime that is Communist in official ideology and Leninist in organization? How do they treat their employees, whose declining economic status has been in great contrast with that of their employers'? What do all these questions mean for the political development of China? These are the questions, all centred on the political role of capitalists in a Communist regime, that I try to answer in this book.

To simply report what has happened may be informative with facts, as many publications in the genre of 'area studies' are, but it will not be informative in revealing and explaining the actual process. Like its predecessor, this book keeps the ambition of shedding some theoretical and analytical light on the empirical investigations. But social scientists have not been able to develop a widely accepted procedure in connecting the two research activities together, very likely because there are many types of 'academic excellence' and many ways of achieving it. The general advice would be to make the best use (and sense) of whatever is at your disposal. I have done as much empirical work as my resources allow for finding out what's going on in reality, but I hope that it is the work's relevance to more general issues – the relationships between economic and political development, between businesses and the state, and between wealth and political power, the function and survival of a dominating political party, social classes and democratization, and so on – that makes this book worth reading. I am aware how controversial it would be to distinguish 'the social science of China' from 'the area study of China'. There is no doubt that the two are inherently and tightly intertwined, but I do not think that enough effort has been made to inject a dose of analysis into the area study of China. The country, or any particular structure or process in it, is too often treated as a special or even a peculiar case, and it seems that all we need is detailed knowledge rather than theoretically guided and empirically informed analysis. It is my wish that this book will offer a few analytical insights without losing its empirical rigour.

This approach is clearly reflected in the book's title. In it I purposefully use the word 'Communist' because the book is mostly concerned with the nation's political system, not its culture, population, or even the economy per se. Similarly, I use the word 'capitalists' rather than 'private business owners' or 'private entrepreneurs'. Although these terms will be used interchangeably in this book, it is their status as a distinctive economic and political group that this study is about. I must add immediately that I am clearly aware of the diversity *within* this group, but I do not think that the diversity has been so overwhelming that it renders the treatment of the group as a whole useless. The reader will find further elaborations on the concepts in the first chapter. Some people have suggested that a more 'eye-catching' title and subtitle be adopted. I did think about some possibilities, such as *The Politics of Business*, *Squaring Business into the Circle of Politics*, and others. But in the end, I gave up. I know that we often, perhaps too often, see such titles in the social science publications, but it puzzles me why it is believed that the reader will be more tempted to buy or even to read a book by the title only, having to find what the book is really about by checking the subtitle. Why don't we tell our readers what the book is about without any subtitle? To me, a clumsy but accurate title is more desirable than a catchy but ambiguous title followed by a long and explanatory subtitle. As academic researchers, we are expected to present the results of scientific research, and we should not do this in a style akin to selling mobile phone apps. The current practice seems to come from a trick widely employed in the advertising industry: make a grand promise to lure the customers but leave the details in fine print.

# Acknowledgements

I am very grateful for the financial support of the UK's Economic and Social Research Council (ESRC), without which I could not have imagined finishing this project and writing up this book. It is only a small grant but large enough for allowing me to do almost all I want. The School of Applied Social Sciences at the University of Durham has also provided a financial and administrative contribution to this project, which I appreciate very much. The contributions and co-operation of business owners, government officials, ordinary workers, and academics that I interviewed or conversed with in China have also been crucial for the completion of this project. Their identities are to be concealed in this book, a request by all of them that I shall respect. I would like to thank my editor at Palgrave Macmillan, Alexandra Webster, and Timothy Shaw, the editor of the International Political Economy (IPE) Series, for accepting this book. I am very grateful to the anonymous reviewers of my book proposal for their time, suggestions, and encouragement. Some of my colleagues at the School of Applied Social Sciences, University of Durham, Dave Byrne, Richard Giulianotti, and Juan Morilas, provided some useful suggestions and comments on the proposal. I was very lucky to have Angela Emerson as our finance secretary, who processed so many requests promptly and retired at the end of this project. I reported some preliminary results and ideas at Zhou Enlai School of Government (Nankai University), The Central Bureau of Translation and Compilation, and other research institutions in Beijing, Tianjin, Shanghai, and Shenzhen, and I thank the thoughtful and critical comments made by the social scientists in these institutions. Parts of Chapter 5 have been reproduced in J. Hsu and R. Hasmath (eds) (2012) *The Chinese Corporatist State: Adaptation, Survival and Resistance*. New York and Oxford, UK: Routledge.

Finally, I have dedicated my first book to my parents, my second to my family, and I dedicate this book to all my teachers, from those at The Second Primary School at Xiaoguan Street in the 1970s to the prominent sociologists at Columbia University in the late 1990s, for whose generosity, encouragement, and inspiration I am so grateful.

# Note on Chinese Characters and Sources

When referring to Chinese names of persons, places, or events, the current practice is to provide the pinyin alongside the corresponding English words. However, I have found such arrangement not very helpful even though the pinyin system is an effective aid to learning Chinese pronunciations. This is so because many Chinese characters share exactly the same pronunciation, a major cause of much inconvenience for the learner and the reader. If the reader does not know Chinese at all, then the pinyin will not mean anything to them. If they know how to use pinyin to say Chinese characters, they would struggle in guessing the right meaning of the characters purely based on the pronunciation, particularly so given the fact that the pinyin used in the English literature has no connotation, which is crucial for Chinese pronunciation. If the reader is able to read Chinese characters or is a native speaker, guessing the connotation and deciding on the right character of several possibilities is much easier as knowledge of the context will help. In such situation, however, the pinyin becomes redundant to knowing the correct Chinese characters. Therefore, I came to the conclusion that it would be more straightforward and useful simply to attach Chinese characters to English words. If the reader wants to know how to pronounce these Chinese characters, the learning should be (should have been) done somewhere else. This is the practice for using other languages without a system like the pinyin, so why don't we put down the Chinese characters directly? In fact, some academics, such as Julia Strauss, the editor of *The China Quarterly*, have adopted such practice, which I shall follow here in this book. But I shall still put the pinyin beside the Chinese characters as some readers may have become used to it. Items in the References will be listed by the alphabetical order of the surname of the author (or the first author); when an item is published in Chinese, pinyin is only given to the author's name but not to the title of the publication, but I have provided the English translation of the title.

# 1
# The Political Significance of Capitalists in Communist China

The fate of industrial capitalists in China could not have been more dramatic: They were latecomers and underdogs in the world history of capitalism, starting to experience notable growth under the auspices of the last feudalist dynasties in the seventeenth century. As recently as the Second World War, only a small minority of them enjoyed some kind of independence and influence in the Chinese society at large, while the vast majority were truly 'petty capitalists'. During the wars in the first half of the twentieth century, their voice was rarely taken seriously by warlords or political leaders. When the Communists came to power in 1949, they treated the capitalists in a friendly manner for a while but only for the purpose of helping the new regime win some time before removing the whole class economically, politically, and even to a certain extent physically from this regime. It could not be more ironic that several decades later the Communists found themselves with no alternative but to show their respect to the remaining capitalists and more importantly to create a new generation of capitalists, some of whom have even been selected to join the political elites. What has been going on? It is the objective of this book to make sense of such vicissitudes. As my intention is to give an analytical account rather than a comprehensive description of the whole process, it is necessary at the outset to clarify a few conceptual and theoretical issues before delving into the details in the following chapters.

## Why do I call the new generation of private business owners 'capitalists'?

This book is about the political life of capitalists in China, a nation politically dominated by a Communist party. In this chapter we shall leave

1

aside the question of how communist the Chinese Communist Party (CCP) is, because to a certain extent the whole book can be taken as an answer to that question. Suffice it to say that the CCP still claims, at least in public, to follow the ideological principles of Communism – although how its leaders interpret the core principles of this ideology is another matter – and to monopolize the power of ruling.

An explanation is required here, however, for using the word 'capitalists', since the corresponding Chinese phrase, 资本家 (zi ben jia), is not commonly used in today's China, at least not in official or public media. It first became a contested issue soon after the Communists took power in 1949. In the spring of that year, two-thirds of capitalist enterprises in the City of Tianjin (the industrial and financial centre in North China) were not running normally due to political alienation between the local Communist leaders and the capitalists. When Liu Shaoqi (刘少奇), then a top CCP leader, went there in an attempt to revive the local economy, some capitalists asked him whether people could stop calling them 'capitalists' because by definition capitalists 'exploit' the workers, which was evil. Liu did not find a better title for them but had a clear intention of encouraging them to keep their factories up and running. His solution was to redefine the nature of exploitation, saying, '[t]oday's capitalist exploitation not only is not a crime but actually is a contribution' (Li Zhancai, 李占才, 2009: 124). As we shall see in the next chapter, the validity of Liu's conforming words was short-lived – only four years after Liu's speech, Mao Zedong launched a series of campaigns against the capitalists, which eventually removed the whole class from the new regime's economic and political structures.

Even after the old generation of capitalists disappeared, fear of the disastrous consequences of carrying the title 'capitalist' – humiliation in public, physical tortures, confiscation of personal properties, and so on – has stayed in the minds of the people who remember those days. So when a group of people started off their journey of making profits from the end of the 1970s, with the approval of the CCP, it becomes a political question whether it is appropriate to call them 'capitalists'. I am not aware of any documents issued by the CCP on this issue, but it is very clear that the official answer is a negative one. In the 1990s there was a small group of people who did believe that the new generation of private business owners had formed a new class of capitalists, but their voice was soon suppressed.[1] A few social scientists in China, very likely representing the views of the CCP, have tried to explain why the title 'capitalist' is not applicable to the new generation of people who profit through their employees' work. For example,

Zhang Houyi (张厚义)[2] and Zhu Guanglei (朱光磊),[3] have argued that this new stratum had nothing to do with the old generation of capitalists – those who survived the regime transition around 1949 but didn't survive the subsequent political campaigns; China has socio-economic strata but no classes and therefore, China has no capitalists.

I do not find such explanation convincing, because I do not understand why this new generation of private business owners – let's use this title before the issue is settled – have to have any connections with the old capitalists in order to be qualified as capitalists. In other words, why can't they become capitalists in their own right? Whether they are capitalists or not should not depend on their connections with the old generation of capitalists but depend on what they do. Doubtlessly, these two generations are different in some important ways. Most members of the new generation are not the offspring of the old one; rather, they come from a variety of social backgrounds and the institutional environments are entirely different. However, they do share a fundamental property that defines what a capitalist is, that is, investing capital in products or services so that profits could be made as personal gains. I have no intention of getting into a debate over the definition of capitalist. Here, Karl Marx's specification should be sufficient and familiar to many Chinese social scientists: the capitalist is the personal embodiment of the capitalist production process, that is, the process of using capital to generate surplus values:

> The objective content of the circulation [money starting and returning to his pocket] ... is his subjective purpose, and it is only in so far as the appropriation of ever more wealth in the abstract is the sole driving force behind his operations that he functions as a capitalist, i.e. as capital personified and endowed with consciousness and a will. Use-values must therefore never be treated as the immediate aim of the capitalist; nor must the profit on any single transaction. His aim is rather the unceasing movement of profit-making. This boundless drive for enrichment, this passionate chase after value, is common to the capitalist and the miser.
>
> (1977: 254)

> As a capitalist, he is only capital personified. His soul is the soul of capital. But capital has one sole driving force, the drive to valorize itself, to create surplus-value, to make its constant part, the means of production, absorb the greatest possible amount of surplus labour.... . The time during which the worker works is the time during which

the capitalist consumes the labour-power he has bought from him. If the worker consumes disposable time for himself, he robs the capitalist.

(Ibid.: 342)

In short, a person is a capitalist if he invests in the process of generating profits by employing workers' labour. Except for those strictly self-employed, this is exactly what the new generation of business owners have been doing. They may not obtain the initial financial support for starting the process from any member of the old generation of capitalists, but as we shall see further in Chapter 3, they could use their own savings or borrow money from their relatives and friends. They may come from all walks of life, including peasants, blue-collar workers, teachers, fresh graduates, red guards returning to the home cities, government employees and even officials, but so did the previous generation. They all can turn themselves into capitalists by making profits out of the surplus value produced by their employees. The majority of them pay their employees the lowest wages possible in order to maximize their profit, most of which is then reinvested in the process. It would be extremely difficult to explain how some of them have expanded their businesses without such process. With regard to the pursuit of profit and the expansion of business by reinvesting the profits produced by workers' labour, there are essentially no fundamental differences between the two generations; therefore, there should be no doubt whatsoever that this newly emerging group of business owners are capitalists. Some academics in the West do not hesitate to use 'capitalist' in their publications; for example, Bruce Dickson calls those private business owners who are also members of the CCP 'Red Capitalists' – they are red because of their CCP membership, but Dickson didn't explain why we could still call them 'capitalists' – it is very likely that he took it for granted.[4] Private business owners in today's China would not mind the word 'red', but I seriously doubt they would be happy to hear people calling them 'capitalists'.

The reason for not accepting this commonality and therefore not using the word 'capitalist' must be political. This is a politically charged issue in China because capitalists constitute a class, and if they do exist in today's China, there will be class struggles between the capitalists and the workers' class. Since Deng Xiaoping became the paramount leader of the CCP, the Party wants the Chinese people to forget class struggles and focus their attention on improving their material life. In relation to 'capitalists', the word 剥削 (bo xue, exploitation) is not used in public discourse either after Deng announced that no debating (on issues such as exploitation or capitalism vs socialism) was one of his innovations. CCP leaders after Mao learnt the lesson that the legitimacy of their political dominance would benefit from political harmonies, not contentions. Given such mandate, it is no wonder that social scientists in China would argue for the disappearance of capitalists.

It is truly remarkable that a political party holding Marxism as its guiding ideology is working very hard to avoid Marxist terminologies. A series of alternatives to 'capitalist' is available. Jiang Zemin, the CCP's former General Secretary, made the announcement that 'the newly rich', like all their fellow citizens, were 'constructors of socialism'; they are also called 'business owners' (企业主, qi ye zhu), 'private entrepreneurs' (私营企业家, qi ye jia),[5] or 'the newly wealthy stratum' (新富阶层, xin fu jie ceng). Clearly, the stability of ruling overrides ideological commitment. And private business owners in China welcome such strategy because they are very conscious of their image in the society. On the one hand, the most influential members of this group have worked very hard to legalize and legitimize private property; for example, All China Federation of Industries and Commerce (quan guo gong shang lian) made several requests to the National People's Congress to add an article protecting 'private properties' in the Constitution. On the other hand, they realize that even the newly obtained amendment to the Constitution cannot provide the assurance that they would not be discriminated against anymore. One strategy is to call themselves or their organizations 'min ying' (civil) (民营) rather than 'si ying' (private) (私营), such as the National Research Association of Min Ying Enterprises. The capitalists in today's China know they are capitalists, but they don't want to carry such a title before their political, economic and social statuses are firmly established. They may enjoy the wealth, but they cannot show their pride at being a capitalist.

Further evidence of the commonality of the two generations of capitalists, although being notorious, is the fact that all of the evils that the CCP identified with regards to the old generation in campaigns such as 五反 (wu fan, five-anti), including bribing government officials, tax evasions, cheating on materials, and so on, can be found among today's private business owners as well, and is actually of a much more serious nature and on a much larger scale. It is indeed very difficult not to call them 'capitalists' if we do not have to appear politically correct within the framework of the CCP's official ideology.

A final justification for calling the private business owners 'capitalists' is related to the foreign firms that have been operating in today's China.

There is no objection in China to calling the bosses of these foreign firms 'capitalists', but there are no fundamental differences between their pursuit of profits and that of the domestic private business owners – as a matter of fact, the Chinese business owners have made a strong demand for being treated in the same way as the foreigners. If so, there is every reason for treating them all the same as 'capitalists'. Obviously, the CCP would find it very inconvenient to explain how a new generation of capitalists has grown under its leadership.

## Capitalists and Communists: friends or foes?

China's capitalists have never had their day. This is remarkable given that most other major civilizations in the world, at one historical moment or another, have witnessed a rigorous growth of a class of capitalists. Indeed, the immaturity and powerlessness of the Chinese capitalists has long been the subject of a research enterprise for Chinese economic historians,[6] and tackling this question is seen as an en route towards explaining China's almost unique lag in the processes of modernization and democratization. The scope and the focus of this study are much narrower – it examines the history of capitalists in China in the most recent six decades and in the context of the Chinese Communist Party (CCP) being the dominant political party. My aim is to understand the interaction between the two fronts of development, economic and political, through the lens of the changing political statuses of the capitalists.

Historically speaking, the relationship between the capitalists and the communists was characterized by mutual suspicion and mistrust, to say the least. Even today, with the CCP having adopted a series of strategies of co-opting the new capitalists (Dickson, 2008), it would be naïve to believe that there shall be no more tensions between the two sides, although the CCP-controlled public media have tried to portray a rather harmonious picture. While to characterize such a relationship and to determine the implications of the relationship for China's political development are the tasks for the whole project, it is useful here to start by giving a brief account of the ups and downs of their relations before introducing the specific questions to be answered in the rest of this book.

The CCP was born in a time of wars (the War of Northern Expedition, the Anti-Japanese War and the Civil War). It was after winning the last war, a civil war against the Nationalist Party (Guo Min Dang) that it became the sole ruling party. For the Communists, fighting these wars was not merely a military struggle; they fought with a very strong ideology in mind – Marxism, Leninism, and later Mao Zedong Thought. But fighting the wars was only a special phase in the whole process of establishing a socialist and ultimately communist society. The Nationalists were the enemy not just in the military sense; ideologically, they represented the interests of the landlords in the rural areas and the capitalists in the cities, together constituting a retrogressive force in the history of China and the whole of human history. According to the version of Marxism adopted by the Chinese Communists at that time, human history moves in the following historical phases: primitive, slavery, feudalism, capitalism, socialism, and finally communism. Therefore, that they eventually won the war was not simply because they gained support from the peasantry or because of Mao's and his marshals' military genius, but most importantly because they represented the more advanced force of human history. Such an ideology of historical development was also behind the CCP's policies of transforming the capitalist enterprises after they became the ruling party in China, even though the desire of keeping the whole national economy under control was a strong motivation as well.

As capitalists followed the principles of capitalism, they were the enemy of the communists, ideologically if not militarily. During the civil war, some influential capitalists, particularly those with close personal or business connections with the then incumbent Nationalist government, such as the notorious Four Big Families (Jiang, Song, Kong and Chen), were indeed on the side of the Guo Min Dang. However, the vast majority of capitalists had neither interest nor clout in engaging in any politics; all they wanted was a peaceful environment in which they could run their businesses smoothly. Among them, even the politically most ambitious ones, such as the leaders of the Democratic Construction Party, desired no more than remaking China a powerful nation through their economic contributions. Before the communists finally took power in 1949, they realized, or at least heard, that their businesses and assets would be under the risk of being confiscated by the new regime. To leave, or to stay? That was the question for many capitalists when it became clear that the Nationalists would soon lose the war and start moving to Taiwan. Either because they didn't like the Nationalists, or because they did not see a future in Taiwan, or because they believed what the communists promised, or for the lack of alternative choices, ultimately most of them stayed at the mainland to meet the advancing communists.

'Who are our friends and who are our foes? This is the primary question for our revolution.' This is one of the most well-known quotations of Mao Zedong, but how to deal with the capitalists was not an easy question for Mao and his colleagues. The difficulty comes from the contradiction between ideological principles and pragmatic tactics of consolidating political power. Ideologically, capitalists should have no status whatsoever as they are the embodiment of capitalist principles. In its essence, Marxism is a moral philosophy. To the communists, as Karl Marx taught them, it is morally wrong and economically inefficient for the capitalists to reap profits from the workers' labour simply by possessing the means of production. On the other hand, the CCP leaders were wise enough to realize that it would not be to their interests to nationalize the capitalists' properties, as demonstrated by the economic and employment problems in the early years of the Soviet Russia soon after the Russian communists came into the position of managing the national economy. No incumbent governments want to see any unrest because they would be the only ones to blame. The communists were poorly prepared for taking over the huge task of running the nation's economy as few of them were equipped with economist knowledge.

In the end, the contradiction between ideology and pragmatism was resolved again by 'the phase theory of revolution', a notion of the philosophy of history that the Communists readily fall back on when they must be pragmatic. During the early years of the new regime, China would have to experience a period of 'New Democratic Revolution', meaning capitalism would stay, before the 'Socialist Revolution', when capitalism would be eventually extinguished. Such a compromised and temporal solution was reflected in the composition of the ministers in the new government: a significant proportion of them were from non-Communist political parties (see details in the next chapter). While the CCP's leadership dominated, the government, on appearance, was a coalition. Politically speaking, China's capitalists enjoyed the highest status they could have hoped for during the initial years of the People's Republic.

The relatively friendly relationship – it was never a honeymoon – between the communists and the capitalists lasted a much shorter period than expected. Initially, the Communists were prepared to wait for at least ten to fifteen years before the Socialist Revolution could start. However, in just three years (1953–6) the nationalization of capitalist businesses was completed. The swiftness of the process could be explained with two reasons. First, most capitalist businesses became heavily or even completely dependent on the state as almost all materials of production and distribution channels were under state control; second, at the end of political campaigns, especially the 'Five-Anti', capitalists as a whole class lost status, power, and any respect in 'The New Society' (see the next chapter). It soon became clear to the capitalists that, no matter how shocking, humiliating, or saddening it might be, submitting the ownership of their private enterprises to the Communist state would be a smaller price to pay compared with their lives and those of their family members. Their economic as well as political existence came to an end from the mid 1950s to the 1960s.

Ironically, following the disappearance of the capitalists, China spiralled into economic and political disaster. Perhaps even more ironical is that the nation started to pick itself up from the end of the 1970s by introducing elements of capitalism (a wholesale introduction was deemed to be not only ideologically unacceptable but practically too radical and politically risky): private properties (albeit very small scale at the beginning) and free transactions in the market. In the next 30 years or so the growth of private enterprises has been one of the pillars of the nation's economic growth as a whole (the others are town-and-village enterprises and joint-ventures). I have explained how they grew so quickly in an unfriendly environment in another book (Yang, 2007). This book is mostly about what happens politically after such enterprises have become a powerful force in China's economy. While the growth of private businesses and that of their owners is a mutual occurrence that could not be more natural, the two processes have very different implications. The significance of private businesses is mostly if not exclusively economic, or at least it can be dealt with as such. However, the significance of the growth of their owners goes far beyond the economy. To assess what this political significance exactly means is the major task of this study.

## Wealth and political power

The situation briefly described above can be characterized in the following more general terms. According to the ideological principles that the first generation of the CCP leadership deeply believed, the capitalists and the Communists must be political opponents. Nevertheless, there were three reasons that made it clear to both sides that it would be an optimal choice to work together politically, with the concern for how long they would be political allies – no matter how unequal – being put aside until the CCP was ready to throw down the gauntlet:

(1) The majority of the capitalists did not stand up directly as an enemy of the communists; except for a small minority, most of them did

not offer direct help to the Nationalist government or armies. As a matter of fact, many prominent capitalists tried their best to keep political neutrality between the Communists and the Nationalists. In other words, the adversity between capitalists and communists was more ideological than actual.

(2) The communists needed the support of the capitalists for obtaining and maintaining political power, especially in the early years when the CCP finally became the ruling party. On the other hand, many capitalists started to develop high hopes for the Communists thanks to the peace at the end of the war, the rampant corruptions in the former National government, and a growing sense of nationalism and patriotism.

(3) Political parties representing the capitalists, which were so weak compared with the CCP, had no better alternatives to endorsing the Communist regime. It is no surprise that such a symbiotic relationship broke down when the Communists gained an upper hand over the national economy, the very basis of the capitalists' political status in the new regime.

In short, for the capitalists, their control of the means of production is the only basis of the power in their hands. This was true when the CCP firstly came to power and it is still true after the CCP has stayed in power for more than six decades. No matter how the CCP has adapted itself, there will always be a potential hostility towards the capitalists unless the Party openly and completely gives up its Communist ideology. The winning of wars legitimized the coercive power in the new Communist state, which then allowed them to take the control of means of productions away from the capitalists later on. Ideological principles were brought back as justifications for nationalizing the capitalists' assets and properties. Once they lost their control of industrial production, it was only a matter of time that the capitalists as a class would be obliterated both economically and politically, and it was fortunate that most of them were not removed physically. About two decades later, a new generation of capitalists created their own wealth and control of production under the Communist leadership, which forms the basis of a certain political power. If Karl Marx was right in pointing out the economic foundation of political power, he is right only on the condition that political power has nothing to do with the majority of the people's consent and has everything to do with ruthless coercion.

As the logic applies to both the old and the new generation of capitalists, the political relationship between the capitalists and the communists has become a very important as well as delicate issue. How far can the new capitalists go in transforming their newly created wealth into genuine political power? Or would there always be a limit on their political influence no matter how powerful they become economically? A third possibility is to maintain a mutually beneficial relationship, but what are the conditions for sustaining such a relationship? What would make the capitalists compatible with a communist political system? How has this been done in practice? What does this mean for the Chinese state, the capitalists, and the nation's future political development? What does it mean for other social groups in China? In the rest of the book I shall tackle these questions – sometimes a few at the same time – from a variety of perspectives and by drawing on a variety of sources.

All in all, behind all these questions is the attempt to infer a social group's political status and power based on its economic status and financial wealth against the state's coercive powers. From the perspective of the wealthy, it is tempting to believe that wealth should somehow transform into political power because running the economy is part of politics, the wealthy have a strong desire to protect their wealth via political and legal mechanisms, and the wealthy have the capacity to do so. For example, even a prominent political scientist in China would agree with Lord John Emerich Edward Dalberg Acton that one would want to speak out and seek political power once becoming wealthy (Fang, 2006). If this is true, the new capitalists will become a potential competitor to the CCP, although what they want to say may not be a direct challenge to the CCP's political dominance. However, while acknowledging the influence of wealth, other prominent social thinkers point to the limits, sooner or later, that wealth would have to reach. As Max Weber pointed out, '"Economically conditioned" power is not, of course, identical with "power" as such. On the contrary, the emergence of economic power may be the consequence of power existing on other grounds' (1978: 926). Bertrand Russell was more direct: 'Economic power within a State, although ultimately derived from law and public opinion, easily acquires a certain independence. It can influence law by corruption and public opinion by propaganda. It can put politicians under obligations which interfere with their freedom. It can threaten to cause a financial crisis. But there are very definite limits to what it can achieve' (1938: 128). He did not proceed to explain why there must be limits, which is probably obvious to him: most of the times the state, being in control of a variety of coercive power, is normally more powerful than the possessors of wealth. If these observations are valid, it remains unclear, however, what the conditions are for economic power to be transformed into political power or to what extent wealth can be used for influencing politicians. We should not expect that the influence that wealth exercises on an authoritarian Communist regime is necessarily more limited than its influence in a democratic system simply because the regime is more likely to use coercive power. It could be the very opposite since such regime is more vulnerable to the influence of wealth when the top politicians are desperate to legitimize and consolidate their political power. Therefore, how far wealth can go in turning itself into political power is highly contingent on not only the relative weight of the wealth to political coercion but also to other factors such as the dependence on the resources controlled by the state and the power of other social groups. It is my objective to address this general issue in the specific context of China.

## Economic development and political change: the Chinese context

Ultimately, the above questions lead to an even more general question of the relationship between economic development and political change – when an authoritarian Communist regime has experienced more than three decades of fast economic growth and a large group of private business owners have become very influential in the national economy, what, if anything, could we expect to happen to the nation's political development? China has drawn an increasing amount of attention from social scientists across the world since the 1970s not simply because it is becoming more prosperous and powerful but no less because it comes as an unusual case that defies the common wisdom of social sciences. It has embraced most capitalist economic principles while still maintaining an authoritarian and Leninist political system, challenging the tight connection and compatibility of economic and political systems. The co-existence of a fast-growing largely market economy[7] and the lack of any foreseeable signs that such a regime will fall apart soon must be perplexing or perhaps even frustrating to many experts of Chinese affairs – it seems that the regime could sustain its political dominance indefinitely. Either the experts have missed out something fundamentally important in the connection between market economy, economic growth, and political change, or the life expectancy of such a regime is too long for the current generation of China specialists to witness the regime's transformation. A brief review of such academic conundrum will help us understand why it would be informative to learn about the political life of the capitalists.

Some years after China embarked on economic reforms more than 30 years ago scholars of Chinese affairs claimed to have discovered an inherent contradiction in the logic of the whole process. Astutely using the Chinese idiom 骑虎难下 (caught in the dilemma of dismounting from a tiger or riding along), Gordon White asserted that the reforms would only lead to 'a political deadlock, reflecting serious contradictions which lie at the roots of the "market socialism" programme' (1993: 77). Other prominent China scholars have reached the same verdict: either the liberal economic policies will induce a democratic political system, or the Communist regime will suffocate the economic growth for the sake of its political dominance (Goldman & MacFarquhar, 1999; Guo and Yang, 2003; Pei, 1994; Walder, 1995; Zheng, 1994). Some even make a bold prediction that China will adopt a western-style democratic political system in a foreseeable future (Gilley, 2005; Pei, 2008). However, the reality has shown a different picture: with the economy having grown at the fastest speed in the world consecutively for three decades, the CCP has not only survived but become 'more powerful than ever' (McGregor, 2007). Like it or not, the CCP has been largely successful in keeping the economy growing on the one hand and sustaining or perhaps even enhancing its political power on the other.

Consequently, China scholars have become less venturous of making predictions about China's political future. More fundamentally, this shows their declined confidence in the connection between economic development and democratization (Baum, 1996; Bueno de Mesquita and Downs, 2005). Recently, Andrew Walder has urged his fellow researchers on China to give up metaphysics and turn to the hard work of collecting empirical evidence (2010: xxiv–xxv):

> China's growing pains are problems of governance, but not necessarily problems of democratization. From a metaphysical perspective, China's transition is 'trapped' because the democratization of national political institutions has been delayed and perhaps blocked indefinitely. A democratic transition is surely appealing on normative grounds, but the implied assumption is that competitive elections will create a government that can effectively address the institution-building agenda identified in this book. It is not immediately clear whether a new multiparty electoral system would craft better health-care policy, environmental safeguards, and consumer protection laws, or could successfully gather the political will and

consensus to implement bold new strategies. Multiparty electoral systems have proved highly compatible with incompetent national administration and all manner of corruption, both historically and today. Among the dozens of post-Communist states around the world, one of the least common paths for a post-Communist regime to follow is that of a well-functioning democracy. A small minority of these states are consolidated, effective democratic regimes – but most are corrupt dictatorships or unstable democracies. China's current state and future trajectory should not be defined by abstract conceptions of the alleged logic that underlies different political and economic systems. Rather, China must be assessed for what it is – a rapidly developing market economy with an authoritarian political system, which faces the same problems of institution building as every rising economic power in recent world history. The devil is in the details – not in the metaphysics.

In short, effective governance (functioning institutions and implementation of policies) is more valuable than democracy; democracy is worth pursuing only if it comes with effective governance. Since so many newly democratized nations have been suffering from poor governance, which could be partly explained by instabilities brought out in the process of pursuing democracy, it is not appealing anymore to pursue democracy as a normative ideal. If all regimes face the same challenges (improving the effectiveness of governance) regardless of whether they are democratic or authoritarian, it is pragmatism that will prevail. Just like Deng Xiaoping's theory of 'white cat, black cat', a regime, either democratic or authoritarian, will be desirable as long as it can solve a series of governance problems.[8] This all sounds very realistic but defeatist as well.

While this 'governance-focused' approach does make some sense – China's authoritarian regime could sustain itself for a very long time, if not indefinitely, as long as it could deliver a decent record of governance – it however has effectively moved away from the question of whether we can make a meaningful connection between economic growth and political development. Implied in Walder's sober advice is the defeatist call to give up the attempt to make sensible connections between economic development and democratization. Let's follow his advice and stop treating democracy as a normative ideal and treat it as one of the possible scenarios of political development, but does that mean we should shift our attention from democratization to governance? I do not think that the relationship between the two types of development, economic and political, is so complicated that it is out of

the reach of our intellectual capacity. The relationship is quite complicated, of course, because there are always exceptions that defy general
claims. But that may be what we should find out in the first place: What
is the source of such complication? How many scenarios are there?
What may be behind those scenarios?

To address – I dare not say answer – these questions, one strategy is
to find an empirical case that could represent the abstract relationship.
This study of the political life of the capitalists in China follows this
approach. Rather than predicting what will happen to China's political
system in the twenty-first century, it is more sensible and realistic to
carefully study a critical component that has significant implications
for understanding the country's political development. I believe that
the political participation of private business owners can well serve such
function. The seemingly ironic nature of the phenomenon – the political involvement of capitalists in a Communist regime – perfectly illustrates the unique position of this group of wealthy people in China's
social, economic, and political structures. That is, *they stand at the intersection of China's economic and political developments.* On the economic
side, China has become a private-sector economy, with 70 per cent
of GDP now in private hands (*BusinessWeek*, 22/8/2005). In addition,
private enterprises offer jobs to more than 40 million people (Zhang,
2006). On the political side, the CCP has attempted to incorporate
private business owners into the power structure by allowing them to
join the Party (banned in 1989 but lifted in 2002) and even to take positions in the legislative bodies (People's Congress and People's Political
Consultative Assembly). By 2004, 35 per cent of private business owners were members of the CCP (Dickson, 2007: 837), and by June 2007
about 3.2 million CCP members were working in private companies
(McGregor, 2007b). Of the two thousand plus members of the national
Congress or the Assembly, more than 60 are private business owners,
and much more at the local levels (Zhang, 2006).

It is crucial to understand the context in which the new generation
of capitalists are developing in order to appreciate the significance of
their increasing visibility, influence, and formal participation in China's
political system; that is, whether they would become the harbingers of
democratization or keep colluding with local officials, or something
in between. In the context of China, if rapid economic development
may not necessarily lead to democratization, we must understand the
mechanisms that are responsible for such disconnection. If economic
development is necessary but not sufficient, what else has to be there
but is not there yet in China? Is the growing political independence

of these entrepreneurs vital for China to become more democratic? How has such transformation from a marginal economic contributor to a potentially political force happened? How far can it go within the institutional boundaries delineated by the Communist regime? Having completed a major study on the institutional origins of private entrepreneurship in China (Yang, 2007), I come to the conclusion that I should work on these questions with regard to the political significance of the private enterprises' growth. More specifically, to what extent has the private entrepreneurs' economic power been actually translated into political power? And in what sense, if any, can such translation be taken as a form of democratization, no matter how loosely the term is defined? Are memberships of the CCP and legislative institutions valid indicators of political participation in political decision-making, or are they part of the CCP's tactic of pre-empting private business owners from forming an organized opposition? Why do some private entrepreneurs participate in politics while others not? How do they interpret and what do they expect of their role in China's political structure? How do their financial performance and personal connections with politicians influence their political participation?

Most current studies on private business owners in China have portrayed them as having little sense of political responsibilities and colluding with local officials to promote their own financial interests (Chen, 2002; Dickson, 2007; Pearson, 1997; Tsai, 2005; Wank, 1999). A common conclusion is that the shared interests by entrepreneurs and local officials in making profits, often enhanced by their personal relations, have diminished the likelihood of introducing democratic procedures in China. These studies have reached such a conclusion because their empirical targets are at the local level and because the issues studied are only related to daily business operations. It is therefore very difficult to assess the actual degree and the prospect of political participation of private entrepreneurs as these studies do not contain the information needed for evaluating how much difference private entrepreneurs can and would like to make within China's political structure as a whole. To assess the political significance of the capitalists on the trajectory of China's political development, we must examine the process from a variety of perspectives and make use of all sources of evidence available to us.

## Sources of empirical evidence

Given the scope of this study, although I did go to China and collect data of my own, I must draw on the research outputs produced by many other researchers both in and outside China, which I am extremely grateful for. This is particularly true for Chapter 2 (the history of capitalists during the early years of the People's Republic of China PRC), national survey datasets, and the case studies on places or people I cannot possibly reach.

The details of my fieldwork are as follows. I took two fieldtrips in the summers of 2009 and 2010 to a few big cities in China, two in the North and two in the South. I interviewed more than 30 private business owners and ten government officials. On my research trips, I also visited the University Service Centre at The Chinese University of Hong Kong and China's National Library in Beijing to collect published and unpublished reports. Besides this qualitative data, I shall make use of the quantitative data collected by social scientists at the Chinese Academy of Social Sciences, that is, the National Survey of Private Business Owners (NSPBO).[9] I shall analyse these datasets whenever it is appropriate in some chapters of this book. NSPBO is a repeated cross-sectional survey that started in 1993 and then was repeated in 1995, 1997, 2000, 2002, 2004, and 2006. The surveys were organized and administered by a team of researchers affiliated with some resourceful institutions in China, including The Institute of Sociology at The Academy of Social Sciences, State Administration for Industry and Commerce (*guo jia gong shang zong jiu*), All-China Federation of Industry and Commerce (*quan guo gong shang lian*), and the CCP's The Department of United Front (*tong zhan bu*). The target population was all domestic businesses that were officially registered as 'private enterprise' at the time of the survey.[10] All samples were drawn by following a multi-stage quota sampling procedure, starting from the provincial level to counties or equivalent levels. Such procedure and the lack of weighting would not allow reliable inference to be made to the whole population of private business owners. Therefore, statistics presented in the following chapters are only applicable to the sample itself, and I shall avoid statistical inference whenever I can. Instead, I shall mostly employ descriptive statistics and graphs when presenting the results. Response rates were very high (more than 90 per cent). The sample size for each survey was as follows: 1440 (1993), 2869 (1995), 1947 (1997), 3073 (2000), and 3258 (2002).

## Synopsis

To examine the political life of capitalists in China's communist regime, the establishment of the People's Republic is both the natural and the logical starting point. The next chapter is not meant to be a comprehensive survey of the history of capitalists since 1949, a task not only beyond the scope of this book but also unnecessary for its purposes. However, in Chapter 2 I will provide a large amount of details in order to illustrate the vicissitudes in the relationship between the Communist regime and the old generation of capitalists. How did they see each other at the time when it became clear that the Communists would be the next ruling political party? How could we explain the changing fate of the capitalists during the first four or five years of the new regime? I will show that the answers depend very much on how the Communists dealt with the tension between ideological commitment and the immediate demand of consolidating their power in the new regime. Through a series of economic and political campaigns, the new regime eventually gained an upper hand; at the same time, the capitalists finally realized that they had no role to play in 'the new society'.

The 22 years from the virtual disappearance of the old generation of capitalists (1956) to the launch of economic reforms in China (1978) turned out to be the darkest era of the People's Republic. I am not aware of anyone who has been as radical as to attribute all the economic and political disasters in this period to the eradication of capitalists and to interpret the launch of economic reforms as a plan of revising capitalism. Nevertheless, the demise and revival of capitalists in China signals the changing ideologies of the CCP. If their demise means the success of orthodox Maoism, then their revival results from the triumph of economic pragmatism in the party's leadership that has been much friendlier (but no more!) to the new capitalists. Chapter 3 aims to describe the context in which the new generation of capitalists grew up and what kind of people they are, thereby setting up a background for the following chapters that will focus on each of the important aspects of their political life.

The starting point of this study, or the very fact that makes this study possible, is the growing importance of the private sector in China's national economy. This is a classical example of 'unanticipated consequences of social action' (Merton, 1936). The decision made by the Central Committee of the CCP to allow the return of private businesses was intended to solve the urgent problem of finding jobs for millions of young people and to rescue the national economy from the brink of collapse (for details, see Yang, 2007: 75–83); the subsequent fast growth and growing weight of the private sector was not part of the plan at all. More importantly, such growth has posed a series of *political* questions to the top leaders of the CCP. How should the CCP define the political identity of this relatively wealthy group of people? How should the relationship between the new capitalists and the government be defined and regulated? How far should the CCP go in allowing the newly created wealth to be transformed into political assets? Chapter 4 will focus on these questions.

Chapter 5 extends the previous chapter by examining the role of associations of private enterprise owners. It is a specific case of a general challenge that the CCP has been facing – how to contain the new capitalists politically without suffocating their economic life. The fact that the CCP has employed the organizational mechanisms of the United Front suggests that they do not have complete political trust in the new capitalists. To use the jargon in Chinese media, the new capitalists remain 'outside the system (not part of the official institutions)'. In this sense, the business associations are on the boundaries of the system; therefore, their positions are very much precarious. From a different perspective, they can be seen as a ground of competing control of private enterprises between the Chinese state and private businesses. This chapter shall explore the situations to date.

If we accept that people might develop a strong desire to exercise more political influence once they become economically powerful, then we can be quite certain that many of the new capitalists in China have been disappointed by the lack of opportunities to increase their political influence, because so far only several thousand of them have been able to win an opportunity to join the political elite, although in most of the cases this does not mean political power (see Chapter 4 for details). It is true that many other new capitalists exercise their influence on local politicians through informal channels. But even so, the number of opportunities is in great shortage compared with the millions of private business owners. Local elections in villages, towns, and residential communities come as additional opportunities. Again, this is an unanticipated consequence of a purposeful action – top leaders of the CCP promote local elections as a way of governing local communities, and the decision was made far before private enterprises was legitimized. In Chapter 6 I shall investigate which new capitalists have participated in local political competitions, how they have tried to win, and how far they can go in that direction.

In Chapter 7 we come to the most difficult aspect of the subject of this study: how the new capitalists confront the Communist state, the situations in which private business owners would stand up not only for their own interests but for other social groups and ideological principles as well. It is difficult because such confrontations are relatively rare and they are rarely reported, at least not fully, after they have occurred, creating a difficulty for me as an investigator. On the other hand, it is absolutely worth our attention and effort because how these cases were handled politically will effectively reveal the mechanisms and the extent to which the business owners have participated in China's politics. The prominent example is the role private entrepreneurs played in the political turmoil in June 1989, but other recent incidents, albeit politically less contentious, such as dealing with predatory behaviours and discriminating state policies, will be studied as well.

In Chapter 8 we shall shift our attention to a group of people who are related to the new capitalists but stand opposite to them: their employees. Employment relations have often been studied as a subject of human resource management, especially in business schools, but it is an issue of high political significance in China. With the growing political status, influence or even power enjoyed by the new employers is the dramatic decline of the workers status'. Such change of relative status for the two groups poses a difficult question for the Communist state: which side are you on? In this chapter I shall explore the evolving relations among the three parties and discuss how this triangular relationship may have an impact on the nation's political development.

In the concluding chapter, I shall summarize key findings and major arguments presented in the previous chapters, connect them to a set of wider issues, including the relationship between money and power, between economic and political development, between the elite and the ordinary masses, the conditions for democratization, and offer a few observations on the possible scenarios of China's economic and political developments.

# 2
# The Demise of the Old Capitalists in the New Society

In China, an important message that children must learn from their history lessons is that there are two societies in contemporary China: the old and the new, set apart by the transition of power from the Nationalists to the Communists. Drawing on the experience of the French Revolution, Tocqueville ([1856] 2008) long ago demonstrated that any new regime could not escape the marks left by the preceding regimes. But how many marks there might be and how deep they are vary from one context to another. While the new People's Republic carried with it many historical legacies from the previous Republic (the indispensability of a powerful central authority, the ways the ordinary masses are mobilized, the social mobility mechanisms, and so on), the changes from the old to the new society in China are undeniable.[1] The new regime upheld an opposing ideology to the previous regime, the national economy was quickly transformed from a capitalist system to a planned socialist economy, China's relations with other countries took a U-turn, people even addressed each other with different titles or names, and so on. As we shall see later in this chapter, one of the fundamental changes was the relationship between the capitalists and the workers and their relative positions in the Chinese society.

Paradoxically, such changes can be explained by a kind of continuity with regards to the role of the capitalists; that is, their dependence on the Chinese state. The fall of China's last feudalist dynasty (Qing) in 1911 seemed to have provided 'a golden age' for the capitalists to become a leading political force (Bergère, 1989). So why did they fail to carry on exercising some real influence on China's political development? John Fairbank has provided a sensible answer: capitalism failed to grow in China during the late nineteenth and early twentieth century because the capitalist class either could not or would not break away from its dependence on officialdom. The entrepreneurs, merchants, or any businessmen could not keep themselves free from the 'control of the gentry and their representatives in the bureaucracy' (1983: 51). Having lost the golden opportunity in the early 1910s, the Chinese capitalists have never been able to break away from their dependence on the state regardless of the nature of the state, which perhaps is one of the most frustrating events in Chinese history.[2] The autonomy and the liberty gained as a consequence of breaking away from the state never seemed to be attractive enough. On the contrary, the capitalists and other businessmen saw the definite and clear benefits of being attached to the state. It is such dependence that explains their declining status in the new society once the new regime could afford to sever the mutually dependent relationship.

Seen from another perspective, the Communist Party was very effective in making all social groups – not merely the capitalists but the workers as well – dependent on it, a key strategy for consolidating the Party's power and its ruling legitimacy in the early years of the new regime. The legitimacy it enjoyed, no matter how short-lived in historical perspective, will have long-lasting effects. This chapter will identify the foundations of the political legitimacy of the Communist State when it was established in 1949. The legitimacy at the beginning of the regime, no matter how fragile it became later, allowed the Chinese Communist Party (CCP) to construct a corporatist state that has penetrated Chinese society. The Communist state's legitimacy encountered its most serious crisis at the end of the Great Cultural Revolution. This could have been a moment for China to take a dramatic move in the direction of democratization, but it did not happen because the CCP leaders took the opposite lesson seriously: mass democracy leads to anarchy. Coupled with the desire to maintain its power and its penetrating organizational system, the CCP successfully found new grounds for staying in power. Analyzing these processes will help us better understand the institutional environment in which private entrepreneurs start their businesses and how they perceive their political status in the country's political system in the following chapters.

## Class, power, and democracy

When the Chinese Communist Party was formally established in 1921, the Nationalist Party (国民党), as the ruling and much more powerful party, was in the process of winning the war against the warlords in the North. Although the Communists made a great contribution to the unification of China in 1928, overall they remained an underdog in the nation's political landscape. During the ten years between 1928 to the Japanese invasion in 1938, the Communists expanded their political base but were still struggling for survival due to the increasing hostility of the Nationalists towards them. That the CCP survived was mainly thanks to Mao Zedong's strategy of 'encircling the cities from the rural areas'. The ruling party always occupies the cities; to avoid their strongholds while attacking their weakness was definitely a wise strategy.

A consequence – expected or not – of such strategy was the connection of each of the two political parties with their respective social base. Most capitalists were living in the major cities, such as Shanghai, Tianjin, Wuhan, and running their businesses there. While the capitalists and the Nationalists were living in the urban areas for respectively different reasons, the very fact that they lived together naturally led to frequent interactions and tighter connections among them. In the meantime, the Communists were busy gaining support from the peasants in the rural areas through a series of land reforms. By taking away the land from the landlords and then distributing it to the peasants, the Communists established their reputation as a political party for the peasants and the poor working class in general. In contrast, the Nationalists were on the side of the capitalists and the rich, even though they might not have wanted to be perceived as such. This is ironical since the political ideology set up by the founding father of the Nationalist Party, Sun Zhongshan (孙中山), was 'The Three Principles of People' (三民主义, people's rights, lives and governments).

This historical process of the two major political parties becoming affiliated to the respective polarized social classes posed serious problems to both parties: the Nationalists would find themselves gradually alienated from the vast majority of the population, while the Communists would find themselves poorly prepared for interacting with the capitalists – and the workers as well although to a lesser extent – when it was their turn to take over the cities. It seems that the Nationalists did not pay much attention to such 'natural' affiliation and the implications of such class affiliations for their political future in the process of holding on to power. After taking over the leadership of the Nationalist Party from Sun Zhongshan, Jiang Kai-shek (Jiang Jieshi) seemed to have lost his enthusiasm and commitment to any ideology, becoming concerned only with expanding his military and political power. In contrast, Mao Zedong took ideology very seriously and in a series of articles worked hard to create his own theories of social structures, the state, and political revolutions in the Chinese context. His analyses of the class structure in China became the guiding principles for most of the CCP's political decisions and policies.

While facing the same external enemy during the Anti-Japanese War (1938–45), the two major political parties had no choice but to temporarily put their confrontations aside. However, when it became clear that the Japanese would soon lose the war, the gravity of a subsequent civil war became more serious than ever before. This is why all major 'capitalist democratic parties' were established around the year 1945, including The Alliance for Democracy (民主同盟会), The Association for Democratic Construction (民主建国会), The Association for the Promotion of Democracy (民主促进会), and some others.[3] It is straightforward to see why they were 'democratic' – all of them called for preventing the civil war and taking the opportunity to turn China into a democracy. Ironically, by calling these parties 'democratic', the Communists seemed to have no problem accepting the implication that the CCP was *not* a party for democracy. On the other hand, these democratic parties were capitalist only to a minor extent; that is, except for The Association for Democratic Construction (民建), of which most of the members were capitalists in the sense of owning their own businesses, most members of other political parties were intellectuals and professionals.

What matters here are not the titles but the belief held by the Communists that democracy was a political idea to be associated with capitalists – democracy is a capitalist thing, very likely because democracy existed mostly in capitalist societies; according to a widely held Marxist notion, democracy is simply a political tool used by the capitalists for protecting their own economic interests. Those intellectuals and professionals might not have been industrial capitalists but they were members of a much wider capitalist class ('bourgeoisies' or 'petty bourgeoisies', and these terms were used interchangeably in the Chinese language). According to the logic of connecting social class to political system, which started to be widely accepted by the Communists at that time, something supported by the capitalists and the bourgeoisies must not be to the interests of the peasants (and later of the workers as well).

To completely dismiss democracy, however, would be to seriously damage their political legitimacy – anyway, most of the Communist leaders were strong supporters of democracy during the May Fourth Movement in 1919. But on the other hand they did not want to stand together with the capitalists to promote democracy. Mao Zedong's solution to this problem was to make democracy class-specific: there is a democracy for the capitalist class, which copies the Western style, and there is a democracy for the working classes (workers and peasants), which is essentially a tool for mobilizing the masses for a political mission, such as fighting the Anti-Japanese War.[4] Accordingly, the democracy called for by the capitalists was 'The Old Democratic Revolution' while in contrast, the democracy led by the Communists was 'The New Democratic Revolution'. According to this classification, democracy can, and should, never be a universal system to be desired and achieved in all societies because democracy is always a particular class's democracy. One class's democracy is another's totalitarianism, all depending on which class is in power.

This is something that the democratic parties failed to appreciate. Indeed, their ignorance of the crucial importance of class and power was the source of their political naivety. They thought that the end of the Second World War provided 'a precious historical moment to build China into a completely genuine democratic nation' (Wang, Jinwu, 1985: 616). To them, the value of democracy could not be overestimated because the root cause of civil war 'was a single political party's authoritarian regime and individual dictatorship' (ibid.). What they did not realize was that if they did not possess the power to force the two political parties to give up the plan for authoritarian rule, if the two parties did not pursue democracy at the same time, and if the winning party after cruel competition for power had no intention to give up some of its power in order to construct a democracy, there would be no realistic conditions for building a democracy. Indeed, had the Nationalists and the Communists taken their words seriously, such as stopping the government from using military force to interfere in people's political activities, respecting people's rights of free speech, press and association, nationalizing military forces, and so on, China would have been a two-party democracy like that of the US or the UK, with the Nationalists representing the capitalists and the Communists the working classes.

Democracy is a political system that provides an institutional arrangement through which different political groups compete for power *peacefully* because the competition operates according to a set of rules agreed by the participating parties who are prepared to accept *any* result. It requires compromise, respect of the political system, and the acceptance of defeat in political competitions without resorting to violence. Nevertheless, to the two major political parties in China at the end of the Anti-Japanese War, nothing but violence would determine the outcome of political competition. Whoever persuades them to put down their weapons is either politically naïve or on the side of the opponent.

Among the capitalist pro-democracy activists, the only person who realized this at that time was Liang Shuming (梁漱溟), who urged the Communists to tolerate the existence of the Nationalists as political adversaries. 'Military force and democracy', he pointed out, 'are not compatible; there shall be no democracy after unification by force' (ibid.: 704). According to Edmund Fung, 'Chinese liberals and democrats were neither a product of capitalist development nor, in the main, associated with big business, which was almost nonexistent. From their standpoint, they could not see the need for a struggle between the capitalists and the working class because both were weak' (2000: 225). While whether there was any big business at that time is a matter of subjective judgement, it is indeed true that few of the most influential capitalists had any significant connections with the democratic movements or political parties: the biggest capitalists were almost all connected with the 'Four Big Families', both politically and personally, and others simply kept themselves clear of any political activities.

When the Communists seized Peking and then started to attack Nanjing (the capital city of the Nationalist government), it became clear to almost everyone that it was a matter of time before the Communists would win the war. However, as a sign that the Communists had done everything to preserve peace, Mao Zedong published eight conditions for ending the war, including dismissing the Nationalist government and taking over the Nationalist armies, clearly more a winner's ultimatum than a plea for peace. It soon became clear at the end of the civil war that what the Communists wanted to establish was not a political system that would give all political parties an equal chance of competing for power; rather, it would be *their* system – they might give the political parties friendly or even loyal to the CCP a chance to participate in the political system, but the leading or dominating role of the CCP would not be something to be questioned, let alone challenged. Almost two years before the establishment of the People's Republic in October 1949, Mao Zedong already decided to establish a political system in which the CCP would be the sole ruling party indefinitely. On 30 November 1947, he told Joseph Stalin that '[a]fter the complete victory of the Chinese revolution, China should be like the Soviet Union and Yugoslavia, that is, except for the Chinese Communist Party, all other political parties leave the political stage, which will greatly strengthen the Chinese revolution' (Yang, Kuisong, 2009: 467).

For the Communists, such political dominance was legitimized by their undisputable contributions and great sacrifices made in the process of winning the wars and by the support by the majority of the population, that is, the peasants. In other words, they deserved to be the dominating party because it was they who brought peace to China by winning the wars and who enjoyed the support of the largest social group. Whether their power was mostly based on force, whether the new system was an example of the tyranny of the majority, and whether it was fair to leave no hope for other political parties to compete with them, these were the questions that the Communists had no intention to face up to, at least not openly. It would be only a matter of time before they would transform China into a society in which there would be no place for the capitalists. It was completely out of pragmatic considerations that the Communists would appear friendly to the capitalists when they first had to interact with each other; that is, they had no choice but to bow to the economic power of the capitalists. The early years of the new regime was a history of ultimately eliminating the capitalist class from the landscape of the new society although such an ideology-and-power-driven process sometimes had to yield to the pragmatic demand of keeping the national economy up and running.

When Mao Zedong made the announcement of the establishment of the Central Government of the People's Republic of China (PRC), what allowed him to do that? In other words, what made the ruling of the new regime legitimate? If legitimacy refers to the acceptance of the ruling by the ruled without the use of force by the former, that is, the acceptance is voluntary by the ruled based on some principles or norms they believe (Weber, 1978: 212–5), then we must find the reasons behind that acceptance from the perspective of the ruled. In the specific context of China at the end of the Civil War, it should not be difficult to find such reasons:

- The Communists had accumulated a wide-range support in the majority of the rural areas since the 1930s. It was achieved by carrying out a series of campaigns of land reforms, which land was redistributed from the hands of landlords to peasants.
- After so many years of wars and political struggles, the Communists finally offered a real hope of peace to the Chinese people. It became very clear that they were the only political force that could deliver a vision of a prosperous and respectable China and the capacity for realizing the vision.
- Across almost all social groups in China there had been a strong desire to replace the Nationalist Government due to rampant corruption, hyperinflation, unethical suppression of liberal movements, close connections to American government, and so on. This government was the worst example of what a Chinese government could

be: isolated from the vast Chinese population, a government only for a minority of wealthy and powerful families, selling China's interest to foreign governments for the sake of keeping themselves in power. In contrast, the new Communist government tried its best to work with the ordinary people as closely as they could, they wouldn't allow family relations to interfere with the functioning of the government, let alone allowing political succession through generations, as Chiang Kai-shek and North Korea's leader did.

- There was no other political organization that was powerful and capable enough to stand as an alternative to the Communist Party. All the other political parties either had not earned enough credits for becoming a ruling party or simply were too weak even to protect themselves.

Given these contextual factors, the corollary would be that the relationship between the Communists and the majority of the capitalists – except those tightly connected to the Nationalist Government and even Jiang Kai-shek himself – would be an awkward one. On the one hand, 'the petty bourgeoisie and the national bourgeoisie', to use Mao's terminology, should welcome the new regime because like other social groups they had been longing for peace, most of them had been fed up with the industrial monopoly by the small number of Nationalist companies, tumultuous financial situations, and ill-treatments by the Nationalist government, especially approaching the end of the Civil War, and they would be very happy to have a strong state in which they could expand their businesses. Finally, the political parties that claimed to represent their economic interests, such as the Democratic Construction Association, the Democratic Alliance, and so on, were unable to make any direct contributions to the military campaigns, and their basis of political support was highly limited. In short, the capitalists were both pulled and pushed into accepting the inevitable rule by the Communists.

But on the other hand, such acceptance was only half-hearted. The capitalists and the bourgeoisies didn't know very much about the Communists as they were living in big cities while the Communists were building their base of support in the countryside. Most importantly, they later came to learn that the Communists followed an ideology that was hostile to the fundamental principles of their life. Although the Communists made a great effort when their military success became irreversible to convince the most influential capitalists that they would protect the national industries and commerce, the Communists' ideological commitment to nationalizing all private enterprises was undeniable, which meant that sooner or later the capitalists would lose their properties and businesses. Another important and political concern was the monopoly of political power by the Communists in the new regime – most capitalist political parties would have liked to see the new China a genuine democracy. Strangely, this dimension of the hostility between the capitalists and the Communists never fully expressed itself, very likely because the task of finishing the Civil War was so overwhelming and because the Communists had made a promise to protect the domestic capitalists (as long as they supported the new regime). There were a few other relatively minor reasons for the capitalists not to welcome the Communists whole-heartedly: some influential capitalists had worked with or for the Nationalist Government before and so might have been seen as political enemies by the new regime, the Communists would stand on the side of the workers in opposition to their capitalist employers, and capitalists did not like the ways in which many mid-level Communist leaders handled their matters.

## To stay, or to leave? That is the question!

This question was haunting most of the capitalists when the Communists were about to take over the cities. Except for a few high-profile capitalists, most capitalists had no experience of directly interacting with the Communists due to the reasons specified above. On the other hand, the capitalist democratic parties were very weak not only politically but organizationally as well – they were mostly out of touch with what they hoped to represent, that is, the majority of the capitalists. For most of the time, these parties were confined to a small number of active and high-profile members. Their influence came from their personal statuses, their personal connections with leaders of the two major political parties, and their views published in the public media, but not from their representation of the capitalists as a class. When the civil war was approaching its end, some prominent figures of these capitalist parties had already became 'friends' of the Communists, while the vast majority of the capitalists had no clue of what was happening. Had the capitalist party leaders been the least effective in introducing the Communists or at least their ideas to the capitalists, the capitalists would not have found it so difficult to decide whether to leave or to stay.

When the Communists were approaching the cities, the capitalists had three options: (1a) to leave for Taiwan with the Nationalist government; (1b) to leave for Hong Kong or any place outside China but other than Taiwan; (2) to stay at the mainland. There is no reliable information for finding out what kind of capitalists and how many of them chose a particular option, but it would make sense to expect the following: a small number of 'comprador or bureaucratic capitalists', that is, those with tight connections to the Nationalist government, took option 1a; a large number of 'big capitalists' who would keep themselves away from both the Nationalists and the Communists took option 1b, but the majority of capitalists took option 2 for a variety of reasons (the difficulty of moving equipment overseas, the lack of friends or relatives overseas, the uncertainties in a new place, the lack of support from family members, and so on). Except for the first group who knew they were unquestionably the enemies of the Communists, few among the other two groups knew very much about the Communists, but they had heard that the Communists were committed to an ideology that was pretty much against their own interests. For example, Chen Guangpu (陈光甫, a banker in Shanghai) was heavily disappointed with what the Nationalists had done but on the other hand found it very difficult to appreciate the Communist behaviour as well. On 12 December 1948 he wrote in his diary:

> The Communist Party called themselves People's Liberation Army, starting by letting the workers to rule. For the example of banking industry, they firstly expelled the managers, then set up a worker's council, and started to check records [of each capitalist]. At that time should I stay in Shanghai, or should I not stay? Such set of tactics I find very hard to appreciate, so better not to see at all.
>
> (Li Zhanzai, 2009: 83)

I am not aware of any systematic evidence for showing how many capitalists thought in the same way as Chen Guangpu did. Cases collected by Chinese researchers (for example, Li Zhancai) do indicate, however, most of them had mixed feelings towards the Communists. In the end, it was what they could to, not what they preferred to do, that determined eventually whether they stayed or left. They would stay, of course, if everything would become favourable to their business operations. Those who left were not convinced that this would happen and were able to move their assets overseas. Chen Guangpu never came back to the mainland because he was a financier rather than an industrialist. Indeed, later events show that the Communists would keep most of the manufacturing industries but not capitalist financial institutions (Zhang, 张徐乐, 2006).

Many other capitalists were not certain of the situation and found it difficult to move their assets overseas. It would have been preferable if they could have stayed somewhere outside China, such as Hong Kong, to watch how things evolved before making a final decision. As Rong Desheng (荣德生), a well-known capitalist in Shanghai and father of Rong Yiren (荣毅仁) witnessed, from the second half of 1948 many capitalists started to move their assets (equipments and capital) outside China, mostly to Taiwan, Hong Kong, Southeast Asia, the US, and so on (Li Zhancai, 2009: 18–20). The top leaders of the Communists were clearly aware of their concerns and suspicions. They knew that once they were in power, they must rely on the capitalists to keep the national economy up and running, at least initially. It therefore became an urgent matter for them to keep as many capitalists inside the mainland as they could or urge them to return to the mainland if they had already gone, especially the undecided big capitalists who had no history of supporting the Nationalists. Mao Zedong told many people that the economic policies of the new regime would balance the interests of the capitalists and the workers, and Zhou Enlai wrote a personal letter to some of the biggest capitalists with a promise that they should see their businesses grow rather than shrink in the new regime. For example, Lu Zuofu (卢作孚) was a deputy Minister of Transportation in the Nationalist Government in 1938, but the Communist leader knew he was only a technocrat. Capitalists like him became the target for both the Communists and the Nationalists. Zhou Enlai personally sent a message to Lu promising financial help such as loans for his trouble-laden company, which eventually convinced Lu to come back to 'the new society'. The return was followed by about three years of settling down, celebration of peace, and some business development. Zhou Enlai was successful in persuading some other influential capitalists either to stay or to come back. Another prominent example is Liu Hongsheng (刘洪生), who went to Taiwan but decided not to move there. Then he moved to Hong Kong, but obviously he would have preferred to stay in the mainland if the regime would give him the assurance that his businesses would not be affected. He got such assurance personally from Zhou Enlai, and one of his sons, who secretly worked for the CCP, assured him as well. Indeed, for the first two years after he moved back to Shanghai from Hong Kong he was strongly convinced that the new Communist regime was sincere in supporting capitalist enterprises and treating the capitalists surprisingly well (Cochran, 2007).

However, as we shall see later, these capitalists soon would find out that these happy days would be short-lived.

## The tension between Communism and pragmatism

A fundamental problem that the Communists have been constantly looking to resolve is the discrepancies between the principles of their committed ideology (Communism, Marxism, Leninism, or a mixture of all of these) and the problems at hand (wars, relations with different classes, economic development, international relations, and so on). This problem is clearly manifested in the way the Communists interacted with the capitalists. One of the fundamental questions was how the new regime would reconcile the interests of the workers and the capitalists. There was no clear answer then and I do not think there is a definite answer today. Essentially, it is a contradiction between the Communist ideology and the practical demand of developing the nation's economy. The ideology dictates that the Communists must be on the side of the workers, but to develop the economy the state must allow the capitalists to continue to exploit the workers' labour. Ideologically, the Communists are the pioneering group of the proletariats with the mission to overthrow the capitalist economic and political structures. In reality, it was much more difficult to build a base of support among the industrial workers than to gain support from the peasants. And once they occupied urban areas, the Communists had no choice but bow to the demanding task of reviving the economy. They must be pragmatic; they did have the power to eliminate the capitalists physically, as the Soviets did after they came to power, but that would make their task of running the economy even more challenging, if manageable at all. The Communist state decided to stick to their ideology in the 1950s by turning all private (equivalent to capitalist) enterprises into socialist (state-owned) ones. About 25 years later, they found that the strategy was not working and switched back to the option of developing the nation's economy by introducing elements of capitalism, but left how to care for the workers' interest untouched. In almost no time they succeeded in striking a good balance between making full commitments to their ideology and solving a practical problem.

On the political front, the Communists changed their commitments throughout the years of their struggle for political power. All opposition political parties in the world know how to use the tactic of accusing the ruling party in the name of grand political ideals, such as freedom, justice, democracy, human rights, and so on. The Communists are of no exception: they called for democracy and people's rights when the Nationalists were in power; but once they were certain they would be soon in power, they started to use the word 'democracy' less frequently or used it with a different meaning. They said very little about other political parties' right to participate in the competition for power after they became the ruling party, nor did they establish any institutional arrangements to ensure the fairness of competitions for political power. If the CCP would be the first ruling party in the new regime, how long would it stay as the ruling party, under what conditions would other political parties have the chance to replace it? These questions were not even asked, at least not openly, let alone answered.

Leaders of the CCP were clearly aware that they must show how serious they were about sharing the new government with other 'capitalist democratic parties'. The first government of the PRC presented itself as a coalition government, with the CCP taking the leading role, of course. With Mao Zedong as the Chairman, there were six Vice-Chairmen, three of which were non-Communists. Zhou Enlai was the first Prime Minister or head of the national government; among the four Deputy Prime Ministers, two were non-Communists; and among the thirty ministerial level leaders, thirteen were from outside the CCP.[5] Another friendly gesture was to bring some prominent capitalists into national or regional governments. For example, Rong Desheng (荣德生), Rong Yiren's (荣毅仁) father, nicknamed 'King of Cotton and Wheat Flour', was selected to be a member of the National People's Political Consultative Assembly, a member of the Military and Political Council of Eastern China, and a Deputy Director of the Public Administration of South Jiangsu Province. When the Communists were approaching Shanghai, many of his relatives and friends tried to convince him to leave for Hong Kong. His reaction was: 'I don't believe the Communists are even worse than the Nationalists!'

However, how long would such institutional framework stay as such? What would be the procedures of changing the government? Would the non-Communist parties be able to grow freely and compete for power with the Communists in the future? In short, did the capitalist political parties have a future as a ruling party in the People's Republic? As Yang Kuisong (杨奎松), a professor of the history of the PRC, pointed out, leaders of the Chinese Communist Party understood that they 'would need the cooperation of the capitalist class.... However, based on the theory of revolutionary phases, it was very clear to every Communist that after the democratic revolution against imperialism and feudalism, the task for the next phase of the revolution, that is, the socialist revolution against capitalism and realizing socialism, would be brought up as a top priority. Their pursuit of socialism requires that it would be inevitable for them to see the capitalist class as their next enemy and therefore to hold a hostile attitude toward capitalism' (2009: 464). In a meeting of the Politbureau in September 1948, Liu Shaoqi clearly pointed out that after the CCP became the ruling party, the main problem would be 'the confrontation between the proletariat class and the capitalist class.... Right from the first day of temporal cooperation, we must watch out for it to defect' (ibid.: 468).

While things might have looked very friendly on the surface at the national government, most ordinary capitalists felt that they were political aliens to the coming Communists. Although Mao Zedong and Zhou Enlai had repeatedly reassured some leading capitalists that they would respect private properties and allow everyone to develop their own interests, such as what Mao told Li Zhuchen (李烛尘, Li Zhancai, 2009: 112), most local Communist leaders, such as those in Tianjin, the industrial and financial centre in northern China, either kept a distance from the capitalists or even encouraged the workers to steal assets from the capitalists (Hershatter, 1986). Clearly, what the capitalists heard was quite different from what the Communist cadres heard. In a meeting of the Central Committee of the CCP held in January 1949, Mao told his senior members of staff that the relationship between the CCP and the representative delegates of the capitalist class would be the most important political challenge. The fundamental principle when dealing with this challenge, according to Mao, was to stick to the perspective of class analysis: 'When you write an article or a piece of news, never forget the perspective of class. All articles focusing on the class issue are deep, and those unable to address this issue clearly are superficial.' (Yang, Kuisong, 2009: 469) However, when the new regime started to suffer from low production, shrinking markets, a large number of closures and bankruptcies, and hundreds of thousands of unemployed workers, Mao started to criticize his comrades for causing these problems by treating the capitalists as class enemies. About two-thirds of capitalists in Tianjin stopped running their businesses; some even moved to other places or overseas. It was in this context that Liu Zhaoqi made a visit to Tianjin and gave a well-known but controversial speech with an aim of ironing out the conflicts between the workers and the capitalists.

However, the ambivalent or undecided attitudes of the CCP towards the capitalists were no more clearly shown than Liu Shaoqi's own. At the end of 1947, he clearly instructed his fellow Communists to reply on the workers and the proletariats after they occupied the cities. They could make alliances with petty capitalists but not the capitalist class in general (ibid.: 464). However, once he and Mao learnt that many capitalists had left Tianjin, because the Communists had encouraged the workers to take away personal properties from many capitalists, leaving about 70 per cent of capitalist firms in Tianjin defunct, he had to tell the workers that the time had not yet come to grab capitalist properties. In the meantime, he told the capitalists not to be afraid of exploiting the workers; as a matter of fact, he encouraged the capitalists to continue to exploit them because the factories would not be up and running without the exploitation and consequently the workers would lose their jobs: 'Today, the capitalist exploitation is not a crime; on the contrary, it deserves credits' (ibid.: 474). Liu's speech aroused some critiques within the CCP and he had to moderate his views later. I cannot find a better example for illustrating the tension between Communist ideology and pragmatism among the top CCP leaders.

## The Five-Antis (五反) campaign: the first step towards eliminating the capitalist class[6]

Why did the Communist regime keep capitalism – and the capitalists – alive during its first few years? Barry Richman (1969: 912) supplied a fairly long list of reasons:

(1) The capitalists' experience, knowledge, and skill in running industry and business were seen as, and have proved to be, highly beneficial in Red China.
(2) The Red Chinese have probably felt that the numerous capitalists could be trusted because they were basically nationalistic [patriotic].
(3) The Chinese Communists also felt secure about their revolution in the early stages because Russia was around to give them protection.
(4) [T]o lure back many of the capitalists, professionals, and other talented people who had fled the country.
(5) The regime felt that there could be good general propaganda value in displaying an image of a humane and fair government that allowed capitalists to coexist with Communists, at least in the short run.
(6) By having the capitalists around, people can be kept 'fighting' to wipe out all elements of bourgeois mentality and behaviour. The capitalists give the regime a good, though largely impersonal, target for carrying out the class struggle and moving forward to the pure Maoist communist society.
(7) Finally, it is likely that only very few of the Chinese capitalists' children will lay claim to the inheritances left by their fathers. Therefore, the wealth and remaining assets of the capitalists will be taken over by the state in any case in the not-too-distant future.

All these represent a softening approach to ideological commitments for the pragmatic reason of keeping the new regime afloat. But the signals concomitantly sent out to the various groups of the society were not consistent, to say the least, but depended on the level of confidence of the CCP leadership, therefore leaving many people confused. The capitalists were sometimes encouraged by state policies or a top leader's speech, while other times they were badly treated by local officials and workers. Over time, the capitalists became apprehensive of what would happen to them with an unconfirmed hope that the whole environment would eventually become more favourable.

The Five-Antis campaign was the turning point for the fate of the capitalists in the new Communist regime, the beginning of ending the Communists' reluctant but pragmatic relationship with the capitalists. Although it lasted only for about ten months (the end of January to October, 1952), it was a devastating blow from which the capitalists would never recover. It started from the Three-Antis campaign (san fan, anti-corruption, anti-waste, and anti-bureaucracy), with a brief Four-Antis in between, mostly in Shanghai.

The target of the Three-Antis was Communist cadres who were perceived to have gone astray from their Communist principles: taking bribes, having an affair with a capitalist's daughter, using public money for personal use, indulging themselves in luxury lifestyles, and so on. The most serious cases were two Party Secretaries of Tianjin, who took bribes of about a million yuan, an astronomical number in 1951. In Beijing, from the spring of 1949 to the autumn of 1951, 650 government agents or enterprise staff members were found to have a history of corruption. Further, at the Ministry of Trade and the Ministry of Finance, about half of the 300,000 employees were involved in corruption. Corruption was also found in the armies (Yang, Kuisong, 2009: 484). These cases were particularly unacceptable to Mao because he had repeatedly warned his fellow Communists of such regime-threatening crimes even before taking power. Mao was extremely worried that these problems were repetitions of Li Zicheng's fall from power at the end of the Ming dynasty – the leader of peasant rebellions in the Ming dynasty lost his hard won ruling power due to rampant corruption, arrogance and other undisciplined behaviour among his colleagues. Mao's nightmare would be the CCP turned into a political party no better than the Nationalists as a consequence of this corrupt behaviour.

Before the Three-Antis campaign was completed, which lasted only a little more than a month from the beginning of December 1951 to 26 January 1952, it was revealed that most of the cadres' malfeasances were connected to the capitalists, which was why the Three-Antis were soon extended to Five-Antis – there were 'five poisons' among the capitalist class: bribery, tax evasion, stealing state property, shoddy work and inferior materials, and stealing state economic information.[7] On 26 January 1952, the CCP's Central Committee issued an instruction to launch the Five-Antis campaign, calling for an attack on 'the unlawful capitalist class',[8] because Mao believed that the capitalists were behind the three crimes committed by some of his cadres and therefore posed a more serious threat to his new regime. Those state agents, cadres, or military officers were corrupted because they were contaminated by the thoughts and lifestyles of the capitalist class. As it was the capitalists who took initiative in bribing the state agents, Mao believed that the capitalists were launching a purposeful attack on his new regime.[9] Mr Sheng Pihua (盛丕华), who was a capitalist himself but selected to be a Deputy Major of Shanghai, called for all other capitalists to cooperate with the Communist state.

This is an early but excellent example of 'class struggle', Mao's favourite political method of mobilizing the ordinary people ('the masses') to fight against 'a class enemy', through which his political power became consolidated. The process works as follows: after investigating some state agents' misbehaviour such as taking bribes or helping a relative to get a job, it became clear that some of these agents had close relations with the capitalists. Mao dubbed the actions taken by the capitalists 'sugar-coated bullets and bombs', for example, it was reported that some capitalists encouraged their daughters to have affairs with local leaders (Yang, Kuisong, 2009: Chapter 6). While these may actually have been desperate strategies adopted by the capitalists to survive the new regime, Mao saw them as intentional attacks launched by the capitalists on the new proletariat regime. The question was: how to find them out? The Communists developed a very effective tactic, which was to create an atmosphere in which you felt as if someone was watching over your shoulder and there were only two options in front of you: (1) to confess; or (2) not to confess. To take the first option, the benefit would be to gain leniency from the authority, but the potential cost would be that you might lose most of your 'unlawful assets' and it would be a very humiliating experience. To take the second option, the potential benefit would be a slim chance that you might get away with it, but this would be a very risky choice because if you were found out you would be severely punished. What the Communist authorities would do was make the capitalists go for option one rather than option two. The key was to show that some of the bad behaviours were indeed found out, even though the number of such cases might have been very small, they were enough to create a starting point and the momentum for a snowball or chain effect. This was achieved with the help of the workers, that is, the employees of the capitalists.[10]

Before the Communists entered the cities and became the ruling power, the workers had some mixed feelings about their bosses, all because of their relatively inferior status. On the one hand, the workers hated the capitalists because they did the hard work while it was their employers who reaped the profits, a phenomenon that later they learnt to call 'exploitation'. But on the other hand, the workers admired or envied the high quality of material life and the education enjoyed by the capitalists; they wished some day to live a life like that. With the Communists behind them, the Five-Antis offered the workers a great opportunity to make their dreams come true. Organized in labour unions, the workers had both a legitimate reason – the capitalists had committed crimes of exploiting the workers – and actual power to demand that the capitalists comply with their orders. Obviously, some workers took the opportunity too enthusiastically – the supposedly investigating process to a large extent turned into a campaign of personal attacks. In Tianjin, for example, the workers took the campaign as an opportunity to demand higher pay and better benefits (Lieberthal, 1980: 41). Soon the Communists leaders realized that over reactions on the part of the workers would damage the confidence of the capitalists in the new regime and eventually drag the whole economy down (Zhang Xule, 2006: 61). It is truly puzzling that top CCP leaders never seemed to worry about the possibility that the participants would take a political campaign into their own hands, which I think is responsible for the later disaster of the Cultural Revolution.

Although for the sake of keeping the economy running some moderation was applied to the fierce attacking articles in the media,[11] it was extremely clear that it was politically correct for the workers and other employees to turn the existing social structure upside down. The moderation was applied mostly at the ideological and the highest level. On the ground, the workers enjoyed the process of becoming the masters of their former bosses, and it was almost a given that some workers would humiliate their employers in the name of fighting back against the capitalist attack on the new regime. Reading the history of this campaign, I cannot help but thinking this was a preliminary Great Proletariat Cultural Revolution! A variety of interrogating and humiliating tactics were employed, including beating, slapping in the face, spitting in the face, forced kneeling on a hard floor or bench, pinching fingers with needles, and so on. Marshal Chen Yi, then the Mayor of Shanghai, issued an order to stop these actions, but it was ignored. (Yang, Kuisong, 2009: 496). The underlying rationale behind the workers' behaviour should be very clear, although it was never publicly spelled out: the capitalists were the political enemy; as they had committed evil crimes, we as the masters of the new society had every right to treat them in whatever way we felt necessary and happy with. There was no law for protecting the rights of the capitalists as they should have no rights in the first place. The new regime was on its way to becoming a tyranny of the majority. Before and in the rural areas, the tyranny was of the peasants against the landlords, and now it was repeated in the cities with the workers against the capitalists. While the workers might have enjoyed a temporary revenging sense of superiority to their former bosses, it soon turned out that such a campaign was to nobody's interest – the workers would suffer as well once their bosses could not run the factories or shops anymore. However, in such an authoritarian environment, no one would realize or dare to point out that it was the philosophy of class struggle that was at the root of such political torture.

Once the workers were mobilized and a few cases were established either through small meetings or secret letters, rallies were called where the two classes confronted each other, with the capitalists being the targets, of course. During the ten months of the campaign, it was estimated that on average a worker attended 30 such rallies while a cadre attended 40 (Zhang, Xule, 2006: 76). In these rallies, the capitalists realized immediately that it would be too risky to think they could survive the whole process without voluntarily reporting and confessing 'the crimes' they had committed. My interest here is not in the details of the strategies adopted by each side; rather, I was struck by the way in which the capitalists identified the nature and the causes of their crimes. As an example, below is my translation of the confession by Mr Wang, a bank manager in Shanghai, in February 1952 (Yang, Kuisong, 2009: 337):

> I came from a family of the capitalist class and developed the habit of chasing after luxuries since my childhood. At the age of eighteen I started to do business in a comprador insurance company and all I learnt was the false and deceiving management methods and corrupted life styles adopted by the capitalist class. From the age of twenty-four, I started to organize my own business, taking the pursuit of profits as the centre of my life and personal enjoyment as the purpose of life ... When our firm was taken over by the new China, I was very upset. But why was I so upset? Doubtlessly, it was

because I hated to lose an important territory of the capitalist class and a central institution of the capitalist class. My thoughts appeared to go off the right track and for some time I was very resentful. Consequently, I made an active attempt to regain my status of the capitalist class and to keep my interests of the capitalist class...so I have displayed much shameful and despicably selfish conduct...

Now I hate the capitalist poisons brought with me from the old society, which made me commit those corrupt, shameful, and despicable behaviours, and led me to a road of corruption and destruction. Now I want to make a complete confession so that I can get rid of this heavy and filthy baggage and clean up the sordid crimes all over my body. I am thankful to the great Chairman Mao. The education that this campaign has given me is unforgettable as it saved me from a filthy abyss. If I don't tell all what I did, then I will be a ghost for ever, leaving a ghost in my heart for ever, I won't be able to appear in front of human beings for ever, and ultimately I will be punished by the people. Now I want to transform myself to be a new person, so I hope people would point out as many crimes and dirty spots as they could. Today I take off my trousers, but my tail is still there, so I hope the people would do an operation for me by cutting off my tail in order to transform myself into a new person. I have committed so many evil conducts that did so much harm to the people and the nation, so I should confess completely. At this moment I do not worry about any losses anymore, only to wait for the penalties meted out by the authorities.

Even a capitalist as prominent as Mr Zi Yaohua (资耀华), who was a member of the National People's Assembly of Political Consultation and a member of the government of the City of Tianjin, would have to bow to the pressure, claiming that all he learnt in the US was 'the methods of exploiting the workers and helping the capitalist maximize their profits' and he would 'be determined to accept the leadership of the workers' class, transform thoughts and confess past mistakes' (Zhang Xule, 2006: 71). There are two striking properties of these 'confessing' letters or speeches submitted by capitalists: (1) the level of self-humiliation is so high that one must wonder whether the Communist authorities truly believed the sincerity of these words; they would be foolish if they did believe; they did not believe most of what the capitalists said but still pretended to believe because otherwise the whole campaign would have become meaningless; (2) all confessions were phrased in a highly political fashion, especially in the language of class and class struggle.

The Five-Antis was a campaign to destroy the whole capitalist class at all levels (political, economic, social, and personal). At the end of the campaign, although most capitalists were physically still alive, they had already been destroyed financially, politically, socially, and psychologically. They were perceived as a group of people who would try every dirty trick to squeeze profit from the workers' hard labour. They were shameless and despicable without any sense of morality and therefore deserved no social and political status in 'the new society'. All they should and could do was to sever themselves from their past, transform themselves into labourers and hope the new regime would be generous enough to accept their effort. Take the example of Lu Zuofu, the capitalist I mentioned before. Zhou Enlai's promise to Lu Zuofu of offering financial support to his troubled company was not realized because during the Five-Antis campaign the Communist state announced the cessation of loans to and investments in private companies. Although the central government later would have liked to make an exception to the new policy, eventually Lu became highly disappointed and devastated. He was humiliated during the campaign through repeated personal accusations and attacks by his employees. Someone he treated as a son and who lived in his house for many years openly accused Lu of embezzling public property by taking two sofas back home and later declared he was moving out of the house as a way of drawing a line between himself as a worker and Lu as a capitalist (Li, Zhancai, 2009: 58). To Lu, the humiliation was not bearable anymore and suicide was the only way out.

The capitalists admitted that bribing, tax evasion, and profiteering were normal among them – everyone had done one or more of these things before. The most famous case was Wang Kangnian (汪康年), who sold fake medicines to the Chinese armies fighting in the Korean War. This case was taken as a major piece of evidence that all capitalists were evil and pursued profits at all costs and without any sense of morality and social justice. These accusations might not have affected the petty shop owners, but it was a serious blow to those big capitalists who saw themselves not only as capitalists but also as decent and respectable people of high social status. In the Chinese culture, any damage to social status was taken extremely seriously – a matter of 'losing face', which could result in suicide. According to Yang Kuisong's research, during the month from 18 January to 19 February, 49 people committed suicide with an additional 16 failing. In February alone, there were 73 suicides (Yang, Kuisong, 2009: 321). During half of March, 53 committed suicide (ibid.: 329). In the eight days from the 2nd to the

8th of April, 67 capitalists and their family members committed suicide (ibid.: 345). An incomplete count during 25 January to 1 April (66 days) shows there were 876 people who committed suicide; that is, on average, there were more than 13 people who killed themselves each day (ibid.: 498). Among them, suicide was committed by a couple or even the whole family. Even Rong Yiren, a red capitalist favoured by top CCP leaders, was as despairing as to consider hanging himself when there were no more alternatives. In such circumstances, who would not simply hand out their assets in order to save their lives? That the subsequent nationalization of capitalist enterprises was completed much faster than expected was at least partly because the capitalists were all scared and had no choice but to follow suit. Obviously, this was a much wiser choice than to resist because they could keep their life and even got paid interest by the state.

Even Bo Yibo (薄一波), who was in charge of the National Committee of Promoting Production and Austerity, reported to Mao that many local cadres had very confusing ideas about what the campaign was about and among the workers and shop employees the campaign was 'anti-everything ... anti-exploitation, anti-suppression, anti-capitalist corrupted lifestyles, and so on ... some arrested capitalists without any order. A capitalist usually had twenty to thirty organizations doing investigations on him, some took turns to hold rallies on their crimes...' (ibid.: 322). To stop such undisciplined campaigns against the capitalists, Bo suggested putting all capitalists in Shanghai into five categories (lawful, basically lawful, half lawful and half unlawful, seriously unlawful, and completely unlawful). Then came the arbitrary criteria on who should belong to which category: for example, the CCP leaders in Shanghai announced that the percentage of seriously unlawful and completely unlawful capitalists would be no more than 5 per cent of all capitalists, but it was never explained where this figure came from. Also, the criterion of 'basically lawful' varied from place to place: in Beijing, a capitalist with unlawful profit under two million yuan would be labelled as 'basically unlawful' but in Shanghai this figure was raised to ten million. In Tianjin, the 'seriously law-breaking' and 'completely law-breaking' capitalists were 5.3 per cent (Lieberthal, 1980: 168). It is not a coincidence that they all happened to be around 5 per cent – Mao Zedong and Bo Yibo set up a quota for each of the five categories of capitalists.

In such circumstances, some Communist intellectuals no longer hesitated in revealing the CCP's true stand in organizing the coalition government. As an ideological support to the Five-Anti campaign, intellectuals responsible to the CCP, especially those working at the Bureau of Theory of the CCP's Department of Propaganda, published a series of newspaper articles documenting how the capitalists had attacked the new regime. In these articles some of the CCP's views towards the capitalists started to become known to the public. Of these points, the following are the most noteworthy: that although the CCP had made an alliance with domestic capitalists, the four classes (workers, peasants, intellectuals, and domestic capitalists) in the new society were not politically equal; the leadership status of the workers' class must not be challenged; although some representatives of the capitalist class could take a position in political institutions and governments, they would not be permitted to occupy any major roles in these organizations (ibid.: 489), a policy that would return a few decades later after a new generation of capitalists emerged.

## The nationalization: the second step towards eliminating the capitalist class

What the capitalists in China feared most about the Chinese Communist Party is exactly what the Party's name means: *gong chan* (共产), literally, sharing assets. They feared that the CCP would share their assets with the workers, as the Party took away the properties of the landlords in the rural areas and distributed them to the peasants. When taking over the cities, the Communists assured the capitalists that, in the name of developing the national economy, they would not do that. Indeed, the new regime even adopted some policies for supporting the capitalist enterprises during the first few years of the PRC, such as ordering products from private enterprises and smoothing labour–capital relations (Dong, Furen, 董辅礽, 2001: 50–6). The Five-Antis was a political campaign; to the capitalists, the price was to pay back 'the unlawful profits', suspension of production and personal humiliation, but not the taking over businesses from the capitalists.

Although the CCP adopted the accommodating policies for the purpose of preventing the economy from slipping into recession, to socializing the whole economy was only a matter of time. Seen in this light, the Five-Antis was only a prelude to the ultimate nationalization of private ownership of means of production. The campaign sent out a clear message to the capitalists: the capitalists' possession of wealth could in no way match the coercive power of the Communist state; therefore, the capitalists would be wise to comply with whatever the Communist state demands. Jeremy Brown and Paul Pickowicz's notion of 'culture of accommodation' captures what this meant to the capitalists very well (2007: 10–11):

> Fear mixed with hopeful idealism fostered what we call a 'culture of accommodation'. Instead of resisting or simply fleeing China, many non-party figures bent over backwards to collaborate in their own demise. Capitalists handed over their money, leaders of social welfare organizations gave up their autonomy, and performers and scientists relinquished their artistic and academic freedom. Their hope was that coming to an accommodation with the new regime would, at best, lead to political and material rewards. At the least, those who collaborated hoped to spare themselves and their families unnecessary violence and turbulence. For some the strategy worked: cooperative businessmen were granted official positions, and even if they were no longer filthy rich, they were still guaranteed comfortable lives. By 1953, many people had survived the campaigns of the preceding years. They were perhaps bowed, but they were unbroken. How many could say the same in 1957 or 1966 or 1976? The gradually intensifying atmosphere of paranoia fostered before 1953 did not preordain the later tragedies of the Mao years, but the seeds of catastrophe had been planted.

Top leaders of the CCP believed the time for nationalizing capitalist enterprises came when private enterprises became almost completely dependent on the Communist state and the socialization of agriculture was achieved in the rural areas. Barry Richman explained how the Chinese state made the capitalists dependent on it (1969: 896):

- Capitalist enterprises gradually became dependent on the Communist state on getting orders of their products; all retail and whole sale enterprises had to rely on state allocations for their merchandise;
- The Communist state had the authority of determining the price, wage rates, working conditions and other managerial issues;
- The State was also behind worker's councils that were set up within private enterprises and played a major role in management;
- 'In reality, private industrial enterprises became essentially processing plants for the state, and commercial organizations became state distribution channels.'

In essence, the Communist state actually controlled almost every aspect of management. In 1955, this made the nationalization of some capitalist enterprises the only option, which set up an example for all other capitalist enterprises. By the end of that year, Mao Zedong thought this could be done nationally. And it took only one year to nationalize almost all capitalist enterprises – the contribution to the national GDP by capitalist enterprises became negligible (less than 0.1 per cent); even the individual businesses counted for only 7 per cent, and all the rest came from either state-owned, collective-owned, or state-controlled co-operations (Dong, Furen, 2001: 196–7). The year of 1956 appeared to be a time of celebration – the official media was full of photos and reports that high-profile capitalists were in a rush to report the great news (that their businesses had completed state-private joint ownership) to the top leaders of CCP.

Were they genuinely happy to hand over their enterprises to the Communist state? With most of the capitalists of the old generation having died and with no reliable historical evidence of their thoughts available, we can only speculate on the possible answers. I would think that a minority of them were genuinely happy because their patriotism led them to believe that their personal enterprises could become part of a much more powerful national economy. In addition, their quality of life did not seem to be seriously affected given the interest that the Communist state would pay them. Some of them even gained political credit for 'performing well' in the campaign. According to the estimate by Barry Richman, '[a]bout a hundred and ten capitalists have been members of the National People's Congress in recent years, and twelve of them have been members of the standing committee of this congress. Hundreds more have been members of top-level municipal government bodies in those cities where there are sizable numbers of capitalists' (1969: 901). Li Zhuchen (李烛沉) was a good example in Tianjin, being the leading capitalist in the process of transforming private enterprises into public ownership. He repeatedly told other capitalists to '[l]isten to Chairman Mao's words and follow the Communist Party'. On 15 January 1955, he published an essay in *Tianjin Daily* to show his determination and in November 1955 he brought Mao a silk banner with six characters on it: 'Listen to your words and follow the Party' (Li Zhancai, 2009: 125). Next year (1956) Mao personally asked him to become the Minister of the Department of Food Industries, clearly an award Mao gave to Li Zhuchen in return for his loyalty.

It is very difficult for me to believe that the majority of the capitalists were genuinely happy to yield their ownership to the Communist state, because it is against basic human nature for people to welcome the confiscation of their assets, no matter in how friendly a manner this is done. But, when the capitalists realized that all that was left for them was the nominal ownership of their businesses – which was meaningless without being able to make key managerial decisions – that they would be severely punished if they resisted, but rewarded with life safety and interest if they did not, they were all in a rush to turn their factories and shops over to the Communist state. When people realize they have to lose something one way or another, it would be rational for them to make the event as happy or stress free as they can manage. They could minimize their dissonance by thinking of the rewards (safety, peace of mind, interest, a good relationship with the state and all the subsequent benefits because of the good relationship); these benefits clearly outweigh the option of resistance. The story of Wu Tsung-I[12] (Richman, 1969: 907) well illustrates what was truly in the mind of a capitalist: 'In 1954, because of pressure, and seeing the writing on the wall, the board of directors of the Sung Sing Textile Corporation applied for joint ownership. According to Wu, there were several reasons why the directors decided to apply rapidly for joint ownership. The chief ones were the following:

(a) To avoid worker and union-management conflicts, which they were sure would become serious if they did not soon take such action.
(b) All indications were that the state would hold back material allocations, restrict customers, organize boycotts, and exert other pressures against those private firms – particularly large ones – that delayed in applying for joint ownership. Joint firms, on the other hand, could be expected to receive equal treatment with pure state enterprises. The directors took note that Sung Sing was prohibited in 1954 from supplying commodities to Shanghai's largest private retail department store, Wing On, or to other suppliers of this store, and the store itself was being subject to much mass picketing and boycotts.
(c) Party and government officials, using a variety of arguments and approaches, persuaded the directors that to apply for joint ownership as soon as possible was in their own and their corporation's best interests.
(d) The directors felt that joint ownership was inevitable anyway, and by showing acceptance and even active support of the regime's aims early they could expect to be much better off in the long run.'

Perhaps the capitalists should have been grateful for the leniency of the Communists: after all, the capitalists received interest for giving away their enterprises, although the value of their assets was likely undervalued.[13] The legality of such transformation was never challenged, at least not that I am aware of. From the perspective of the CCP, the only problem in this process is that it was done in too much of a rush.[14]

# 3
# The Growth of the New Capitalists

The history of the People's Republic of China (PRC) evolved just as a natural experiment. Initially, people strongly believed that a good theory (Marxism, Leninism, and Mao Zedong Thought) would bring a particular result (a powerful nation). Some time (nearly 30 years) later, the result was however neither expected nor desirable (political instability, social disintegration, poverty, and economic recession); therefore, a new theory (pragmatism) replaced the old, and some new results have emerged, one of which, still unexpected but more desirable, is the growth of a new generation of capitalists. The desirability of the results, particularly the increased wealth, lends much support to the new theory, although the side-effects of the contributing factor (increased inequality and social unrest, and so on) have been sidelined. As I have explained how China's institutional contexts brought about entrepreneurial strategies in another book (Yang, 2007), in this chapter I focus on the ideological principles that are responsible for the emergence and growth of the new generation of capitalists. Without a proper understanding of these principles, it would be difficult for us to study how the Communist state interacts with the new capitalists in the following chapters. Then I shall produce a profile of these capitalists so that the reader will know who they are before we discuss their political life.

## The triumph of economic pragmatism and its limitations

All states must deal with the tension between ideological commitment and political tactics for solving specific problems at hand. Ideology is an effective tool for justifying the rule and mobilizing the populace, which is particularly so for authoritarian and totalitarian regimes because their legitimacy is not gained through public consent. Ideology can thus lend the extra support desperately needed by such regimes for sustaining their political dominance. Ideally, the tactics designed and employed for keeping the regime functioning should be in line with the ideological principles. To keep the consistency, however, may become an enormous challenge to the state when surviving a particular crisis requires tactics that are at odds with the advocated ideology. In this sense, the likelihood of the survival of an authoritarian regime depends on the capacity and flexibility to deal with such tension.

As described in the previous chapter, capitalist enterprises as a whole experienced some very difficult times in the process of socializing the new People's Republic's national economy. Following the route of Soviet Russia, the Chinese Communist state established a highly controlled political and economic system. From production to distribution, nearly every sector was operated according to state plans; hence the term 'planned economy'. By the mid 1950s, major 'capitalist' enterprises virtually disappeared from China's industrial landscape. During the Cultural Revolution (1966–76), even the small and tiny private businesses were shut down or confiscated as 'capitalist tails', the charge being that they hindered the progress of the socialist movement, they were economically less efficient than the mass production organized by the state, and their mode of production was morally wrong because it exploited the working class.

It turned out that the 20 years or so after the demise of capitalist enterprises (approximately 1957 to 1978) were the most difficult times for the People's Republic. The good days for the workers, even as 'the masters of the new society', did not last long as they were demoralized when not rewarded for hard work (Unger and Chan, 2007). The morale soon declined dramatically despite the fact that the Communist state frequently set up model workers, such as Lei Feng (雷锋) and Wang Jinxi (王进喜), with an aim to boost production. On top of the inefficiencies of state-run enterprises, disruptions caused by a series of political campaigns, with the most well-known being The Great Leap Forward and The Great Proletariat Cultural Revolution, eventually brought the economy to the brink of collapse.

Ironically, the only solution appeared to be to bring back the capitalists, firstly by restoring the status of the surviving old capitalists,[1] then inviting capitalists from overseas (initially overseas Chinese capitalists in Hong Kong, Taiwan, or Southeast Asia but later from all major industrialized countries), and finally by creating a new generation of capitalists from within China. But the return of capitalist businesses was nowhere to be found in state plans. Rather, the Communist state had no other alternative but to allow a new generation of capitalists to grow in order to solve the urgent problems of stimulating production, supplying essential goods and services to people's daily lives, and providing employment opportunities to millions of urban youth at the end of the 1970s, who were anxiously waiting to find a job, especially those returning to their urban homes from the 'Up to the Mountain, Down to the Village' (上山下乡) movement. It was reported that more than 15 million people, or about 6 per cent of the working population in cities and towns, were looking for jobs (Dong, Fureng, 2001, vol. 2: 245; Gold, 1989). State enterprises were already overstaffed, thus the only feasible solution was to allow these young people to help themselves, including the option of setting up their own businesses. To avoid any ideological controversy, a limit on the maximum number of employees (eight) was imposed.[2]

The first volte-face against the old generation of capitalists in the first half of the 1950s, no matter how ruthlessly it was executed, was somehow expected, because the rationale behind the campaigns was in line with the general Communist ideology. However, the second one at the end of the 1970s and early 1980s was unexpected – it was an option as a result of running out of options; therefore, an ideological justification was required. This was no easy task, which explains why much of the 1980s was perhaps the most liberal as well the most confusing decade in the history of PRC; the old ideology was being abandoned but a new one was yet to be found. With the split among the top leaders of the CCP, the Chinese state as whole did not have a coherent strategy for squaring their ideological commitments with the immediate challenge of recovering the economy; the only principle seemed to be 'proceed cautiously' ('crossing the river by grappling to find the stones'). Deng Xiaoping's invention of 'no debate' (over whether the reform policies were capitalist or socialist in nature) was equivalent to suspending the CCP's ideological commitment and the responsibility of providing a vision of what kind of nation the PRC should be. Under his authority, most of the Party leaders soon accepted that the tangible improvements of quality of life would provide a much stronger support to the legitimacy of the Communist state than its orthodox theories.

The demise and revival of capitalists in China resulted from the Communists' yield to the urgent need of sustaining the legitimacy of their rule and in the meantime compromising their ideological commitment. If the demise of capitalists means the success of orthodox Maoism, then their revival has resulted from the triumph of economic pragmatism in the party's leadership. To understand the political status of the new capitalists, it is crucial to learn where Deng Xiaoping's confidence comes from – how could he be so certain that letting the capitalists grow would only enhance rather than jeopardize the legitimacy of the CCP? The rationale behind such confidence tells us the principles by which the CCP deals with the new capitalists. Deng claimed that China would not see a new generation of capitalists as a result of economic reforms because the CCP 'would not encourage polarization. The wealth created will firstly go to the nation and secondly go to the people, so *no new capitalist class will emerge.*' (Deng, Xiaoping, 1993: 123–4, emphasis added) However, he didn't explain how this would happen: did he mean that the profits created by private businesses would all be taken away by the state? If so, in what way and by how much? Furthermore, would the profits earned be a big enough incentive for these people to set up businesses in the first place? The only feasible and sensible way to implement this would be to collect more tax from these people to redistribute the newly created wealth across the whole society, a mechanism Deng rarely, if ever, mentioned. Even today, the CCP has never come up with a coherent long term policy for taxation. Although the tax rate is high enough for redistributing the newly created wealth to the needy, tax evasion is so prevalent that it is perhaps even more serious than in those years of the Five-Antis campaign (Thornton, 2004). The lack of a clear and widely accepted tax policy and the corrupt enforcement of tax laws are responsible for the unprecedented increase of inequality in China – in less than 30 years, China has turned from one of the most egalitarian societies to one of the most unequal societies in the world.[3]

The consequence is that most people do not pay serious attention to ideology anymore; the unstoppable, large number of corruption cases indicates that even state officials only pay it lip service. Nevertheless, it would be either naïve or irresponsible for CCP leaders to think that ideology is not relevant anymore. That the CCP's ideology has lost its relevance to most ordinary Chinese people's daily life does not mean that there shall be no ideological issues anymore. The termination of debates over capitalism or socialism should not mean that ideology is irrelevant anymore to the economy and the politics of China. Related to the changing social structure and employment relations, the most visible consequence is the ban of some sensitive words in public discourses, such as exploitation, capitalist, discrimination, and so on. The Communist state does not want to be blamed for creating a new polarized social structure. It is to their interest to downplay the significance of employment disputes and the increased gap between the newly wealthy capitalists and the working poor. In this sense, Deng's pragmatism of economic development is very irresponsible as effectively it either deals with any problems only when they come up or leaves the task to the next generation of political leaders. For example, while letting some people get rich first, there are no policies on controlling inequalities and setting up mechanisms of 'getting rich together', which has been claimed to be one of the ultimate goals of the reforms. While each of these two goals is desirable on its own, specific policies that are designed to strike the delicate balance between the two demands have long fallen behind the call of the general principles. So far younger generations of China's top leaders have offered no vision of how economic growth will be sustained without jeopardizing social justice and equality. Social stability is maintained basically through a stick and carrot strategy and on a case-by-case basis: when there are mass protests or serious incidents, the state will hand out financial compensation on the one hand and suppress the activists on the other.

## Deng Xioping and capitalists

The rise of the new generation of capitalists has made the CCP gradually retreat from its orthodox ideological positions. Initially, the Party saw the self-employed and the petty business owners as a marginal group in the social structure, just as the position of the whole private sector in the national economy. They existed to help the state solve the employment problem and to offer some convenience to people's daily lives. In the meantime, they needed to be monitored and contained within the parameters of state regulations – there has always been a sense of suspicion as this group of people are doing something alien to the socialist and communist principles. Up to the early 1990s, local state officials felt no remorse when they openly showed their contempt for street peddlers and petty business owners.[4] Such distrustful and even spiteful attitudes towards the new capitalists lasted until 1992 when Deng Xiaoping made it clear that the Party should not care about capitalism – and therefore capitalists – anymore as long as the economy was growing. Given the green light to growth of the private sector and the privatization of state-owned enterprises, the CCP must define the political identity of the increasing number of capitalists – while the CCP welcomes the contributions made by the capitalists because economic growth will enhance the legitimacy of the CCP's ruling, how would they fit into the current Communist political structure?

One of Deng Xiaoping's major contributions to China's development was transforming such a temporary solution into a long-term national policy. Under his leadership, constraints on private businesses, including market entry, price, employment, and so on, were cautiously but steadily lifted. Economic progress was then used to show the rigidity of orthodox Marxist principles, to legitimize the more liberal policies, and to downplay ideological controversies such as exploitation and the nature of the reforms. The case of 'The Fool's Melon Seeds' can well illustrate the confrontation between two competing ideologies. Nicknamed 'The Fool', the businessman's real name was Nian Guangjiu. He started his business of producing and selling toasted melon seeds, a popular snack in China, as early as 1972. In the early 1980s, he employed more than 100 people, clearly far more than the maximum officially permitted. Local officials, who initially encouraged him to grow as an example of individual business, later discovered that 'The Fool' earned an annual income of more than a million yuan and employed many people, indisputable evidence of 'capitalist exploitation'. Some local officials proposed to put him in jail. It was Deng Xiaoping's direct intervention that stopped the prosecution. Under the encouragement of Deng and other CCP leaders (Zhao Ziyang, Hu Yaobang, Wan Li, and so on), private enterprises have experienced dramatic growth. But before giving the details, it is necessary to clarify the meaning of the word 'capitalist' that I shall use in this book.

As early as 1979, Deng Xiaoping said the following with regard to the political identify of the old capitalists: 'These people stopped receiving a fixed rate of interest long ago. As long as they no longer exploit others, we have no reason to continue to label them "capitalists"'.[5] Almost at the same time, the United Front received instruction to redeem the life of the capitalists, which included the fact that all personal properties taken away during the Cultural Revolution must be returned and salaries repaid plus interest. In the summer of 1979 Deng said:

> The means of production formerly owned by the Chinese capitalist class came under state control long ago, and the payment of a fixed rate of interest ended 13 years ago. The overwhelming majority of the capitalists with the capacity to work have transformed themselves into working people who earn their own living in our socialist society... . Today, as working people, they are contributing their share to our socialist modernization.[6]

In a nutshell, according to Deng, the crucial reason for removing the term 'capitalist' from China's political vocabulary is because they do not exploit others anymore; instead, they live on their own work, just as others in China. The issue of exploitation is however a tricky one: how would we know if someone has exploited others? Would the term 'capitalist' be revived if someone who has nothing to do with the old capitalists starts to exploit others? Obviously, Deng's objective was to remove the antagonism between the capitalists and the workers so that there would be no political obstacle to economic reconstruction. This became the key rationale behind all specific policies of the United Front for the reform period. The irony is that *exploitation becomes the very mechanism through which economic reconstruction is to be realized.* Consequently, the reform process and the process of recreating a new generation of capitalists were two sides of the same coin. It was purely for political reasons that this could not be openly acknowledged. The only solution was to use a different title for the new capitalists, anything other than the word 'capitalist' itself.

## What kind of people are the new capitalists in China?

### Definition and classifications

In this book, the expression 'the new capitalists' refers to the owners of domestic private enterprises. Therefore, it is necessary to explain the meaning of 'domestic private enterprises' before learning about their owners. The meaning of 'private enterprise' should become clearer after we make two distinctions. First, all commercial organizations in China can be broadly classified as 'private enterprises' and 'public enterprises'. The latter refer to enterprises owned by the Chinese state (state-owned enterprises, or SOEs), local governments, and communities (or collectively-owned enterprises, including town-and-village enterprises, or TVEs). Second, there are different types of private enterprises, but we can set the international private enterprises (purely owned by a foreign investor or controlled by a foreign investor) apart from the domestic ones. This study focuses on the domestic private enterprises regardless of the form of the ownership (sole-ownership, family owned, share holding, partnership, and so on). More precisely, they are officially registered as 'private enterprises' at government agencies. Owners of 'individual household business' may be included as long as they employ a certain number of employees no matter how small the number, but self-employed people are not seen as 'capitalists' and therefore they are not included in this study.[7]

Both in and outside China, the term 'The New Rich' (or the 'nouveaux riches', xian fu 先富) has been used. Obviously, this is a much broader and ambivalent concept – it does not define how rich is rich or how new is new; furthermore, although many private business owners belong to this 'new rich' group, some of them may not be rich enough to be included. On the other hand, some among 'the new rich' may not own any business, such as top executives, lawyers, doctors, those earning a large amount of money by trading stocks or properties, and those who have gained a large amount of money through illegal or immoral channels. People in China do not seem to realize (or do not mind) the negative connotation of the term – it suggests one who displays the new wealth in 'an ostentatious or vulgar fashion' (*Oxford Dictionary of English*) – because they seem to have conflicting feelings towards the new rich. On the one hand, they admire them, especially those who appear to have become rich through hard work, technological competence, or smart marketing ideas, but on the other hand, they are always suspicious of how the new rich could get so rich and so quickly. The new generation of capitalists, like their predecessors, have not been able to keep themselves clean, and frequent revelation of serious cases in the media, such as bribing, using materials of extremely low quality or even poisonous materials, being ruthless towards employees, and so on, has confirmed public suspicion. This is the source of a wide discussion of 'the original sins' of these new capitalists who have been operating under moral suspicion.

The new capitalists can be classified in different ways. A useful scheme is to put them into three major groups (Li, 2001: 222): '(1) "self-made entrepreneurs" – peasants-turned-industrialists in rural areas and owners of small business firms in cities; (2) "bureaucratic entrepreneurs" – government officials, either former or incumbent, and their relatives who have made fortunes by various forms of using their power in the process of marketization and privatization; and (3) "technical entrepreneurs" – computer and Internet specialists who have become wealthy as a result of rapid technological development and the impact of economic globalization'. Note that the second type are not really entrepreneurs because they didn't invest their own money or bank loans in setting up a business; all they do is to make use of the power in their hand for obtaining illegal or inappropriate personal gains, such as taking bribes after giving away state assets (raw materials, energy, land, insider's information, and so on) to someone at a low price. These are corrupted state officials, not entrepreneurs, although their transactions involve business activities. Joseph Fewsmith is absolutely correct in pointing out that such involvement of the Chinese governments in business activities is the main source of corruption (1999: 69): 'Potentially the most important weakness in China's central state capacity derives from the entrepreneurial activities of the central government itself. ... What such bureaucratic involvement in the economy suggests is an institutionalization of corruption... .' We shall come back to this issue in Chapter 7.

## The growth of private enterprises

To depict a relatively accurate picture of the growth of private enterprises is nevertheless not easy, especially for the 1980s when the legitimacy of private enterprises was not yet firmly established. To protect themselves from potential prosecution and harassment by local officials, some private businesses put on a 'red hat', namely, concealing their true identity by registering themselves as collective enterprises or operating as a part of a state-owned enterprise. The secretive nature of this strategy of survival means that it is next to impossible to estimate the number of these 'red hat' companies. It is reasonable to expect, however, that the total number of these disguised companies has decreased significantly with the CCP's gradual recognition of the legitimacy of private enterprises, which started from the end of the 1980s. In 2002, Jiang Zemin, then the CCP's General Secretary, declared that private business owners, like other social groups in China – peasants, workers, and soldiers – should be regarded as 'contributors to the socialist mission' as well and should therefore be welcome to join the CCP.

Against the above background, it is very likely that the numbers in Figure 3.1 have underestimated the size of the private sector, although it is difficult to determine the level of the underestimation. There are two lines in the chart. The upper line shows the number of private enterprises in hundreds of thousands, and the lower one shows the number of employees in the private sector in millions. A few specific figures will help the reader obtain a better sense of how fast private enterprises have grown. In 1989, there were only 90,000 private enterprises officially registered in China, employing 1.6 million people, which constituted a little more than 3 per cent of all employees. Only 14 years later in 2003, the private sector grew into a force of 3.4 million firms with 47 million employees; in other words, it employed approximately 12 per cent of the country's total labour force. Different units are used here in order to show that the two lines grow at about the same speed. Today, the figure has reached nearly 70 per cent. Their divergence since the early 1990s has been quite gentle, indicating that the increase of employees comes gradually more from the increase of the number of enterprises than from the increase of their size.

This brings us to the question of how large on average a private enterprise is in terms of the number of employees. Based on results

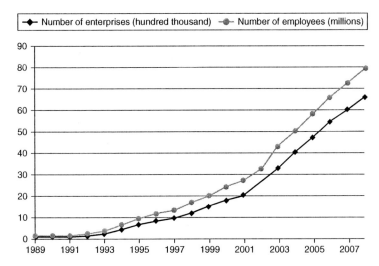

*Figure 3.1* The growth of Private enterprises in china, 1989–2008
*Source*: Annual Report of Private Enterprises in China, various issues.

from the National Survey of Private Business Owners (NSPBO, introduced in Chapter 1), Table 3.1 shows the median of employee numbers
from 1992 to 2005.[8] It was only about 30 from 1992 to 1996, and by
the end of the last century it increased considerably to 60, but it then
declined a bit afterwards. Overall, it shows that the vast majority of
private businesses in China remain very small. On the other hand, the
IQR (inter-quartile range)[9] clearly indicates that although there were
some fluctuations up to 1996, it was from 1999 that the variation of
the employment size started to increase dramatically, which was very
likely due to the increased number of very large firms (more than 1000
employees). Today, private firms in China are much more diverse than
they were initially. Indeed, the year 1999 could be seen as a landmark
for the development of private enterprises in China, in which the
Fifteenth Congress of the CCP openly recognized the private sector as
'an important component of China's socialist economy', not a dispen-
sable element at the margin of the economy anymore. Subsequently,
China's *Constitution* was amended with a clear statement protecting the
legal rights and interests of private businesses.

## A profile of the new capitalists in China[10]

Previously I argued that the private business owners that started to grow
after the launch of economic reforms were the same as the capitalists

*Table 3.1*  Median of employees with IQR among private enterprises in China, 1992–2005

| Year | Median number of employees | IQR |
|------|---------------------------|-----|
| 1992 | 30 | 50 |
| 1994 | 30 | 70 |
| 1996 | 30 | 66 |
| 1999 | 60 | 100 |
| 2001 | 60 | 127 |
| 2003 | 48 | 105 |
| 2005 | 50 | 109 |

when the CCP came to power in terms of the nature of their business and the way that business was operated. That is, today's private business owners are new capitalists. I do agree with some Chinese researchers, however, that these new capitalists have little to do with the old generation. There is nothing surprising in this if the reader has read the previous chapter – nearly all capitalist enterprises were nationalized and many old capitalists have since died. It is possible that some of them were lucky enough to survive the Great Cultural Revolution and managed to save some assets for their off-spring, which could be used for setting up a new business, but the number of such old capitalists should be extremely small.

This means that the new capitalists could only emerge from the existing social groups – workers, technicians and managers of state-owned enterprises, peasants, school and university graduates, youth returning from countryside, and so on – and they emerged in the special institutional context at the end of the 1970s and the early 1980s. Starting up a new business requires some initial conditions (start-up capital, materials, premises, and so on) and personal attributes (knowledge of the product and the market, willingness to take risk, and so on). Therefore, it will be only those who possess the needed resources and personal characteristics that stand out. It is thus sensible to expect 'the typical first generation of the new capitalist' to be a young to middle-aged man who has already had some experience of working in a particular industry or market through either working in a state or collective enterprise, or running an individual business, or dealing with related matters as a government official. Here, I shall paint a rough picture of these new capitalists.[11]

First of all, in spite of what the Communists have done to promote the position of women in the People's Republic, including Mao Zedong's well-known slogan 'Women could hold up half of the sky' and the establishment of Women's Federations, in no economic and political arena have women in the PRC even come close to being in a position to compete with their male counterparts. To set up a business is still predominantly men's business. The survey results from 1993 to 2002 indicate that among the new capitalists only 11 per cent were female. This figure increased to 14 per cent in 2004 and 2006, and this may be already a sign of historical progress given that there were almost no female businessmen in pre-1949 China.

Figure 3.2 confirms my above expectation of the new capitalists' ages, but it offers some additional and interesting information as well. In the 1990s, the median age of new capitalists was on the rise from early 40s to late 60s; there were few above the age of 60, but in the meantime a number of 'younger generation' new capitalists started to emerge from 1995. It is very likely that some of them are not only young but also 'the second generation' of new capitalists, most of which are the off-spring of the first generation capitalists as most private businesses in China are family-owned and managed. The median age became very stable around 40 from the turn of the millennium, but the differentiation of

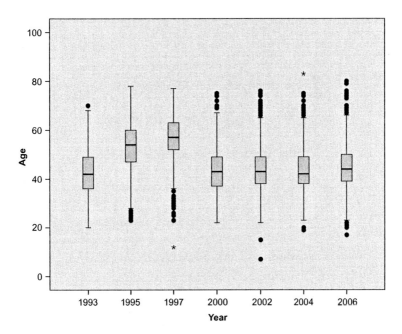

*Figure 3.2* Age of Private Business Owners in China, 1993–2006
*Source*: National Survey of Private Business Owners, 1993–2006.

the two generations becomes more notable as well. On the one hand, there were many more 'old capitalists' among the first generation (those black dots at the top), who reached their retiring age (65 and above). On the other hand and at the same time, a small number of 'teenage capitalists' started to emerge (the black dots below the boxes). It is no wonder that the transition of business from the first generation to the second or even the third generation has become a common concern among the new capitalists in China.

Given the enormous government spending on higher education and the improved quality of life, the younger generation of new capitalists should be better educated. This is indeed the case, as shown in the Figure 3.3.[12]

It is very clear that the percentages of new capitalists with only primary or secondary school educations have shrunk over the years – in 1993 they constituted nearly half (47 per cent) of all private business owners interviewed in the survey, but in 2006, they counted only about 14 per cent. The percentages for high school and professional colleges have increased, but at a mild rate. The increase of those with university

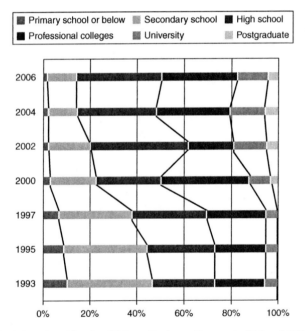

*Figure 3.3*   Educational levels of Private Business Owners in China, 1993–2006
*Source*: National Survey of Private Business Owners, 1993–2006.

and postgraduate degrees is considerable: in the 1990s, those with a university degree counted less than 5 per cent and those with a post-graduate degree less than 1 per cent, but they increased to around 14 per cent and 5 per cent, respectively, in this century. Put together, we can say that today's capitalists in China are normally middle-aged (35 to 50) and well educated men.

Administrators of NSPBO stopped including questions on the family background of private business owners since the year 2000, very likely because their respondents did not like to reveal so much personal information and the questionnaires were not very accessible. The following information is therefore confined to the years of 1993, 1995 and 1997 only.[13]

One cannot miss the message in Figure 3.4. The most common family background (measured by father's occupation) of the new capitalists in China is ordinary rural household, and the percentage increased in those years – from about a third to 45 per cent, more precisely. This was followed by cadres of various institutions (government, state enterprises, or public sector institutions, just below 20 per cent) and ordinary workers (12 to 15 per cent). Besides these, about 15 to 20 per cent of private business owners' fathers carried a professional/academic title.[14] All in all, we can identify three major family backgrounds from where the first

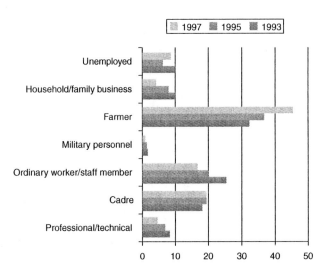

*Figure 3.4*  Father's occupation of Private Business Owners in China, 1993–7
*Source*: National Survey of Private Business Owners, 1993–7.

generation of the new capitalists in China came. The first and the largest group was those ordinary farmers, workers, and members of staff in all kinds of business organizations; the second was those families who could, one way or another, offer better support to the process of setting up a new business, including cadres of state institutions, professionals, technicians, and specialists; and the final and smallest group was those unemployed.

Would their father's occupation have any influence on the new capitalists' own occupation? In statistical terminology, how strong is the association between the new capitalists' own occupation and their father's occupation?[15] While the results do turn out to be statistically significant, I prefer to use a few graphs for presenting them.

We can draw at least three conclusions by reading these two figures for understanding the relationship between private business owners' occupations and their fathers' occupations in the mid 1990s: (1) the father's occupation did seem to be strongly correlated with the son's – for example, given the father's occupation being professional, the percentage for the son's being professional as well is the highest among all categories[17]; (2) however, there are many situations in which the son took an occupation very different from the father's – even when the father's occupation was unemployed or farmer or worker, the percentages of the sons being a professional or cadre were quite high, indicating a considerable level of upward social mobility; (3) these observations are valid for both 1993 and 1995 as the two sets of results do not differ significantly.

## Motivations of becoming a business owner

Why did these people want to set up their own businesses? The answer is not straightforward because, without examining empirical data, there is no commonsense answer. We could pose a series of hypotheses that go in either direction, that is, while some of them will lead to reasons for setting up one's own business, others point to the hurdles or risks of doing so. Institutional and social environments would be a major hurdle. It took a decade for private businesses in China to become legitimate economic organizations; even in 1993 when the first wave of the NSPBO started and Deng Xiaoping openly brushed away the debate, among the CCP leaders, over capitalism vs socialism and urged his colleagues to speed up the pace of economic reforms, there were still many restrictions on the development of the private sector. This was particularly prohibitive for those who were trying to expand their businesses quickly. On top of that, few of the general public had much respect for the 'newly rich' even though they might be jealous of the money

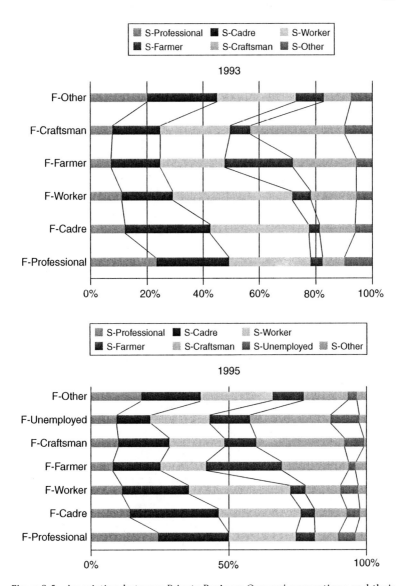

*Figure 3.5* Association between Private Business Owners' occupations and their fathers' occupations, 1993 and 1995
*Source*: National Survey of Private Business Owners, 1993 and 1995.

the rich enjoyed. For the vast majority who simply wanted to open a small businesses, market uncertainties, unpredictable state policies, difficulties in dealing with local officials, the lack of access to resources essential for opening a new business (credit, raw materials, sales channels, technology know-how, and so on) all could jeopardize the initial plan. On the other hand, setting up one's business was a very attractive option for a variety of reasons: better material life, interesting life-style, a sense of achievement, and so on, and it has been increasingly so with the slow but gradual legitimization of private enterprises over time. It is sensible to expect that to increase income would be the most common motivation before private enterprises were granted a legitimate status, and after that non-monetary motivation should prevail. The year of 1992 was a turning point since the status of private enterprises was established not only on paper but in practice as well because most state officials, realizing that their political careers were tightly connected to the performance of the private enterprises in their jurisdiction, became actively involved in promoting these enterprises.

Now let's take a look at what the data collected from NSPBO tell us about entrepreneurial motivations.[18] As I expected the motivations vary according to the year in which a private business was established,[19] I present the motivations listed by the survey organizations over the following time periods (Figure 3.6): before 1978 (prior to the economic reforms), 1978–88 (from the start of economic reforms to the 1989 protests), 1989–91 (from the 1989 protests to Deng Xiaoping's speech in his South China tour), and from 1992 to 2005 (the last year listed in the data). The number of private businesses established before the economic reforms is extremely small, confirming that the reform policies did open up a great institutional space for private businesses. The number of private enterprises decreased dramatically, however, in the three years after the 1989 incidents due to the CCP's suspicion of the role of private business owners in these incidents and the corresponding policies adopted by the Chinese government for restoring market order. Of all the motivations listed in the survey questionnaire, 'to realize one's value' turns out to be the most frequent motivation of setting up a private business for time periods, followed by 'to make use of one's abilities', which is not very different from realizing one's value. Therefore, the majority of the new capitalists, at least for those participating in the surveys, consistently claimed that they started their own business for some kind of psychological satisfaction rather than for material gain. The desire to make money (increase income) was never a dominating factor over the years. Nevertheless, these two motivations could be compatible with each

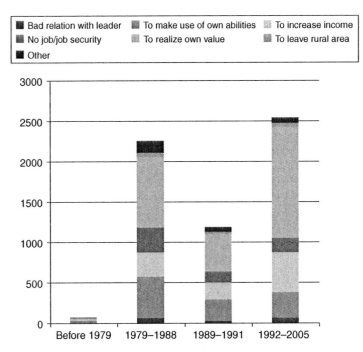

*Figure 3.6* Motivations of setting up own business by time period
*Source*: National Survey of Private Business Owners, 1993–2006.

other: earning more money and gaining a sense of achievement could be two outcomes of the same action of setting up and running one's own business; in addition, the second motivation sounds much more legitimate politically and socially. Many years ago Karl Marx pointed out that 'in so far as he [the capitalist] is capital personified, his motivating force is not the acquisition and enjoyment of use-values, but the acquisition and augmentation of exchange-values' (1977: 739). But why wouldn't the capitalist pursue both? Both use-values and exchange-values bring the same benefit to the capitalist: the joy and satisfaction of seeing one's desires and dreams being fulfilled.

Here is a good place to find out just how rich the new capitalists are. Income distribution is almost invariably skewed anywhere in the world, and this is likely to be the case among the new rich in China. As we saw above, the new capitalists in China all come from a highly egalitarian social structure. Nevertheless, in order to provide incentives for entrepreneurship, the CCP has created an institutional space in which access to valuable resources is unevenly distributed across and within different social groups. We therefore should expect a great diversity among the new capitalists in terms of their financial situation, even though on average they should be better off than most of the other social groups. Overall, data from NSPBO confirm such expectations but also show some relatively surprising results (Table 3.2). Their median income remained the same in the 1990s, picking up only at the end in 1999; it was in the first half of this century that the median income increased steadily from fifty to eighty thousand yuan. I have presented the mean income as well because the mean is sensitive to extreme values, therefore, we could gain a sense of how much the mean has been pulled by such extremely high incomes. Comparing the mean and the median, we can see that the effect of these high incomes declined over the years – the mean is about five to seven times the median in the 1990s but it comes down to about three times the median in this century. The '5 per cent trimmed mean' is the mean recalculated after eliminating the 5 per cent largest and the 5 per cent smallest incomes, which obviously is much closer to the median. Finally, the inter-quartile range remained stable in the 1990s but then increased in the 2000s. Overall, we can say that while the personal income of the new capitalists increased during the period from 1992 to 2005, their income became more unequal as well, particularly after the turn of the century.

Given that some people have found their current jobs not able to fulfil their potentials, or they have a strong desire to improve their financial situation, or they have no other means of making a living than opening up their own businesses, in short, given that they are strongly motivated to start up a new business and they know what they would do, where do they get initial capital, the most essential condition for a new businesses? Understandably, such information is quite sensitive. Besides, the survey instruments used in NSPBO for soliciting relevant information were constantly changing over the years, making

*Table 3.2*   Central tendency of personal income of Private Business Owners in China, 1992–2005 (ten thousand Chinese yuan)

|  | 1992 | 1994 | 1996 | 1999 | 2001 | 2003 | 2005 |
|---|---|---|---|---|---|---|---|
| Mean | 15.3 | 11.2 | 9.2 | 13.8 | 13.7 | 20.2 | 18.6 |
| 5% Trimmed mean | 4.8 | 4.1 | 3.7 | 5.2 | 7.9 | 11.6 | 11.0 |
| Median | 2.0 | 2.0 | 2.0 | 3.0 | 5.0 | 6.0 | 8.0 |
| IQR | 6.2 | 4.2 | 4.0 | 6.4 | 8.0 | 12.0 | 12.0 |

*Source:* National Survey of Private Business Owners, 1993–2006.

it extremely difficult to obtain a clear idea. Preliminary results (not shown here) indicate that the most common ways of obtaining the initial capital include the earnings saved from a variety of sources (salaries, profits made from previous small businesses, such as getihu or family business, or trading bonds and stocks) and money borrowed from relatives, friends, or other related persons (other personally known private business owners, colleagues, neighbours, and so on). Investments from banks and overseas investors are very rare. In short, the majority of the new capitalists have relied on an enormous but largely unregistered 'civil financial market' in China, that is, which operates outside the financial system under the control of the Chinese state.

In 2004 and 2006 surveys, private enterprises participating in NSPBO were asked whether the private enterprise came from the sales of a state or collective enterprise (gain zhi). In 2004, 18.5 per cent gave a positive answer, which then increased to 20.3 per cent in 2006. If such figures could represent the whole population of enterprises in China, around 20 per cent of today's private enterprises in China are former state or collective enterprises. Of these privatized enterprises, about 35 per cent were previously state-owned, and the rest were either urban or rural collective enterprises. Perhaps the most important question is: how were these public companies sold to private owners? The survey results show that only 26 to 28 per cent were sold through auctions open to contenders. In addition, 12 per cent of them were sold to someone under the direct instructions from the local government. Most of the times (40 to 43 per cent) the firms were simply sold to the managers, although sometimes employees were given some shares as well. In other words, there were a large number of formerly state or collective enterprise managers who were transformed into capitalists overnight. Most remarkably, the capital needed for purchasing the state or collective enterprises came mostly from personal savings (69 to 75 per cent). As the median selling price was 1.6 million Chinese yuan (2006), this means two thirds of former managers were already multimillionaires! Around 38 per cent of them reported that they borrowed money from relatives and friends, which again indicated how much money there was waiting for opportunities of investment, while bank loans counted only 31 per cent to 47 per cent (in combination with personal investment).

What did China's new capitalists do when they started their new businesses? More precisely, which industries did they enter? Did they change the sectors of business over time? Table 3.3 provides an answer. Manufacturing stands out as the most popular industry – with the exception of 2003, about 40 per cent of private enterprises were in

*Table 3.3*   Major industries of private enterprises in China, 1995–2005[20]

| Industry | 1994 | 1996 | 1999 | 2001 | 2003 | 2005 |
|---|---|---|---|---|---|---|
| Agriculture | 4.1 | 4.1 | 4.7 | 5.6 | 6.1 | 6.3 |
| Mining | 1.2 | 2.0 | 1.2 | 1.3 | 1.4 | 2.0 |
| Manufacturing | 40.4 | 42.3 | 39.8 | 38.3 | 34.9 | 43.5 |
| Power | .9 | 1.0 | 1.1 | .7 | 1.2 | 1.1 |
| Construction | 5.5 | 8.9 | 6.4 | 5.9 | 7.5 | 5.4 |
| Geology and watering | .0 | .1 | .0 | .1 | .1 | .0 |
| Transportation | 2.4 | 3.5 | 2.3 | 2.5 | 2.4 | 2.5 |
| Service and catering | 27.4 | 16.2 | 20.6 | 21.4 | 20.7 | 26.0 |
| Finance and insurance | .3 | .2 | .2 | .3 | .2 | .1 |
| Real estate | .9 | 1.4 | 3.2 | 3.8 | 3.5 | 2.5 |
| Social service | 7.2 | 5.8 | 6.2 | 5.6 | 7.5 | 3.9 |
| Hygiene and sports | .5 | .6 | 1.1 | 1.3 | 1.4 | .7 |
| Education and culture | .3 | 2.9 | 1.0 | 1.1 | .8 | .3 |
| Science and technology | 2.5 | 2.1 | 2.6 | 2.1 | 2.3 | 1.5 |
| Others | 6.5 | 9.0 | 9.6 | 9.9 | 10.0 | 4.2 |
| Valid sample size | 2787 | 1775 | 2798 | 3094 | 2831 | 3341 |

*Source:* National Survey of Private Business Owners, 1993–2006.

this industry. If we connect this finding with the median size of these enterprises that was reported previously (Table 3.1), we should have no difficulty in imagining that the most typical private enterprise in China is a small factory (less than 100 employees) manufacturing a huge variety of products. Following this industry is service and catering (except for 1996, they count about 20 to 27 per cent); again, we can imagine that these include a vast number of small shops, stores, and restaurants. Together, these small factories and shops constituted about two-thirds of all private businesses in China. Most strikingly, these percentages do not change much at all over the ten year period of the surveys, which is in great contrast to the rapid growth of the total number of private enterprises (Figure 3.1). It seems clear that while the sheer size of the private sector in China has increased dramatically, perhaps except for a few fortunate ones, the majority of private enterprises remain in labour-intensive business activities. Those high-end and capital-intensive industries, such as finance and technologies, appear to be remote to most private firms (less than 3 per cent over the years). This illustrates 'the glass door' that private business owners have been complaining about in recent years, referring to the institutional barriers that prevent them from entering a few state-controlled industries, an issue we shall come back to in Chapter 7.

# 4
# Wealth and Power, Business and Politics

All governments take the development and promotion of businesses as one of their key responsibilities, but in China the degree to which government and business are intertwined is perhaps the highest among all nations. The introduction of the market and related institutions has hardly weakened the functions of China's authoritarian government agencies. On the contrary, except for a few years of ideological confusion in the 1980s, governments at all levels have become even more powerful than they were before the economic reforms.[1] Not only have they adopted policies to encourage the growth of private businesses but have also directly engaged in the entrepreneurial process. Setting up more and bigger businesses is their business because (1) their political performance is assessed based on the number and the size of local businesses, (2) local governments run their own businesses, such as hotels and trading corporations, and (3) private businesses generate a larger and larger proportion of local revenues and consequently the officials' personal wellbeing heavily relies on the businesses (housing, bonuses, car, and so on).[2] This means that running a private business, especially a large one, has everything to do with politics. One simply cannot have access to valuable opportunities and resources desperately needed for developing a big business without establishing and maintaining close relations with government officials because all the essential resources – land, financial credit, administrative permission, and so on – are in their hands. For many large projects, although the entrepreneur may do the actual management, it is the politician who decides on what can be done and even how it should be done. Effectively, entrepreneurs and local politicians are business partners making different kinds of contributions to the same enterprises.

Such a cooperative relationship, however, has created and will continue to create a political problem for China's top leaders. Most government officials would not be content to play a supporting role in the whole process; as a matter of fact, they think themselves deserving of more rewards than the businessmen, so why should they not make use of the power in their hands to acquire a share of the profits generated from the businesses that they help set up? In other words, the political responsibility of developing local economies turns into an institutional source of corruption, which in turn will threaten the legitimacy of the CCP's ruling. It is this dilemma of developing the economy on the one hand and the erosion of political legitimacy by the interpenetration between money and power on the other that poses a serious threat to the CCP. Furthermore, the increasing diversity among the new capitalists, shown in the later part of the previous chapter, means that the government–entrepreneur relationship is heavily biased towards the big business owners. One consequence is that the actual business partnership spills over into the political arena: dealing with the most influential members of the new capitalists becomes a key, if not the most important, responsibility of the United Front Department of the CCP, and in addition to this, most of the biggest capitalists would be more than happy to join the political elite. However, does this really mean that they have successfully transformed their wealth into political power? Put differently, is there a convergence of political and business elites? In his articles and books, Bruce Dickson (2007, 2008) has offered a positive answer, but I shall show my reservations in this chapter. Please let me remind the reader of the Communists' suspicious and ambivalent attitudes towards the capitalists in the early 1950s as illustrated in Chapter 2. I do not see how the Communists in today's China can brush away their own suspicions of the new capitalists. How far would the CCP let the convergence of business and politics, or of money and political power, go? This is a serious question as the answer will shape China's political future.

## How do the new capitalists see themselves socially, economically, and politically?

To illustrate why the transformation of wealth into political power may not be as straightforward as Dickson has asserted, let's examine some of the results from the National Survey of Private Business Owners. In each of these almost biannual surveys, the selected private business owners were asked to rate their status in each of the social, economic, and political hierarchies with a ten-point scale.[3] First of all, let's take a look at the mean of each scale across the years (Figure 4.1):

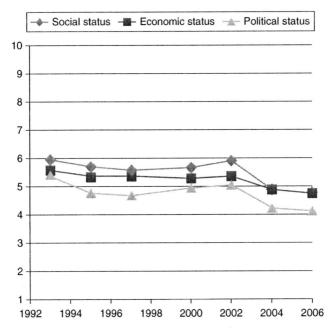

*Figure 4.1* Mean scores of self-reported social, economic, and political statuses among private business owners in China, 1993–2006
*Source*: National Survey of Private Business Owners, 1993–2006.

We can make the following observations of the survey results presented in this figure. During the thirteen years from 1993 to 2006, the overall trend was that for all three statuses, the new capitalists were less and less confident, although the change is mild. The decline of the mean for economic status has been consistent over the years. For social and political statuses, they declined from 1993 to 1997 but then picked up from 2000 and 2002; however, they declined again, and more drastically, in 2004 and 2006. The biggest differences between their social, economic and political statuses were found in 2004 and 2006 as well. The year in which private business owners thought they enjoyed the highest political status was 1993, and after several years of decline it reached another higher point in 2002. This should not be surprising if we realize that Deng Xiaoping's influential speech in his tour to the South was made in 1992 and in 2001 Jiang Zemin, then the General Secretary of the CCP, announced that private business owners could

join the CCP. The most interesting finding is that private business owners consistently thought that their social status was higher than their
economic status, which in turn was higher than their political status.
It was only by 2004 that their self-perceived economic status caught up
with their social status. *On average, they always thought that their political
status was lower than both social and economic statuses.*

The relatively considerable decline of self-confidence among the new
capitalists since 2002 is intriguing; there does not seem to be any major
events such as the publication of state policies that could explain such
decline. The only explanation that I can think of is that the samples
changed from 2004. The surveys up to 2002 were mostly administered
by social scientists through the organizational networks of the All China
Federation of Business and Commerce (ACFBC). The survey organizers then
seemed to realize that the samples could not represent the small private
enterprises because most of the selected enterprises were members of the
ACFBC, which normally accepts medium to large companies. Therefore,
from 2004 they started to draw two samples, one through the ACFBC and
the other through the National Bureau of Business and Commerce, the
government's administrative body in charge of all private businesses. Very
likely it is the inclusion of small private firms that is responsible for the
decline of the overall self-perceived statuses since 2004 because it should
be understandable that owners of small firms were politically less confident than the bigger business owners. To verify such expectation, below
I present the boxplots (Figure 4.2) that show how the self-rated political
status is associated with the size of the firm. Here, I use the total amount
of tax paid in 2005 as the measure of a firm's size because tax is directly
related to the revenue of a local government. Unsurprisingly, the distribution of such a variable is highly skewed toward the higher end; therefore,
the log is taken with base 10 in order to normalize the distribution. After
this transformation, the boxplots show a very clear connection between
the size of a private firm and its owner's political confidence: the more tax
paid, the higher the owner would believe that his or her political position
is in the Chinese society (1 is the highest and 10 the lowest).

Further, let's examine how the new capitalists perceived their political, social, and economic statuses over the years by reading the following heatmaps (Figures 4.3a, b, and c).

In these maps, a whiter colour represents a higher percentage of cases
in that particular category. For example, in all three maps, the category
with the highest percentage of cases is 5, and this is particularly so for
economic status (completely white), followed by political (two light
yellow rectangles) and social status (three light yellow and one darker

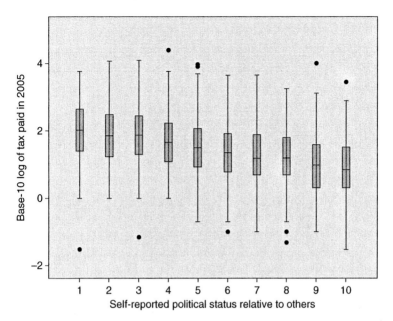

*Figure 4.2* Association between self-reported political status and tax paid by private business owners in China, 2005
*Source*: National Survey of Private Business Owners, 2006.

yellow rectangles). The map for economic status is most concentrated in the middle categories (3 to 6), and that for social status is most concentrated on relatively higher scores (2 to 5). The distribution of the scores for political status appears to be the most diffuse, indicating that private business owners were more divided politically than socially and economically. The distributions in these maps also confirm the above observation that private business owners became less confident from 2004, particularly for social and economic statuses, while such declining confidence was milder for political status.

Finally, let's examine the relationships between these scores and their changes over the years (Table 4.1). First of all, all coefficients are positive and statistically significant at the 0.01 level, indicating overall strong and positive relationships between the three self-perceived statuses. Furthermore, during the survey years from 1993 to 2006, the relationship between the scores of social and political statuses was the strongest, followed by that between economic and social statuses, with the relationship between economic and political statuses the weakest. This, again, challenges the claim that the wealth accumulated by the

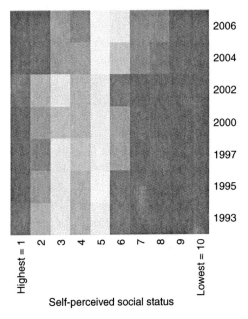

*Figure 4.3a* The distribution of the scores of self-perceived *social* status among private business owners in China, 1993–2006

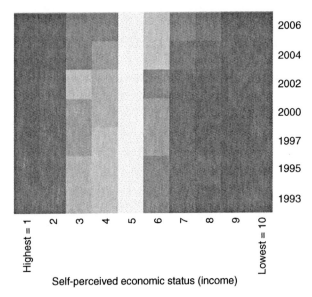

*Figure 4.3b* The distribution of the scores of self-perceived *economic* status among private business owners in China, 1993–2006

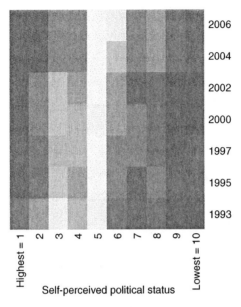

*Figure 4.3c*    The distribution of the scores of self-perceived *political* status among private business owners in China, 1993–2006
*Source*: National Survey of Private Business Owners, 1993–2006.

*Table 4.1*    Correlation coefficients of scores of self-perceived social, economic, and political statuses among private business owners in China, 1993–2006[4]

| Year | Economic and social | Social and political | Economic and political |
|------|--------------------|--------------------|-----------------------|
| 1993 | 0.56** | 0.65** | 0.39** |
| 1995 | 0.57** | 0.60** | 0.36** |
| 1997 | 0.60** | 0.63** | 0.42** |
| 2000 | 0.54** | 0.67** | 0.39** |
| 2002 | 0.57** | 0.64** | 0.42** |
| 2004 | 0.74** | 0.74** | 0.56** |
| 2006 | 0.75** | 0.75** | 0.61** |

**: $p < 0.01$.
*Source*: National Survey of Private Business Owners, 1993–2006.

new capitalists has been transformed into political status or even political power; at least, the new capitalists themselves do not think so. For each pair of relationships, the strength of correlation fluctuates up to 2002 but then all increased substantially in 2004 and 2006. Again, without further evidence to prove otherwise, I would explain such change with the more polarized samples in these two years. That is, given the fact that two samples were drawn (and then combined) from relatively big and small private enterprises, the connections between these three statuses have been reinforced – owners of big businesses enjoy a higher confidence while those small business owners' confidence has declined in all three aspects.

## Power, status, and influence

The above discussions point to a more general question: what is the relationship between power, status, and influence in the political life of private business owners in China? It seems many of the new capitalists do not feel that they have become politically more powerful with the increase of their wealth and social status. This is a fundamental question because it would then become easy for us to understand many phenomena, including those revealed above, with regard to the political participation by the new capitalists in China's Communist political system (still Communist in the sense of official ideology and no chance for political competition). In the next section I shall argue and explain why memberships of the CCP or even memberships of the People's Congress and the People's Political Consultative Assembly are *not* indicators of political power in China. Before doing that, however, I shall present an analytical framework on power, status, and influence – the three dimensions of measuring political participation in order to facilitate the analysis of the political participation by private business owners in China. This is important and necessary because researchers tend to mean different things while using the term 'political participation'. Huntington and Nelson's definition, albeit offered several decades ago (1976), still captures the core elements of the concept:

> By political participation we mean activity by private citizens designed to influence government decision-making. Participation may be individual or collective, organized or spontaneous, sustained or sporadic, peaceful or violent, legal or illegal, effective or ineffective. (p.3) [P]olitical participation may be directed toward changing decisions by current authorities, toward replacing or retaining those authorities, or toward changing or defending the existing organization of the political system and the rules of the political game. All are means of influencing the decisions and the actions of the government.
>
> (p. 6)

In short, political participation is citizens' action with an aim of influencing their government's decisions, regardless of how this is achieved. In a liberal democracy, there exist many ways of exercising such influence, such as those listed in the General Social Survey or the recent European Social Survey, including contacting members of the parliament, protesting, petitioning, publishing letters in the media, boycotting, and voting in political elections, of course. In the context of contemporary China, citizens are deprived of these liberties, which seriously limits the number of channels through which they can influence government decisions. Participation in political elections was not even listed as a question in the National Survey of Private Business Owners. As far as I know, the only information on this issue was collected in a survey organized by Kellee Tsai in 2002 to 2003. Of the 1525 responding private business owners, 30 per cent claimed to participate in elections 'actively', 12 per cent participated 'sometimes' and 14 per cent 'occasionally', with the remaining 32 per cent not participating (Tsai, 2007: 123–4). She believed that the percentage of 'actively participating' was over-reported because that was a politically correct choice in China. To a certain extent, her suspicion was confirmed by a small regional study in Guangdong in 2006 – of the 65 private enterprise owners studied, only 10 (or 16.4 per cent) had the experience of voting in an election for a People's Representative (Sun, 孙永芬, 2007: 162).

For the newly wealthy capitalists, all too often 'political participation' is understood as a matter of formality, which is very misleading as it will miss out two important points. First, formal recognition by the Chinese state does not automatically mean political influence. Second, informal ways of influencing governmental decisions will escape our attention. Here, let me elaborate further on the first point, and I shall return to the second point in Chapter 7.

I do not mean that memberships of official political organizations, such as the CCP, the Youth League, the People's Congress, and so on, will not offer opportunities to influence political decisions; they may, or they may not. Therefore, it is inappropriate to take these memberships as reliable indicators of political participation because they do not necessarily lead to influence on government's decision-making. In the West, there is nothing inappropriate to call members of the legislature 'politicians'. Nevertheless, the title 'politicians' (政治家) is rarely, if ever, used for the members of the People's Congress (PC) or the People's Political Consultative Assembly (PPCA). Perhaps there is nothing surprising here – members of the Congress, Senate, or Parliament in Western countries are professional politicians as it is a full-time career, while in China being a member of the PC or the PPCA is not a full-time job. That is not the key point yet: in China, these memberships are more an honour or a symbol of status than a powerful position. This is not to say that members do not have power; as will be shown in this and the next few chapters, they do have a limited amount of power, and some of them do influence some important decisions, but both the CCP leaders and the members themselves are clearly aware that the membership is a symbol of recognition, not real political power. For example, while being asked to comment on the increasing number of private entrepreneurs as members of the PC and PPCA,[5] Zhang Houyi (张厚义), a leading researcher on private enterprises at the Chinese Academy of Social Sciences, said: 'Some successful entrepreneurs not only make money themselves, but also contribute to society and the state through tax revenues and job creation. Therefore they deserve public respect and should be able to enter China's legislative or advisory bodies'. Nevertheless, he made another more intriguing statement: 'Social groups usually strive for more say in political issues when their economic power increases. So it is with China's private sector'.[6] It becomes very unclear whether private entrepreneurs' membership in the PC or PPCA is a recognition or reward for their economic contributions, or whether it is a result of the private entrepreneurs' striving for more influence in politics. So far there is not much evidence for the latter. It should be very clear that recruiting the capitalists into the legislative bodies is mostly a result of the CCP's overall strategy of cooperating with this newly powerful group (in the economic sense).[7]

Now let's move on to discuss the three concepts that are related to political participation: power, status, and influence. I do not think it is necessary to give a general definition of the three terms used here. My main objective here is to reveal and specify the inconsistencies between the three aspects. As Max Weber pointed out in *Economy and Society*: 'Very frequently the striving for power is also conditioned by the social honour it entails. Not all power, however, entails social honour...' (1978, vol. 2: 926). Similarly, Bertrand Russell also pointed out the limitations of economic power's influence on politics (1978: 128). In this study, in order to avoid constantly distinguishing economic power from political power, power refers to political, executive power, normally indicated by holding a leading position in government or the CCP. Note that as explained before, here, membership of the CCP is not taken as an indicator of political power. On the other hand, being the head of a town or urban residential community or its CCP secretary will be seen as political power. Status is represented by positions held in political bodies other than the government or the CCP, including notably the People's Congress, Political Consultative Assembly, and Gong Shang Lian (Federation of Business and Commerce). Finally, political influence refers to activities with an aim to influence politicians or political decision making through informal relations, institutions, or situations, such as informal conversations with political leaders at dinners. Obviously, each of these three dimensions can be measured with a continuum. However, to facilitate the discussion, here I shall focus on the simplest situation where each has only two binary values: have vs not have; therefore, there are eight possible outcomes:

*Table 4.2* Three dimensions and eight possibilities of political participation by private business owners in China

|  | Have status | | Not have status | |
| --- | --- | --- | --- | --- |
|  | Have power | Not have power | Have power | Not have power |
| Have influence | I | II | III | IV |
| Not have influence | V | VI | VII | VII |

We can be quite certain that most private business owners in China fall into the eighth category: having no influence, no status, let alone power. This is no surprise at all as such things are rare commodities. For the example of political status, out of the nearly five million private business owners at the end of 2006, a bit more than 71,000 (or 1.4 per cent) were selected to be either People's representatives or members of the Political Assembly at various levels.[8] The rate of representation for the private business owners is actually higher than those for other social groups due to the relatively small base of this wealthy group: every representative of private business represents about 18,000 fellow private business owners, while every representative from rural areas represents 960,000 people (mostly farmers and agricultural workers) and every representative from urban areas (mostly workers and employees of service sectors) represents 240,000.

The situation opposite to the eighth cell is the first, where the new capitalists have all of the three. But, are there such capitalists in China? If we employ the definitions given above, the answer has to be negative. Realistically, the best situation for them is the second situation, that is, a small number of the new capitalists enjoy certain statuses and influence but not real political power. This is truly puzzling given the fact that some prominent capitalists were selected to take up leading governmental positions in the early years of the republic, such as Rong Yiren and Sheng Pihua, who were Deputy-Mayors of Shanghai.[9] Rong climbed even as high as Vice President of China in the early 1980s. Note that these were the genuine capitalists in the eyes of the Communists. In contrast, as explained in Chapter 1, the Communists would hesitate to call today's private business owners capitalists; even further, Jiang Zemin argued that they were 'labourers', and some social scientists in China actually assert that these wealthy people are part of 'the People'.[10] In addition, as shown above, more than one-third of today's capitalists are members of the CCP.

In short, they are expected to be closer to the CCP than an average person in China, but why have they been treated much less favourably than those old capitalists several decades ago? As the fundamental difference between them and the ordinary people at large is the money in their hands, one cannot help but think that the CCP is worried over the potential that this money could one day be used for actions against it. A rare piece of evidence that could confirm this 'status without power theory' is a document published by the Government of Guangdong in 2008, in which the government would grant private business owners the following: status in society, glory in politics, and benefits in business.[11] So far the highest status allocated to the new capitalists is Vice Chairman of provincial Political Assembly (zheng xie), one in Zhejiang and the other in Chongqing.

It would not be fair to assert that People's Representatives and members of the Political Assembly have no influence on political decision making at all or that these organizations are purely 'rubber stamps'. That would be a sign of ignorance of today's politics in China. These new capitalists do have some political powers, albeit not as binding as the political powers are in a strong democracy, such as the power of inspecting government works, examining budgets, even dismissing the governors. Institutionally, these powers are there for them to use. In reality, however, it is very difficult to use these powers because every political organization, including People's Congress and Political Assembly, is under the control of the CCP, which is why I would call China's political system 'organizational corporatism'. That there are more private business owners becoming members of these organizations will not change such organizational structure. As the new capitalists constitute only a small percentage of all members in these political organizations, the membership means no more than a status or a 'glorious' title, which has further diluted the power that is supposed to be used in addition to the titles. That is, their use of power is most often indicated by addressing some very specific and usually business-related issues rather than major political problems; they speak as business representatives, not politicians. This is why they appear to be helpless when it comes to a few fundamental problems, such as market entrance to certain industries, rent-seeking behaviours by local politicians, and difficulties in obtaining bank loans. These are not purely business or economic problems; as their solutions require the use of political power, they are political problems. The deadlock of solving these problems confirms that what the private business political representatives have is little more than status. As a Chairman of a local Federation of Business and Commerce (gong shang lian) said:

> What we do is process information. We pass the information to the leaders and see if they pay any serious attention. Whether they pay any attention or whether they want to do anything about the information is beyond our responsibility; that's the job for the Party and the government; our job is to supply the information.
>
> (Wang, Xiaoyan, 2007: 106)

Some Chinese academics have pointed out that most private business owners participate in politics mostly for promoting their own economic interests, suggesting that they should have higher and nobler aims. But how could they, given the current political system? It is very difficult to imagine that no private business owners have any higher and nobler political objectives; especially among those very successful ones, whose number is surely beyond tens of thousands, there must be some, even only a small percentage of these tens of thousands, who do have political ambitions or at least would like to make some changes to the current political system. Obviously, it is the potential unbearable costs that put them off.

The desire of pursuing power rather than being satisfied simply with status refers to the third and the seventh situations in Table 4.2; that is, some of the new capitalists have managed to obtain real political power. However, again due to the constraining political environment, this can only be achieved at very low levels. Although power does not always mean influence on crucial policy decision making, the correlation between the two is expected to be very high; therefore, the seventh situation should have a very small number of observations. The third situation, where private business owners were selected to take a leading position in local governments (usually at the county or xian level), is relatively new; the highest level that they could reach is normally 'chu' (the second from the bottom of the administrative hierarchy). As in most cases the level of position is connected to the amount of payment to the local revenue, this is the most explicit transfer of financial wealth into political power.[12] Officially, such direct exchange between power and money is prohibited, of course. Nevertheless, there is no alternative if one wants to turn the money at hand into political power. At an even lower level, some new capitalists have actively participated in elections for leaderships of villages and towns. I shall discuss this topic separately in Chapter 8.

Let's take a look at the remaining situations in Table 4.2. The fifth situation is not realistic – it is almost impossible that a private business owner has both status and power but has no influence at all. We have discussed the sixth situation above, that is, some private business owners have status but no power and influence, such as the leader of Federation of Business and Commerce quoted above. Their lack of power and influence explains why they rarely draw any attention from the media or academic research in China.

The fourth situation should draw a lot of attention but its very covert nature means it is very difficult to confirm its scale and scope. These are the private business owners who have neither status nor power but have considerable influence on local political leaders. The lack of official status or powerful position means that the influence must have been exercised via informal if not always illegal manners. This does not mean that there are no officially acceptable ways of having political influence. Such officially acceptable ways include being invited to attend a meeting with local leaders, having a conversation with a top political leader while the leader is visiting (actually inspecting) the business, or going on a business trip with a political leader. The reason that they could be close to the political leaders is because doing business is one of the most important tasks for all local leaders in China (Walder, 1995). Local GDP is one of the indicators measuring the performance of each local leader, and local economic development also means improvements of their personal well-being; therefore, they have every motivation to keep the most influential private business owners as part of their inner circles. Consequently, these capitalists could exercise influence on the politicians without having to carry any political titles. Nevertheless, for those not so influential private business owners, when they want to influence the politicians in a way that favours their business interests, they would have to go through other channels, most of which are covert if not illegal. In such situation, the only resources at their disposal are money and perhaps personal connections. For example, Zhou Lijiang reported several instances of such 'sinister intervention into politics' (2006: 239–41). The sugar-coated bullets and bombs are coming back! How to reduce corruption – it seems almost impossible to completely eliminate it – while still making local officials work hard to develop local economies? It should be noted, however, that the sinister intervention exists because there are few other legitimate and effective ways of influencing politics.

How should we explain the variation of the situations discussed above? We can find our explanation in the ways in which the Chinese state and the new capitalists interact with each other strategically. What the Chinese state has been trying to achieve is to make use of the entrepreneurial energy of the new capitalists so that it could consolidate its political legitimacy while in the meantime preventing the new capitalists from developing into a political adversary. To achieve this, the political tactic is 'organizational corporatism', that is, to absorb as many new capitalists, especially the influential ones, into a variety of organizations that are under the control of the state. The political statuses allocated to some private business owners represent such a tactic. Few of these statuses, no matter how high-profile they may appear to be, contain elements of real political power, because of the state's worry over these new capitalists' political potential. The effect of such tactics on the behavioural strategies of the new capitalists is to reinforce their pursuit of wealth without venturing into any political arena – to live a wealthy life is their ultimate goal of life anyway and to be politically humble rather than aggressive would help them achieve such a goal. In short, to make money is the common interest shared by the Chinese state and the new capitalists while to become politically active is something the State would strongly discourage and the capitalists do not want to bother with. Therefore, given politics is well separated from business, or in other words, there are no serious political barriers to doing business, the Communist state and the new capitalists can maintain a peaceful and mostly economical relationship while the state keeps an eye on the capitalists. However, even if this is sustainable for most situations and for a long run, there will still remain a small number of cases where some capitalists would find alternatives to the current political arrangements; that is, they want to exercise political influence by going beyond the current system. We shall see some examples later in this book.

The relationships between political power, social status and money will be a problem for the Communist leaders in many years to come. They have not developed, at least not openly, a set of coherent and sustainable principles for coping with the possible consequences arising out of the imbalance between political and monetary powers. No societies have set up an institutional framework in which the transfer between power and money is completely just, that is, free from any suspicion of injustice. The question is whether the state has tried to create a system in which the chance of achieving justice has been maximized, at least to the extent that citizens and outside observers have been convinced it is so.

In light of the above discussion, I shall answer these two questions by examining the affiliations of the new capitalists with the political parties in China, particularly the CCP. Then I shall shift the focus of my analysis to those capitalists that have some formal connections to the Communist state, that is, who have been selected to join the political elite at both national and local levels. Finally, I shall examine some informal connections between the new capitalists and the Communist state, which the former could make use of and consequently have influence on the latter.

## What are the political identities of the new capitalists?

In theory, CCP membership should be seen as a form of political participation in China because the CCP is the sole ruling political party. However, this makes sense only under the assumption that the membership means effective influence on any political decision making, which obviously does not hold for most rank and file members of the party. For most members, the membership only means attending meetings to learn the party policies, which they have no say in at all, and being obliged to make contributions in any event organized by the CCP. Ironically, if a private business owner does want to participate in politics in China, he or she would have a better chance if he or she is *not* a member of the CCP but a member of a 'democratic party' or a section of the People's Political Consultative Assembly (PPCA). This is so simply because the CCP has a much larger membership (just over eight million by 2010) and consequently the probability of being selected to be a People's Representative or a delegate of is much smaller than in a democratic party that usually has a much smaller membership. The potential benefit that the membership of the CCP brings is a higher chance of being selected into a government or party committee. The irony is that membership of the committee is the executive or ruling power itself rather than political participation. All these indicate that in China you cannot *participate* in politics – either you are ruling or you are ruled, but you cannot *influence* politics without being part of the ruling party.

Such irony is at the root of the row over whether private business owners should be allowed to join the CCP – among some influential

CCP leaders, who may not be at the very top, there is always a serious concern about the possibility that the wealth of the new capitalists will be eventually turned into real political power, that is, some of them become top government or party leaders with genuine executive power. This small group of CCP members published their views in the magazine *The Pursuit of Truth* (zhen li de zhui qiu), which was ordered to close down. Nevertheless, even after Jiang Zemin made the announcement that private business owners could join the CCP in July 2001, *The People's Daily*, the CCP official newspaper, dubbed 'the Party's throat and tongue', declared on 17 September 2001 that: 'We permit the wealthy individuals in the new social strata to join the Party, but that does not mean that we will open our door without any disciplines.' Wang Changjiang, a professor at CCP's Party School, said in 2002 that: 'Permitting private business owners to join the Party is not equivalent to letting anyone of them to join' (the 1st issue of《中国党政干部论坛》, *Forum of Party and Government Officials*). No one has made the point more bluntly than Liu Dehou, who said: 'The legal right of political participation by private business owners is not equivalent to "political ruling power"' (Preface to Ao Daiya, 2005: 5). It is no wonder that the new capitalists are feeling 'a glass ceiling of political influence' – a private business owner in Chengdu was pessimistic about their potential political future: 'The CCP is a party for the poor, therefore, they shall never pay any real respect to the businessmen, even though Jian Zemin tried to turn it into "an all-people party"' (Tsai, 2007: 127).

Results from NSPBO clearly suggest that either the resentment of recruiting the new capitalists into the CCP among the 'conservative' members or the distrust of CCP's sincerity of recruiting them among the new capitalists themselves has failed to catch up with the reality that the percentage of CCP members among the capitalists has been on the rise from 13 per cent in 1993 to more than 40 per cent in 2006 (Table 4.3).

In contrast, the percentage of those being members of one of the eight 'democratic political parties' has remained very stable from 5 per

*Table 4.3* The political identity of private business owners in China, 1993–2006

|  | 1993 | 1995 | 1997 | 2000 | 2002 | 2004 | 2006 |
|---|---|---|---|---|---|---|---|
| % CCP | 13.1 | 17.0 | 23.6 | 19.9 | 30.2 | 34.6 | 40.5 |
| % democratic party | 6.5 | 4.9 | 4.7 | 6.7 | 5.7 | 6.2 | 5.0 |
| Valid N | 1440 | 2869 | 1496 | 3059 | 3222 | 2758 | 3446 |

*Source:* National Survey of Private Business Owners, 1993–2006.

cent to 6.5 per cent, obviously resulting from the CCP's suppression of these parties' expansion. The exception is 2000, when the percentage of CCP members dropped to 20 per cent from the previous year's nearly 24 per cent, while that of democratic party members increased by two percentage points. Overall, however, these results suggest that the CCP has made a great effort to recruit these new capitalists while in the meantime preventing them from joining other political parties even though these parties have no chance of competing with the CCP. While this may be the case, we should realize that the increase may be attributed to the increase of private enterprises that were transformed from former state or collective ones, which I presented in the previous chapter. It is very likely that owners of such enterprises were already members of the CCP before the transformation. This means that the CCP's recruiting effort is only partly responsible for the increase of percentages of CCP members among private business owners.

Another caution against reading too much into the above results is that the percentage of private business owners among all CCP members remains tiny; the CCP remains a party of government and military personnel, not even a party of the workers and the farmers (see Chapter 8 for details). In addition, most ordinary CCP members are clearly aware that the membership does not help at all, perhaps even seeing the membership as a burden, which is why there have been many 'three-no members' (not having organizational connections, not paying party membership, and not participating in party activities), 'pocket members' (members who keep their party certificate in their pocket without showing it to the local party branch), or 'invisible members' (Chen, Jiaxi, 2007: 100–1).[13]

## Participation or control? Communist party committees in capitalist firms

Related to the political identity of the new capitalists is the establishment of a Chinese Communist Party committee in their own firms. With the growth of private enterprises and consequently the increasing number of CCP members working in these enterprises, either as employers or employees, the CCP leaders set their Department of Organization and Department of United Front the task of developing an organizational structure for keeping control of these members. In September 2000, CCP's Department of Organizations issued an official memorandum urging local party committees to set up party cells in private enterprises.[14] In August 2003, the Department organized a conference with a specific aim of promoting the establishment of party cells in private enterprises; they even required that every private enterprise with more than 50 employees have CCP members and every enterprise with three or more CCP members or more than 100 employees have a committee.[15] For the business owners, setting up such a committee could lead to some kind of political participation although the mechanisms might not be straightforward: the committee could serve as an additional bridge between the private business and the local party officials, which in turn offers potential opportunities to influence local leaders that private enterprises without such a committee would have no access to. This does not come without any price, however. Unless the committee is under his or her control, the business owner may not welcome such an 'arrangement' even though the pressure to conform could be unbearably high. In the end, whether to establish such committee or not and if yes who would control it becomes a game of gaining the upper hand over the committee.

Given the above discussion, we would expect to see a relatively considerable increase of the percentage of private enterprises with a CCP committee from 2000. The results from NSPBO confirm such expectation (Table 4.4):

*Table 4.4*  Percentage of private businesses with a CCP committee, 1993–2006[16]

|         | 1993 | 1995 | 2000 | 2002 | 2004 | 2006 |
|---------|------|------|------|------|------|------|
| %       | 4.0  | 7.0  | 17.4 | 27.4 | 30.0 | 34.8 |
| Valid N | 1440 | 2866 | 3027 | 3255 | 2460 | 3240 |

*Source:* National Survey of Private Business Owners, 1993–2006.

The speed of the spread of Communist party committees across private enterprises is no less remarkable than that of China's economic growth. In 1993, only 4 per cent had a CCP committee; ten years later, it increased to 30 per cent in 2004 and more than one in three in 2006! If the reader compares the numbers in this table with those in the previous one (Table 4.3), you would notice that they are quite close, especially for 2000 and onwards. Therefore, it is sensible to hypothesize that the rapid establishment of CCP committees in private enterprises may be largely due to the increasing percentage of Communist business owners. In other words, we would expect a strong association between a private business owner's membership of the CCP and the existence of a CCP committee in the business. The appropriate statistics for measuring the strength of such association is the odds ratio, with the integer one suggesting no association at all and any other value showing association, the further away from one the stronger the association. Table 4.5 presents the odds ratios over the years:

*Table 4.5*   Odds ratio for the association between CCP membership and having a CCP committee in private enterprises, 1993–2006

|            | 1993 | 1995 | 2000 | 2002 | 2004 | 2006 |
|------------|------|------|------|------|------|------|
| Odds ratio | 5.4  | 5.0  | 4.6  | 4.5  | 4.4  | 4.4  |
| Valid N    | 1440 | 2866 | 3017 | 3219 | 2287 | 2949 |

*Source:* National Survey of Private Business Owners, 1993–2006.

These results suggest that the association between being a member of the CCP and having a CCP committee has been very strong from 1993 to 2006. The odds of CCP members having a committee is four to five times the odds of non-CCP members; in other words, if the private business owner is a member of the CCP, then it is far more likely that there will be a CCP committee in that business. Given this finding, turning more private business owners into members of the CCP would indeed be a very effective way of enhancing the CCP's control over these firms by establishing party cells in them.

As shown above, the CCP's Department of Organizations made a tight connection between the number of employees and the urgency (to them) of setting up a party cell in private firms, so let's see if the data lend any evidence of their success. To do this, I have constructed a binary logistic regression model with the log odds of having a CCP committee as the response variable and CCP membership and the natural logarithm of employee number as the two explanatory variables (Table 4.6). A separate model is produced for 1995 and 2006 in order to explore the possible change before and after the Department of Organization's campaign:

*Table 4.6*   Binary logistic regression model of having a CCP committee in private businesses in China, 1995 and 2006

|                | Coefficient with significance | | Odds ratio | | 95% confidence interval for the odds ratio | |
|----------------|--------|--------|--------|--------|------------|------------|
|                | 1995   | 2006   | 1995   | 2006   | 1995       | 2006       |
| CCP membership | 1.7*** | 1.6*** | 5.3*** | 5.0*** | (3.8, 7.4) | (4.2, 6.0) |
| ln(employees)  | 0.9*** | 0.8*** | 2.5*** | 2.2*** | (2.2, 2.9) | (2.0, 2.4) |
| Constant       | −7.0   | −4.7   |        |        |            |            |

***: $p < 0.001$.
*Source:* National Survey of Private Business Owners, 1993 – 2006.

While the results clearly show the significant contributions by CCP membership and the number of employees towards the likelihood of establishing a CCP committee in a private enterprise, there is little change in the eleven years from 1995 to 2006. The CCP's Department of Organizations seems to have drummed up a practice that has already been in operation over the years.

## Honour and status without power: the new capitalists in political institutions

In the first two chapters I focused on the tension between the CCP's ideological commitment and the demand to solve practical problems for understanding the party's changing strategies in dealing with the old capitalists. This tension has been reflected at the organizational level in the way that the CCP allocated political positions among the capitalists. On the one hand, the CCP will put its own party members in the most powerful positions, while on the other hand, partly as a gesture of recognizing the capitalists' economic influence and their contributions to the new regime, partly as a symbol of fulfilling the promise of establishing a coalition government, and partly as a way of containing the non-Communist political forces, the CCP must create an organizational mechanism for reconciling all these demands. The solution is to put some of the most prominent capitalists in positions of great honour and status but without effective political power, and this policy was implemented at both national and regional levels. The most well-known example is of course, Rong Yiren, who was selected as one of the deputy Majors of Shanghai in 1957, one of the deputy Ministers of Textile Industries in 1959, one of the Vice Chairmen of the People's Political Consultative Assembly in 1981, and finally one of the Vice Chairmen of the People's Republic in 1993. The same method has been employed for dealing with the new capitalists. However, so far, none of them has broken Rong's record; the highest position two of them have reached is Vice Chairman of a provincial Political Consultative Assembly (Zhejiang and Chongqing).

The level of the positions is not so much our concern as it will not change their symbolic nature. What I would like to study here is who among the new capitalists have been selected into these positions – the number of these positions is highly limited – and what we can learn from the rationale of the selection process for understanding China's political development. Researchers designing NSPBO started to include questions on memberships of the People's Congress (PC) and the People's Political Consultative Assembly (PPCA) from 1995 (this was not

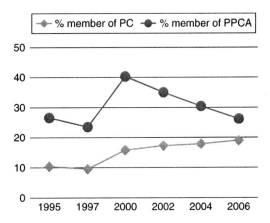

*Figure 4.4*   Respective percentages of members of the PC and the PPCA among private business owners in China, 1995–2006.[17]

an important issue yet in 1993). Figure 4.4 shows how the percentage of members of the PC and of the PPCA, respectively, changed in the survey years:

It is clear that it is more difficult to become a member of the People's Congress, nominally 'the most powerful institution' in China with many important responsibilities of legislation, and the percentage increased only mildly over the years from 10 to 20 per cent. It is difficult to interpret the fluctuation of the percentage for the PPCA, although it kept falling from 2000; it is very likely the figure was heavily influenced by the negotiations between the CCP leaders and the leaders of the Association of Business and Commerce who have the duty of making recommendations.

Now let's take a look at the administrative level of the memberships (Figure 4.5).

Again, over the years from 1995 to 2006, the percentages of membership of the PC are much more stable than those of the PPCA (the categories of District and Township were not included in the 1995 survey), which is very likely due to a much stricter quota system for selecting members of the People's Congress. For membership of the PPCA, there is an enormous increase at the township level and decrease at the county, distribute and provincial levels. This is intriguing as I am not aware of anything that might be responsible for a dramatic change. There must have been an internal policy with regards to the composition of private business owners as members of the PPCA at different

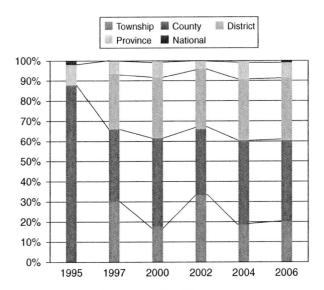

*Figure 4.5a* Level of membership of the PC among private business owner members, 1995–2006

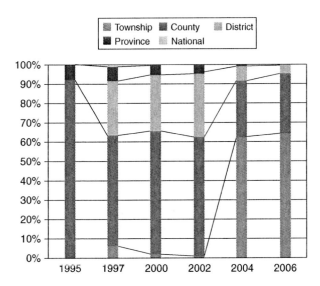

*Figure 4.5b* Level of membership of the PPCA among private business owner members, 1995–2006

administrative levels. Why did the CCP suddenly move many private business owner members of the PPCA to the township level? This is a question that will have to be answered in the future when relevant information is available.

Now let's move on to find out what kind of private business owners have been selected to join the People's Congress and, if they were selected, who were selected to a higher level. Here, I cannot rely on simple graphs anymore but must employ a statistical model for teasing out the contributing factors to the membership. To keep things as simple as possible, firstly I shall analyse only the data collected in 2006, and secondly I shall keep the number of contributing factors ('explanatory variables' in statistical terminology) as small as possible. The target (or response) variable is the membership of the People's Congress, which has six values: not a member (0), township (1), county (2), district (3), province (4), and nation (5). Five explanatory variables are included in the model:[18]

1. Education to indicate the human capital of the private business owner, with values being primary, lower middle school, higher middle school, college, university, and postgraduate; education should be an essential requirement for being a member of the PC as the members are expected to draft, interpret and implement a large number of legal issues;
2. CCP membership (yes or no) to see if it helps as a political asset;
3. The amount of donations to charities as a sign of generosity and a source of social reputation; as the distribution is highly skewed, a natural logarithm is taken, after which the distribution becomes much closer to normality;
4. One indicator of economic contributions to the local economy: the amount of tax paid in 2005; again, the natural log is taken;
5. Natural logarithm of total number of employees in 2005.

With the variables specified, the results of an ordinal multi-category logistic regression model are presented (Table 4.7) in overleaf.

Two surprising findings come out of this model. First, education does not appear to be a statistically significant factor at all levels; in other words, there is no sufficient evidence from the data showing that the educational level of a private business owner has an effect on his or her chance of being selected to be a member of the People's Congress. Perhaps this is not so surprising for two reasons: the members are not professional politicians, and only attend one or two meetings each year,

*Table 4.7* Ordinal logistic regression of membership of People's Congress in China, 2006

| Explanatory variable | Estimate | 95% confidence interval | |
|---|---|---|---|
| Ln(donation) | 0.29*** | 0.22 | 0.36 |
| Ln(tax) | 0.06 | –.02 | 0.14 |
| Ln(employee) | 0.32*** | 0.22 | 0.42 |
| Not CCP member | –0.72*** | –0.92 | –0.51 |
| CCP member | 0 (reference) | | |
| Primary | 0.74 | –0.15 | 1.64 |
| Lower middle school | 0.27 | –0.28 | 0.81 |
| Higher middle school | 0.36 | –0.11 | 0.83 |
| College | 0.32 | –0.15 | 0.79 |
| University | 0.27 | –0.24 | 0.79 |
| Postgraduate | 0 (reference) | | |

–2log Likelihood = 3550.72 (df = 9, $p < 0.001$).
*: $p < 0.001$.
*Source:* National Survey of Private Business Owners, 2006.

leaving all the hard work of drafting legal documents to professionals, and even when they do need to write anything, there is a team of secretaries prepared for the task. Another factor that was expected to be statistically significant but turned out not to be so is the tax paid. In contrast, the amount of donations and the number of employees are both highly significant. It seems when it comes to selecting a private business owner into the People's Congress, local CCP leaders are more concerned with the owners' contributions to public projects and employment than the direct contribution to local revenues. It is likely that these are the two criteria in the local leaders' minds when they were sifting through the profiles of the candidates – these two economic contributions carry more political weight than pure money does.

# 5
# Between the Communist State and Private Enterprises: Private Business Associations

The previous chapter leads us to make the following observation: a distinctive feature of political participation of the new capitalists in China is that it is largely an individual matter. Being selected to join the People's Congress (PA) or the People's Political Consultative Assembly (PPCA) is a symbol of the state's recognition of the selected business owner's individual contribution. Just like some of the most influential old capitalists in the 1940s (the reader may want to go back to Chapter 2 for details), these Communist state's favourite new capitalists do not represent their social group (not to use the word 'class') because they do not act as politicians defending and expanding the interests of the people like themselves; if the old capitalists did not do so during the wars, how could the new capitalists do so now under such a heavy-handed state! An important reason that China remains a Communist regime is the fact that the state monopolizes the power of distributing opportunities to participate in political decision-making across all social groups. Any mobilization of collective action will therefore disturb the nerves of state officials, which is why 'maintaining stability' (wei wen) is at the top of the list of responsibilities for local leaders. 'Civil organizations' – clubs, associations, and many other types of organizations – have mushroomed in the past two decades,[1] but none are of political nature, at least not openly or officially. In addition, some of the important organizations are one way or another under the control or the surveillance of the state, including those of private business owners: the association of getihu, the association of private business owners, All-China Association of Business and Commerce, and many industry-specific organizations that we shall study in this chapter. In short, 'Who should I represent?' becomes a very difficult question for those new capitalists who have become members of the PC or PPCA. On the one hand, they *are* expected to represent the interests of their fellow capitalists; this is particularly so for the PPCA since this institution is composed of people from different sections, which they call 'jie bie', of the society. On the other hand, these elite capitalists find it politically incorrect if they explicitly and loudly speak for private business owners not only because they would be wary of slipping into the dangerous territory of politics but also because they are 'People's' representatives, meaning they are supposed to speak for all the people rather than business owners alone. In practice, however, this question is rarely if ever asked, let alone properly answered.

In this chapter I shall employ this approach of focusing on the tension between economic contributions and political status for understanding the situation of business associations of private enterprises. I shall firstly introduce the types of these associations and discuss their development in China so as to set up the context for the following discussions. Then I point out that a key principle both the Chinese state and the associations have been following is 'keep business to business', that is, maximizing the economic benefits of organizing business associations while staying away from potential political contention at the same time. Drawing on data collected from NSPBO, official documents, and fieldwork, I illustrate the CCP's strategy of containing these associations and private entrepreneurs' desires and efforts to gain more autonomy in the business arena. In the end I characterize such a state–business relationship as 'organizational corporatism', pointing out that such a give-and-take type of arrangement will sooner or later run into its end. It demands greater wisdom, courage, and power from the top leaders of the CCP to replace the United Front with new institutions in order to move beyond the current system.

## Types of business associations and their relations with the Chinese state

Research on business associations in China is usually carried out under the general concern with the growth of civil society against the dominating party-state. Let me make it clear from the outset that I will not infer whether the growth of business associations can be taken as signs of civil society. I believe that this umbrella concept is not effective in describing the complex situations in a large country such as China and therefore is bound to produce more controversy and confusion than knowledge and insights. I agree with Nevitt in shifting our analytical focus away from civil society to the existing institutions of the state–society relations (1996: 37). In addition, inference about civil society is often made with one type of associations or associations in one locality, but with more business associations having emerged and diversified since the 1980s, the state–society interactions also have manifested themselves in different ways, rendering a universal concept unsuitable to cover the variety of situations.

In this section I discuss three types of business associations: (1) All China Federation of Industries and Commerce (ACFIC, *quan guo gong shang lian*, established in 1953); (2) industrial associations that were transformed from governmental ministries, bureaus, and agents, and (3) business associations that are in administrative terms much more detached from the government although that does not mean they have no connections with the government. In the Chinese literature of business associations (see Jia et al., 2004, for example), industrial associations (*hang ye xie hui*) are usually distinguished from business associations (*shang hui*), with the former referring to those established by the government and mostly consisting of state-owned-enterprises (SOEs) and the latter mostly set up by local government or firms themselves with a large proportion of private enterprise members and more autonomy to manage themselves. The State Council has issued official documents requesting that all government agents be decoupled from business associations.[2] Nevertheless, as we shall see below, many associations see connections to the government as an advantage, and those without such connections have complained about suffering from institutional discrimination. We now turn to how each type of business association is connected to the Chinese state.

### The Janus-faced ACFIC

During the first half the twentieth century, self-initiated-and-managed business associations with voluntary memberships did exist in China and for some time even enjoyed a lively growth.[3] When the CCP took power in 1949, the new government understood that they must keep the domestic capitalist enterprises up and running in order to maintain stable economic and social orders. As shown in Chapter 2, such a temporarily symbiotic, if not always friendly, relationship between the Communist state and the capitalist firms didn't last for long. Soon after the CCP believed that the national economy was mostly under its control, it launched the campaign to nationalize the capitalist firms into the newly established socialist and planned economy, and the whole campaign was completed in merely three years (1953–6). With the members gone, the business associations disappeared automatically. Even the most prominent of them, the ACFIC, being one of the non-Communist political groups of the PPCA (*zhen xie*), couldn't survive the non-stop waves of political campaigns and movements, with the Great Proletariat Cultural Revolution being the most disastrous.

The most important contribution Deng Xiaoping made to China was to shift the nation's attention from political campaigns to economic reconstruction. In 1979, he met the remaining top business leaders and encouraged them to expand their businesses. Soon afterwards, the ACFIC was resumed and held a national congress. Among all business associations in China, the ACFIC is unique as politically the most powerful. It not only has the largest number of members but also most of its members enjoy leadership and influence in their region or industry. Nevertheless, political prominence does not automatically come with autonomy – the ACFIC seems to have no choice but to take up multiple identities and functions (hence Janus-faced, to use Margaret Pearson's (1994) term although she was studying associations of foreign firms in China). Although recognized as a 'people's organization' under the leadership of the CCP, a document issued by the CCP's Central Committee in 1991 dictated that the ACFIC was 'the bridge connecting the Party and the Government with the people in the non-state economic sectors' and 'the aid of the Government for administrating the non-state economy'. In other words, it is 'non-governmental civil business chamber in China' (Huang, Mengfu, 2005: 3–4), representing the interests of the various types of non-state businesses (individual businesses, partnerships, limited and share-holding firms, all constituting a bit more than 70 per cent of all ACFIC members), while in the meantime helping the CCP keep them under control. It is only possible for one organization to fulfil the dual demands when there are no conflicts between the two sides. How the ACFIC manages to fulfil its essentially conflicting functions will be one of the issues we shall look at in the next section.

Beyond these political requirements, however, as Kennedy correctly points out, 'the Chinese government has never had a fully articulated and coordinated strategy' (2005: 29). One example is the lack of a law of business associations. This is puzzling since it should not be difficult to create such law; as a matter of fact, the State Council on Economic Development and Reforms (*fa gai wei*) started the legislature process years ago but later the task was suspended for reasons unknown to the general public, while some Chinese researchers believe it has been restarted but it will take at least several years for the law to be created, passed, and enforced in practice (Yu, Hui, 2008). Very likely this is an indication that the state has not come up with an acceptable solution to the dilemma of granting the civil right of setting up civil associations on the one hand and controlling them on the other. In the meantime, different governments and associations are creating their own ways of coping with the restraining regulations, a good example of 'institutional holes' (Yang, 2004, 2007) where ambiguous and contradictory institutional rules create opportunities, sometimes involuntarily, for entrepreneurs and organizations to make use of them for their own purposes.

## Government-sponsored business associations

From the early 1980s the Chinese government started to streamline the state-owned enterprises (SOEs): gradually putting most of them into the market to let them survive on their own and opening most of the industries to non-state enterprises to allow them to compete with SOEs. With so many SOEs operating according to market principles, the functions of many government ministries and agents – especially those set up for administering a particular industry, such as the Ministry of the Textile Industries – became unnecessary, providing the central government with an opportunity to shake off the financial burdens of supporting them. The plan was to let the industries and the firms administer themselves. This was not feasible, however, at least for a short period of time because on the one hand, no administering organizations existed yet that could take over the responsibilities and on other hand, the government must find new employment opportunities for those who worked for the ministries or bureaus. A sensible solution was to transform the governmental agents into industrial associations; for example, the Ministry of Light Industries was reorganized into the National Association of Light Industries. Clearly, these associations are far from 'civil organizations' as they were initiated by the government and are dependent on the state in terms of finance and personnel. For many years, they had little autonomy to manage their own matters, but with their connections with the government gradually becoming tenuous, some of them have started to work independently (Jia, Xinjin et al., 2004, Chapters 5 and 6). Although they remain under the direct control of the government, it is not of much use to take them as examples of state corporatism since they do not tend to work independently in the first place. Therefore, in this chapter I shall not discuss this type of association any further as the concern of this chapter is with business associations of the private enterprises.[4]

## Bottom-up business associations

For the Chinese state, a key challenge is to keep the whole nation under control while gingerly opening up as large an institutional space as it can in order to release the productive energies that have been suppressed for too long. This institutional space has nurtured the growth of many non-state enterprises (town-and-village enterprises or TVEs, private enterprises, foreign firms, and joint-ventures) and civil organizations (arts and crafts, technology, literature, and so on). Given the number of private enterprises growing from about ten thousand to more than a few million in just 35 years, it may be natural to expect a similar growth of business associations initiated by private entrepreneurs. However, this is actually not the case. It was only in 1997, almost 20 years after the start of economic reforms that the Economy and Trade Council picked up four cities in the south (Shanghai, Wenzhou, Xiamen and Guangzhou) for exploring ways of administering 'civil business associations'. So far these associations seem to constitute only a minority of all business and industrial associations[5] – most of the new business associations have come under the umbrella of the ACFIC.

Clearly, the importance of this type of association does not come from their number but from their relative detachment to the state – some were initiated by private business owners, others by local officials with the collaboration of business owners. Tao Qing (陶庆, 2008) conducted an ethnographic study of a business association that was completely initiated and managed by entrepreneurs from outside the local area (we may call them 'migrant entrepreneurs'). They came together naturally for the purpose of sharing feelings (normally bad ones), information, and moral support. This association was never formally recognized by the local government because it did not have a sponsor – it could not have one because it consisted of local shop owners in different sectors. Additionally, as indicated above, state regulations require that only one association be established for each industry. Therefore, the local Civil Affairs Bureau refused to register the association as a legal entity.[6] However, it existed de facto for many years; although a local official told them that their association was illegal, the government took no action to disband them. As a matter of fact, the entrepreneurs openly announced the establishment of the association publicly, with the witness of some local officials and journalists. There are two reasons for their illegal survival: first, the members' businesses were increasingly important or sometimes even essential to the local economy; second, the local government needed an organization through which they could communicate with the business owners smoothly and effectively. Local officials eventually could afford to put state regulations aside as the association did not cause any political trouble, as Fa Lung Gong caused so much trouble to the Chinese state, and indeed promoted the growth of the local economy. In other words, their political and economic legitimacy overturned their illegality. Just as the development of the whole private sector largely depends on the unspoken indulgence of local officials that I explained elsewhere (Yang, 2007), many private enterprise associations, especially those in regions they are particularly active or influential, could grow largely thanks to the local officials' acquiescence (Yu et al., 郁建兴等, 2004). This means that although the association could succeed in the sense of keeping itself alive, its status remains precarious without legal approval.

While hardly any organization in China is able to escape from the state agents' supervision or even monitoring, these associations usually enjoy more autonomy and independence – they elect their own leaders, they have their own sources of income (memberships plus fees collected from organizing activities) – than their counterpart members of ACFIC and those transformed from government bureaus. It is thus not true that these associations have less autonomy than 'state associations' (Foster, 2002; Pei, 1998; Saich, 2000) – the very fact that they do not have a government sponsor is a source of autonomy rather than constraint. This is especially true for the case of Wenzhou, where relatively autonomous associations of private enterprises have been established and managed by private business owners themselves (Chen et al., 陈剩勇, 汪锦军, 马斌, 2004; Zhang, 2008).[7] The relative success of private business associations in Wenzhou could be contributed to the following factors: the local government is relatively weak while the private sector is growing rigorously, fierce competition among private enterprises demands self-regulation and coordination, and many private business owners realized that they must organize themselves in order to make their voice heard by local officials.[8] This brings us to the issue of the relationship between the owners of private businesses and their associations.

## Private business owners and business associations

Before discussing whether business associations in China exemplify any version of corporatism or increasing organizational autonomy, it is necessary to learn how their members, that is, private business owners, relate to them. Curiously, this important aspect of business associations is usually missing or only treated with a light touch in the current literature. How many business owners are members of each type of association and how do they perceive these associations? In this section I present and analyse the data collected in the NSPBO (the reader may want to go back to Chapter 1 for details) in order to provide a preliminary answer to these questions and set up a context for further discussion below.

In the questionnaire used in the NSPBO, the respondents were asked to report their political affiliations, memberships of ACFIC and business associations (see definitions below). The questions on political affiliations were consistent throughout the years, but those on memberships of official business associations, including the Association of Individual Businesses (*ge ti hu xie hui*) and the Association of Private Business Owners (*si ying qi ye xie hui*) were not in use anymore after 2002, which reflects the changing situation in China. Instead, questions soliciting the memberships of industrial and trade associations (*hang ye xie hui*) were added. Further, two types of such industrial and trade associations were distinguished: those sponsored by the government and those sponsored by the ACFIC, while the 'bottom-up associations' were not even treated as a separate type of associations, indicating that such associations remained marginal as recently as in 2006.[9] Table 5.1 shows the change over the years:

*Table 5.1*  Percentages of membership of business associations among private business owners in China, 1993–2006

| Year | ACFIC | Association of Getihu | Association of private enterprises | Industry or trade association | N |
|------|-------|------------------------|-------------------------------------|-------------------------------|---|
| 1993 | 90.3 | 40.2 | 39.4 | 9.1 | 1440 |
| 1995 | 75.6 | 26.7 | 41.6 | 6.1 | 2869 |
| 1997 | 53.2 | 23.9 | 45.2 | 5.8 | 1947 |
| 2000 | 85.5 | 19.6 | 41.6 | 9.7 | 3073 |
| 2002 | 83.5 | NA | 48.0 | NA | 3258 |
| 2004 | 60.8 | NA | | 48.7 (gov) 43.4 (ACFIC) | 3012 |
| 2006 | 64.2 | NA | NA | 66.7 (gov) 45.6 (ACFIC) | 3446 |

*Source:* National Survey of Private Business Owners, 1993–2006.

We can make several observations from examining this table. First of all, the rate of membership of the ACFIC experienced some fluctuations from 1993 to 2006, but the overall levels remained very high (above 60 per cent except for 1997). This may reflect a selection bias of the survey towards ACFIC members as the ACFIC has been a sponsor of the survey. Secondly, the percentages of the Association of Individual Businesses (*getihu*) declined from 40 per cent in 1993 to 20 per cent in 2000. This is not surprising with the liberalization of the institutional environment; consequently, many individual businesses grow out of this type of small business. Organizers of the survey stopped collecting data on this membership from 2002 very likely because they started to realize that the data were not informative as the membership was compulsory – an individual business owner would automatically become a member of this association when the business is registered at the Bureau of Industries and Commerce (*gongshang jü*). The situation is the same for the membership of private business enterprises (those with more than eight employees). The majority of those surveyed, however, did not report themselves as members of either association – the percentage for the association of *get ti hu* was as low as about 20 per cent (except for 1993) and that for the larger private enterprises was a bit more than 40 per cent. Either for some reason the business owners did not register themselves as members, which is hard to understand given the membership is compulsory, or they didn't realize they were members even though their businesses were actually registered as such. Notwithstanding the reason, it is clear that these associations are not popular among private business owners, many of whom have complained that these associations are parts of the government who are only interested in collecting memberships and fees without actually doing anything for private businesses (Chen, Jiaxi, 2007). Such resentment seems to have extended to the ACFIC and other business associations as well.[10]

The statistics on the industrial and trade associations are the most interesting but the most puzzling as well. From 1993 to 2000, the percentages remained below 10 per cent, which then increased to more than 40 per cent in 2004 and 2006, which could be an effect of the rapid increase of this kind of business association in the new millennium, but the speed of increase is astonishing as well as puzzling. Moreover, the distinction between those sponsored by the government and those by the ACFIC was brought into the survey. This clearly reflects the survey organizers' attempt to catch up with the changing situation of business associations in China. With more and more former government ministries and bureaus being transformed into industrial and trade associations, these associations keep their relationship with the government through the sponsorship of a governmental department or agent. Naturally, we would wonder which trade association private business owners would join, or do they join both? Table 5.2 presents the answer with data collected from the 2004 and 2006 surveys in overleaf.

First of all, the percentage of private businesses that did not join any trade association decreased from 38 per cent in 2004 to 29 per cent in 2006. For those who did join, there is a clear tendency that they have moved from trade associations sponsored by the ACFIC to those sponsored by government ministries or agents: the percentage of those not a member of

*Table 5.2* Percentage of membership of trade associations sponsored by government agents and by the ACFIC, 2004 and 2006

|  |  | Government-sponsored | |
|---|---|---|---|
|  |  | Member | Non-member |
| ACFIC-sponsored | Member | 37 → 47 | 10 → 5 |
|  | Non-member | 15 → 19 | 38 → 29 |

Valid sample size: 2561 (2004) and 3183 (2006).
*Source:* National Survey of Private Business Owners, 2004 and 2006.

an ACFIC-sponsored association but a member of government-sponsored one increased from 15 per cent to 19 per cent; in contrast, those being a member of an ACFIC-sponsored association but not a member of a sponsored one decreased from 10 to 5 per cent. This suggests that although the percentage of private businesses that join both types of trade associations increased by 10 per cent (from 37 to 47 per cent), the increase is mostly due to those who joined the government-sponsored trade associations rather than those sponsored by ACFIC. That the ACFIC was not even a recognized sponsor of such associations must be responsible for such a shift. While ACFIC leaders may congratulate themselves for introducing an article protecting private property into China's Constitution, they must bow to the power of government agents at the organizational level.

Despite the fact that little information is available for discovering the mechanisms behind these statistics, what becomes clear is that the relationship between the Chinese state and business associations has been experiencing some significant change since the turn of the century. The CCP has stepped up its effort to increase its presence and subsequent control on the private sector by recruiting more members from these newly wealthy business owners, while in the meantime private business owners have been busy finding a powerful governmental sponsor for their associations in order to benefit from a more organized representation of their interest. What is behind these processes? And what has the CCP done in keeping and expanding its power? We now turn to these questions.

## Keep business to business

### Organizational controls on private enterprises

In its early years, the new government of the People's Republic was clearly aware of their reliance on the 'domestic capitalists' for keeping the whole economy running. Although the CCP's ideology of nationalizing the capitalist enterprises was widely known, it was to the new government's own interest to help those enterprises survive the transition of power. However, politically speaking, the capitalists were the 'class enemies' of the workers, one of the social bases of the new regime; therefore, some control must be exercised on them. On 1 August 1952, Xue Muqiao (薛暮桥), then the Director of the Bureau of Private Enterprises, put all industrial chambers under the leadership of the ACFIC, thereby establishing a pyramid-shape organizational structure for the CCP's convenience of supervising all private enterprises. Later, as a top leader with the responsibility of managing the national economy, Chen Yun (陈云) requested that every CCP committee have a subcommittee on business and commerce. When the ACFIC had its second congress in November 1956, it passed a resolution that the association 'was determined to listen to the words of Chairman Mao and to follow the Chinese Communist Party on the road to Socialism' (Huang, Mengfu, 2005: 18).

Such distrust of private business owners and organizational control imposed on them revived after private enterprises grew at an unexpectedly fast rate in the reform era. On 19 October 1979, when the CCP launched the economic reforms, the ACFIC passed an action resolution in its national congress that was '[d]etermined to follow the CCP unwaveringly and achieving the Four Modernizations wholeheartedly with all effort' (ibid: 28). The firms are new, but the methods of controlling them remain as they were decades ago: a hierarchical structure, penetration of party cells in most associations, and complete acceptance of the CCP's leadership as a condition for existence. As shown in the previous chapter, the percentage of private firms with an internal CCP committee has been increasing at a high speed and up until 2006 two out of five private businesses had a such committee.

Another example of the ACFIC's subjection to the CCP's control is its lack of legal authority to supervise its member associations. The Department of Civil Affairs (min zheng bu) has published a list of departments and agents that have the legal authority to sponsor industrial and trade associations. What is surprising and puzzling is that the ACFIC is not on the list, which means that members of the ACFIC are not legal social organizations recognized by the Chinese government, hence the distinction of associations sponsored by government versus those by the ACFIC in the 2004 and 2006 surveys. This overt discrimination has caused huge confusion and resentment[11] because many associations, especially those set up from the bottom up, cannot find a government sponsor and therefore would like to take the ACFIC as their sponsor. Given that the Chairman of the ACFIC is also a Vice Chairman of the PPCA, it is indeed astonishing that such discrimination against private business associations could happen at all. Some local governments have taken the liberty of granting their local ACFIC the authority of sponsoring business associations,[12] but such examples of bending the rules are still a minority. Consequently, the policy must have seriously constrained the ACFIC's power to expand its memberships. The survey results have confirmed such expectation: the percentage of ACFIC members declined since 2000 from about 85 per cent to about 65 per cent. In addition, the percentage of private enterprises as members of government-sponsored associations increased from 48 per cent in 2004 to 66 per cent in 2006, while that of those with the ACFIC as the sponsor remained at the level of 43–5 per cent.

It should be added, however, that it is simply untrue that business associations in general and the ACFIC in particular have not expanded – their membership has increased many fold in merely three decades and they have tried many times to improve the institutional environment for their members. Perhaps the best example that the ACFIC could do something significant to represent the interests of the private business owners is its tireless effort (three times) in proposing the article of protecting private property as an amendment to China's Constitution (Gao and Yang, 2003), which was finally successful. The irony is that political and organizational control exercised by the party-state has not grown at a slower pace.

## Business autonomy with political dependence

All civil associations pose a dilemma to the CCP's political leadership: on the one hand, the CCP has to withdraw from many economic and social arenas so that people have the institutional space to develop the economy and to manage their own affairs, but on the other hand, the new economic and social organizations may develop into a politically threatening force. While the idea of transforming the previous model of 'big-state, small-society' into 'small-government, big-society' sounds attractive for reasons of making the government more efficient and unleashing peoples' energies, it has been a thorny issue for the CCP to determine where the boundaries should be drawn.

Rescarchers in the West have tried to follow the corporatist approach in characterizing the relationship between the Chinese state and business associations. As Dickson points out, 'the state allows a limited number of associations to exist and provides leaders and budgetary support. However, China's capitalists have begun to create their own associations in addition to the official business associations. This complicates the CCP's corporatist strategy but has not led the party to abandon it' (2008: 20). Indeed, evidence collected from fieldwork of my own and other researchers (Kennedy, 2005: 164; Tsai, 2007: 70) has shown that the corporatist relationship is left very much intact *even though business associations have experienced a considerable growth*. This is so very likely because the Chinese state on one side and private entrepreneurs and their associations on the other have reached a tacit principle[13] – 'keep business to business', that is, the entrepreneurs keep their interactions with the CCP and the government in the realm of business operations, focusing on institutions and regulations related to the daily management of business rather than on their political rights and power. Although more than one-third of private entrepreneurs had resorted to business associations to voice their concerns, they didn't tend to make any political demands, a finding that has been confirmed by researchers both in and outside China (Jia Xijin et al., 2004; Tsai, 2007: 205; and my own fieldwork). The reason for adopting this strategy cannot be clearer: it is almost impossible for any private entrepreneur to amass sufficient support for demanding significant political changes without risking disastrous consequences to their businesses. From the perspective of any particular entrepreneur, the most rational strategy of survival is to stay away from confronting the mighty party-state politically.

Nevertheless, the corporatist model has captured only part of the whole picture. It is true that the Chinese state has done whatever it can to ensure that all associations will not grow into any political threat to its political dominance. However, if this is the whole story, it would be very difficult to explain why both the national government and some local governments (Shanghai, Wenzhou and Shenzhen) have repeatedly required that the connection between the government and business associations be severed and that the associations be independent in personnel, finance, and daily management. It has been so difficult to end the connection because the desire to keep it comes not only from government agents but *from the associations as well*; they too have a strong motivation to remain under the auspices of a government agent because the relationship will make their life much easier. Official statistics in 2004 show that of all business associations in Zhejiang, a province with the most vibrant private sector, about 35 per cent invited government officials (mostly retired or about to retire) to be an associated chairman, and 46 per cent invited such officials as the secretary (Chen, Jiaxi, 2007: 162; Yu, Jianxing et al., 郁建兴等, 2004). During my trips to China in the past several years, I have learnt that a large number of private business associations have employed retired government officials as consultants who are ready to help by making a phone call, arranging a business dinner, or introducing a resourceful figure in the government. Personal connections will stay after retirement, which will help the associations find the right person and a right way to solve any issues. This is why running business associations has become a business of the elite of private entrepreneurs (Tsai, 2007: 205), because large and profitable enterprises would be selected as leaders of the associations, and in turn use their associational positions to expand their connections with government officials and to promote their businesses while small and not-so-profitable enterprises are very inactive. An example is the Association of Business and Commerce of Xiaoshan (萧山), whose Chair succeeded in obtaining a piece of land – to construct a building at the city centre for use by the Association and its members – at a price much lower than the market price (Shi et al., 史晋川, 2008, Chapter 11). In the end, it was the largest 36 businesses (with minimum annual sales of more than 200 million RMB) that were able to move in. Almost all of them confessed that to facilitate their communications and connections with local government was one of the most important reasons for contributing to the cost of the building.

Even when the associations stand up against a government agent on behalf of the interest of their members, it does not mean that they would demand significant political change – it is always about a particular case. At best, they would criticize an individual official without attacking the government in general. The most commonly adopted strategy is to use their connection with an important government official to resolve any trouble or confrontation with a particular government agent. For example, Mr Z, one of my informants, who has several small businesses of long-distance shipping by trucks, and is chairman of a district business association of transportation and a member of the local People's Political Consultative Assembly told me:

> Private businesses in our district submitted tens of millions as taxes and fees, but governmental officials still do not take us seriously; there is no respect. It seems they could do whatever they like; if you resist, they would put you in great trouble. I think we must do something to stop this kind of things. Let me give you an example. A businessman has been in the business of shipping fruits for many years. Once he was fined 1400 yuan by a few staff members of the Technology Supervision Bureau (ji shu jian du jü) because they found

only a couple of rotten peaches! In another instance, they stopped one of my trucks and took away several bottles of fine liquor, saying it's for their leaders! How dare they! Now our association will stop this if they do this again.

No matter how upset he was his association would ask no more than a decent solution to such abuse of power. It seems that it is only when their business interests are seriously jeopardized that they would start to realize that this could be a political issue. Another businessman who owns several printing and copying shops, told me:

I joined the Communist Party in 1999, which I thought the only way to do something good for others. But the trouble is, other members may not think so; it's hard to believe we are members of the same party when I saw what they did, especially those leaders of local government. We [the private businesses] turned in so much tax and fees but what have they done? For instance, I asked the head of environmental protection bureau: you collected fees on more than ten items, what for?

## Understanding the difficult position of private business associations in China

Taking business associations as a special case, corporatism represents a situation when civil organizations do not enjoy a high level of autonomy and are hierarchically ordered, membership is compulsory, and individual associations have jurisdictional monopolies (Kennedy, 2005: 36). Kennedy also distinguishes 'societal corporatism' from 'state corporatism', with the former having more autonomy, but he concludes that 'corporatism is a poor description of government–business relations in China' (ibid.: 44). The above discussions in this chapter have suggested that the corporatist model is still effective, but it is only partly effective in describing the situation in China. The corporatist conceptualization is useful in the following ways. First, most business associations, especially the ACFIC and those initiated or tightly supervised by the government, are not autonomous in their key functions (focus of work, personnel, and finance); the number of business associations with high autonomy is growing but at this moment is still a minority. Second, some associations, such as those set up by former government agents and the ACFIC, are hierarchically ordered with local and industrial lower-level associations, while others are not. Third, memberships of a few government-initiated associations are compulsory, including the Association of Individual Businesses and the Association of Private Enterprises, but these associations have never enjoyed any popularity as many private business owners never joined or they do not recognize their memberships. Fourth, many associations have their jurisdictional monopoly either in a particular industry or in a geographical area, an outcome of the state policy that there should be only one association for each industry at each locality (一地一业一会, yi di yi ye yi hui), which is still the case despite the fact that many entrepreneurs have complained about it and some local officials have bent the rules. In sum, the corporatist model does capture some of the features of the government–association relationship in China, and it has been welcomed by social scientists in China as a more realistic conceptual model than the demanding civil society model that requires civil associations' genuine independence of the state.[14]

On the other hand, Kennedy is correct in pointing out the limitations of the criteria for corporatism discussed above, because those criteria tend to suggest that the state will lose control if business associations appear to be autonomous, if their organizational structure is more horizontal, if membership is voluntary, and if they do not monopolize their jurisdiction. The reality in China is that *the Chinese state is still able to exercise increasingly tighter control alongside the emergence of more business associations and even their growing autonomy in business affairs.* Indeed, corporatism in China has its 'Chinese characteristics', one of which is the control achieved by the organizational networks of the CCP – perhaps we could call this version of corporatism 'organizational corporatism' because the party-state's organizational structure is a major institutional mechanism through which corporatism is represented and realized. The organizational structure of the ACFIC shows the most typical example of such organizational corporatism: its Chairman has a background of business and therefore is qualified for representing the interests of other businessmen, but he is only a Vice Secretary of the CCP committee in the ACFIC and therefore works under the leadership of the Secretary who usually is a Deputy Minister of the CCP's Department of United Front. The organizational interconnection between the ACFIC and the CCP's party structure with the latter always one level superior to the association's leadership is copied throughout local and trade-specific federation of industries and commerce. Reading the journalist reports in *China Business Times*, the official newspaper of the ACFIC, one cannot help gathering a strong sense that the CCP has taken some aggressive steps to expand its organizational network throughout the local branches of the ACFIC. One example is the ACFIC at Wuxi, a city in Jiangsu province, who declared their intention, at the end of 2006, to 'set up CCP local organizations whenever conditions allow so as to strengthen the power of the Party in industry and trade associations' (Wuxi ACFIC, 2008: 246). The irony that this is also one of the few cities whose government has granted more autonomy to the ACFIC clearly represents the current situation of business associations in China: you could enjoy more business autonomy but you would be under tighter control – or 'leadership' in the terminology of China's journalism – of the CCP. Due to the lack of data, it remains unclear to us how extensive such organizational control is within the 'bottom-up' business associations. As this type of association is still a minority and the CCP could require the establishment of its branches, it is premature to expect them to be immune to such organizational control.

As some Chinese researchers point out, the fundamental problem with business associations in China is that 'there has been no change to their dependence on the Party and the government' because they are under the leadership of the CCP's Department of The United Front. Therefore, 'it is extremely difficult for the ACFIC to fight for its members' legal rights and interests and it is inevitable to have confrontations with the Party and the government' (Song, Meiyun, 2005: 84–5). It is difficult to understand why the CCP still sees private business owners as being subject to the United Front principle. If they are 'constructors of socialism', as Jiang Zemin claimed at the eightieth anniversary of the CCP, and they have no connection with the older generation of 'domestic capitalist' and are 'part of the people', as some leading academics in China openly asserted, then it does not make sense anymore to make them subject to the United Front policy because the policy assumes that they are not part of the people and should be treated only as temporary allies for fighting the common enemy. The only explanation for the continuation of the United Front policy is the CCP's unspoken distrust, concern, or even fear of any civil forces, including business associations of the private enterprises. Therefore, no matter how its forms or versions change over time, corporatism will always exist and be lively in China as long as there is no significant change to the current political structure.

More disappointingly to those who have held a high hope for business associations' role in China's democratization prospect, some business associations do not like the idea of democracy or they simply run in a more authoritarian manner without any inclination to enhance the effect of these associations on democracy. Even in Wenzhou, where business associations are reported to be ahead of others in obtaining organizational autonomy and following democratic principles, their success is largely dependent on their leaders' personal charisma even though they enjoy a higher level of autonomy (Chen et al., 陈剩勇, 汪锦军, 马斌, 2004); some are even against the idea of democratic decision-making within the associations (He, 1997). The functions of these associations are highly exclusive, open only to businessmen from Wenzhou or even a certain place in Wenzhou (ibid.). When a member makes a request to the association for protecting the association's interest, the association normally follows the principle of keeping business to business, as pointed out in general terms previously in this chapter, including preventing member businesses from irrational competitions and producing fake products, introducing new products and markets to members, organizing product shows or fairs. There are anecdotal stories in which a business association was successful in defending or protecting a member business's interest and had to confront government agents, but even in these situations, which we shall discuss with more detail in Chapter 7, the confrontation is mostly resolved on a case-by-case basis without relating it to any general political issue at all. The association, or more precisely the association chair, has become a negotiator or a mediator between individual enterprise and the government, and all negotiations and mediations are carried out in business rather than political terms. The biggest demand by the association on local government is to become more efficient, to give them more resources (land and financial credits), and to extract less from local businesses.

The political significance of business associations in China is a question of the half-full glass. On the one hand and historically speaking, this is progress in the direction of democratization because more or less they must represent the interests of their members and voice their desires and concerns, even though this is almost always done within the remit of business activities and without challenging the CCP's political dominance. On the other hand and prospectively speaking, it is difficult to see how far these associations can go in the direction of democratization. Perhaps they have already given up any intention to influence the making of political decisions, some of them do not like to run their associations democratically, and most importantly they are very wary of the potential consequences to their personal assets brought about by any political change, either democratic or not. It is not much of an exaggeration to say that private business owners in China have no political ambitions.

# 6
# Capitalist Candidates in Local Elections

Elections may not have anything to do with democracy, but all democracies hold elections. In other words, elections are a necessary but not a sufficient condition for democracy. Therefore, although elections may not automatically transform an authoritarian regime into a democracy, elections may enhance the chance of such transformation. This explains why so many Western organizations including the Carter Foundation, the Ford Foundation, the International Republican Institute, and the EU have been so enthusiastic about sponsoring academic and administrative projects on local elections in China.[1] The implementation of *The Law of Organizing Village Committees*[2] (trial version) starting in 1988 seems to indicate that China's huge authoritarian iceberg is finally starting to thaw from the bottom. Clearly, it is the Western organizations' hope that once the process is in motion, it will gradually move up to the top. We must keep in mind, however, that it is the Chinese Communist Party who made local elections a national policy by drafting the legislation and implementing the process, although residents in a few villages acted on their own initiative in the early stages. In fact, the potential risk of losing control in rural China was a central point of debate throughout the process of legalizing village elections in China, especially after the incidents at Tiananmen Square in 1989, which is also why it took ten years for The Law to come into its full effect.[3] It is simply difficult to imagine that the CCP would allow, let alone encourage, any weakening of its grip on power, even at the lowest level. Any actual deviations from Communist control would be unexpected to the original intention of even the most liberal among the CCP leaders. The whole process of liberalizing political competition in rural China should therefore be understood as one of the CCP's new attempts to strengthen its political dominance, not the first step towards democratizing the nation's political system.[4]

It is not this chapter's objective, however, to examine the historical development of local elections, to evaluate how democratic the elections are although my discussion will relate to this issue, or to speculate on their implications for China's political future. Rather, my main objective here is to focus on the role of the capitalists in local elections. If it is a general regularity that one would become politically active after accumulating a certain amount of financial wealth, as Lord Acton (Sir John Dalberg-Acton) once argued, then for the newly wealthy capitalists in China, to participate in local elections is an effective way of expressing themselves politically, especially given the fact that it remains extremely difficult for the vast majority of new capitalists to become politically noticeable at the higher levels (provincial and national). If this starting point makes sense, we must answer a series of questions: what kinds of capitalists have been active in local elections? What motivates them to do so? Have they made the whole process more or less democratic? How does their wealth play a role in their campaigns, elections, and subsequent career? How do they deal with the local Communist Party? Do all local residents find the capitalist the kind of the leader they want?

Answers to these questions will tell us about the institutional boundaries in which the elections operate. Would the results of the elections challenge the leadership of CCP in villages and townships? How do the local CCP secretaries keep the elections 'under control'? As local residents now have the opportunity to choose their own leader, these elections provide potential opportunities for private business owners to translate their financial wealth into political power, but it remains unclear to what extent this is indeed the case, or whether something other than wealth plays a significant role in the elections. By studying these scenarios we can learn a great deal about the political influence that private business owners can make in localities. Drawing on a large number of reports written by both Chinese and Western researchers, this chapter will analyse a variety of election cases in which the new capitalists attempt to promote their political profile and influence.

## Why would the CCP allow and organize political elections, even at the lowest administrative levels?

Necessity is the mother of invention. In China's authoritarian political system, where local leaders are normally appointed by their superiors, electing the head of a village by the villagers themselves was indeed a political invention. What was the necessity that gave birth to this invention?

According to O'Brien and Li, the first village elections took place in two counties in Guangxi Autonomous Region in the late 1970s and early 1980s when the villages were experiencing crises in the economic and social transformations (2001: 101; see also Tan, 2006: 59–63). With the dismantling of the Communes and the production brigades starting at the end of the 1970s, there was a vacuum of power or even worse anarchy at the local levels. The increasingly anarchic situation was responsible for the deterioration of public security in many local areas;[5] therefore, there was an urgent need for local governments to fulfil the function of providing security. In addition, granting village residents the right to elect their own leaders could help resolve another crisis: the worsening relationship between the villagers and local officials, who have become increasingly predatory since the fiscal reforms began in the mid 1980s. As the local officials found their political career and personal wellbeing increasingly hinged on the performance of the local economy (Whiting, 2001), they have found few other choices than taxing the villagers. However, taxation, especially heavy taxation without justification is bound to entail resentment (Bernstein and Lü, 2003). And in such a situation, the legitimacy of the tax collectors would become very vulnerable. It was very likely the hope of the top CCP leaders that local elections would somehow increase the legitimacy of local officials and therefore ease the tension between the two sides. It was out of such necessity that the affected village residents decided to elect their own village governments. The fact that bottom-up elections started in these villages rather than somewhere else in China suggests at least three conditions for local elections: (1) there was a governing crisis; (2) some village residents had the desire and the capacity to govern themselves; (3) upper level governments have lost their control or even connections with the villages and very likely as a consequence would like to allow or even encourage local residents to govern themselves.

Another governing crisis recognized in the early 1980s, that is, when the CCP was trying to restore order and production throughout the nation, was the deteriorating relations between local officials and the peasants, although few details are available as to how bad the situation was. Peng Zhen (彭真) was the highest state leader (then the Vice Chairman of the National People's Congress Standing Committee) who whole-heartedly promoted village elections (Li and O'Brien, 2001: 101–2). To understand the emergence and development of local elections, we must ask: why was Peng Zhen so enthusiastic about organizing local elections? Did he genuinely want to take the elections as the first steps towards a whole process of democratizing China's political system, or did he simply make use of the local elections as a contingent solution to an immediate crisis, a tactic similar to loosening up the restrictions on self-employment for dealing with the unemployment crisis in the late 1970s? This is very important because, in a country like China, the true nature of the top leader's motivations determines the significance of a national policy. Logical thinking and available evidence tend to suggest that Peng's motivation was more strategic than ideological. Peng must have had access to some internally circulated evidence of the contentious relations between ordinary residents and the local cadres, such as those reports written by officials at the Ministry of Civil Affairs based on fieldwork investigations; otherwise, he would not have argued that to allow rural residents to directly elect their leaders would be the only way to keep the situation under control. Like the household responsibility system, grassroots initiatives in China would not survive without the acknowledgement of a top leader of the CCP. The news about self-elected village committees delighted Peng Zhen because it was exactly the kind of solution he was looking for.[6] In fact, as early as 1982, Peng Zhen already worked very hard to legalize the elected village committees; he was instrumental in making village residents' committees in the newly amended version of China's Constitution. Article 111 of the Constitution states that 'the residents' committees in urban areas and the villagers' committees in rural areas are self-governing organizations of the local people. The Head, Deputy-Head and the members of the committee should be elected by the residents or the villagers'. Later, other top leaders including Song Ping (宋平), Bo Yibo (薄一波), Wan Li (万里), Zhao Ziyang (赵紫阳) provided the much needed support, although the policy was initially expressed as a 'watch-and-see' (Bai, Yihua, 白益华, 1995: 282–309).

Clearly, the challenge to the CCP's top leaders was to strike a balance between stability and party-control. To enhance stability, they must ease the cadre–masses confrontation by giving the masses some autonomy to select their leaders, which would in turn solve the problem of public security at the same time. The potential risk of following this strategy is that once triggered, it would be very difficult for the upper level officials to rule their jurisdictions in the short run and for the Party to stop the momentum in the long run. More fundamentally, since its coming to power in 1949, the CCP has constantly made use of the low levels of education and the desire to accept democratic values among the ordinary people as a key excuse for not opening up political competition, an argument that is usually given a realistic cast – it is widely accepted that most of the Chinese people, especially the peasants, would like to follow behavioural codes that are alien to democracy. How true is this assessment of Chinese people's educational level of democracy? Results from Chinese social scientists have been inconsistent. Zhong Yang (2006) conducted a survey in the summer of 2000 in 12 counties in southern Jiangsu province.[7] The results show (ibid.: 99–100) that the studied respondents clearly held democratic values: for example, 93 per cent of the respondents agreed that all county and township officials should be elected; 82 per cent would like their Party secretaries to be elected; more than 60 per cent disagreed that '[i]t would not be necessary for ordinary people to be involved in the decision-making process if the officials are capable and trusted by the masses'; in other words, they rejected the elitist politics; and 57 per cent disagreed that '[e]lections should be abandoned if they create chaos and instabilities', an excuse used by the CCP persistently throughout the years. Zhong Yang concluded that 'these findings seem to defy the conventional wisdom that Chinese peasants are socially and politically conservative and hold values incompatible with democracy. In fact, on most of these questions, our peasant respondents in Jiangsu fared equally well or even better than the urban residents in our Beijing surveys' (ibid.: 101).[8] In contrast, Chen Shengyong (陈剩勇, 2009) argued that, based on his observation in many inland areas (Guangxi and Shanxi), most peasants are far from being used to democratic values and procedures and consequently village elections have become a movement pushed forward by local elites from townships. No one would deny the enormous regional variation of the readiness for taking up democratic values and procedures in China, so the question becomes how the 'democratically developed' regions (mostly along the coast in the east) could be used as role models for other regions.

They key issue here is that even if there is an element of truth in the above argument, the CCP must answer the following questions: what kind of education is required for the peasants to be ready to follow democratic values? What is the evidence that the peasants would prefer an authoritarian system to a democratic one? Even if they do, what can be done to change their thoughts? The dilemma for the CCP is that it could use its policy of developing local elections to showcase its willingness to move China's political development forward in the direction of democracy, but on the other hand it would be under pressure to do more, that is, to move the elections to higher levels and to other areas, once the current local elections mature and local residents are ready – in

the sense of both educational levels and political maturity – to participate in politics beyond their immediate local context.

## Would money put the new capitalists in an advantageous position in local elections?

When examining the role of the new capitalists in China's political
development, one cannot help noticing the fact that the process of
opening up political competition in villages and the emergence of an
entrepreneurial and wealthy group of people in rural areas have taken
place in tandem. The years of implementing *The Law of Organizing
Village Committees* were also when private businesses experienced the
most dramatic ups and downs in China. There is no evidence to show
that this has been a product of an intentional plan of the CCP. The previous rigid power structure in rural China has been relaxed and opened
to outcomes unexpected at least in theory, giving a dose of dynamics
local politics. At the same time, an army of wealthy business owners
has emerged largely thanks to the privatization of industrial enterprises
in rural China. Regardless of their motivation, whether it is benign or
selfish, the money in hand makes them more resourceful than those
candidates without the money to participate in the competition for
political power. And when other conditions, such as personal ambition and support from fellow villagers, are ripe, it would be difficult to
understand if they did not want to participate. This may have come as
somewhat of a a surprise to the top leaders of the CCP; however, so far
there is no sign that this group of affluent and influential people would
pose any threat to the party's political dominance. As will be shown
later, there are still several ways for the CCP to keep control on power
in rural China despite the emergence of wealthy village heads.

We must be careful, however, of making any direct connection
between money and power. At the aggregate level, for example, when
we look at the level of economic development and the proportion of
the capitalists (the wealthy or the business owners) as village heads,
we do not have systematic data for showing the association between
the two[9], but anecdotal evidence suggests that it is usually in the relatively wealthy areas, such as Zhejiang and Guangdong, that the new
capitalists are politically the most active and have occupied a higher
percentage of village heads. For example, in 2002, of all members of village resident committees in Zhejiang (133,222), about 30 per cent were
these wealthy and capable people[10] (Xiao and Yue, 肖菁，岳海智, 2003),
which has increased even further to more than 60 per cent in 2005 (Ji

et al, 纪圣麟，周炳泉，陈平，2005). While these numbers are worthy of our attention, they beg more questions: are the percentages about the same everywhere in Zhejiang? Do other wealthy provinces such as Shanghai and Shangdong have the same percentages? Even for places where the percentages are as high as 60 per cent, why do the other 40 per cent not have such high levels of wealthy people being elected as village leaders? In one survey conducted in Guangdong province (Fang and Dong, 方柏华，董明，2009), local residents were asked 'In which way do you think the person was elected to be the CCP secretary or head of residents' committee?' (This is a double-barrelled question – it is unclear whether the question is about the CCP secretary or about the head of residents, 2009: 61, n=252): fair competition (52 per cent), exchanged with money (18 per cent), personal charisma (19 per cent), chosen by upper level government (2 per cent), and unclear (9 per cent). So far we are still quite ignorant of the underlying mechanisms.

One possible mechanism is the local officials' desire to develop the local economy; for this purpose, they would very much like to put a big business owner in the position of village head. The CCP has followed a policy of encouraging people to become wealthy, although in the meantime they emphasize 'becoming wealthy together'; local officials have strong desire to put 'the economically capable people' in power as well. For example, in the City of Yong Kang (永康), Zhejiang province, where 90 per cent of commercial organizations are private, the city leaders made a decision as early as 1994 for 'nurturing and establishing a team of entrepreneurial type of Party secretaries'. In 1996, about 40 per cent of all village leaders were private business owners. During the elections in 2002, 60 per cent of the newly elected members of Village Committees belonged to a 'getting rich first group'. In 2005, of the 653 village Party secretaries, 34 per cent were private business owners and of 706 Head of Village Committees, 74 per cent were private business owners.[11] In a district of the metropolitan Chong Qing, local governments launched a campaign to bring 'the capable' (mostly private business owners) to the leading positions (heads or Party secretaries) of villages.

On the other hand, village residents have a strong desire to become rich and affluent, so they would welcome someone who could help to do so. As two Chinese researchers point out, the rural residents are very pragmatic – behind their voting choices is their expectation and desire to enhance their own interests (Fang and Dong, 方柏华，董明, 2009: 40). For example, in the City of Hejin (河津), Shaanxi province, wealthy business owners would almost always get elected if they competed for village heads, because they would normally invest hundreds of thousands in public projects, such as roads, schools and nurseries, sport and culture facilities, and so on (Guo, 郭高中, 2006). The rationale behind this process seems to be that the basis of being elected as village leaders is the ability to help fellow residents become rich or improve their material life, not necessarily other intangible properties, such as personal charisma, policies, or character. Actually, the residents do care about other properties of their elected leaders; for example, they want their leaders to be fair and maintain justice. Therefore, what they really want is the ability to help fellow residents become rich *given that the leader has no other problems* (such as unfairness, corruption, abuse of power, and so on). Although it might be ignored in the beginning due to the economic power of the wealthy candidate, after a while the residents should presumably raise an eyebrow at the 'purchased position'. Certainly, it will take some years for the residents to think through and make up their minds on a set of principles for their choices. At this moment, researchers have reached the conclusion that rural residents do not care about democracy in the whole process; in other words, they would be happy with the result as long as the elected person could help them become richer; whether the person has a 'democratic style of leadership' is not an important matter. In the study by Fang and Dong (2009: 68), only 4.5 per cent of studied residents cared about this, and they claimed that this conclusion was consistent with another research project on the local construction of democracy in Zhejiang.

Things are even more complicated when we try to discover the motivations of the new capitalist candidates. First of all, we cannot

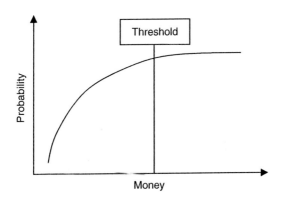

*Figure 6.1* A theoretical relationship between the money spent on election campaigns and the probability of getting elected

be absolutely confident in saying that village elections are all about money. While it is clear that in economically more developed areas, some candidates have spent an increasingly large amount of money to enhance their chance of getting elected, it remains however unclear whether money is the determining factor. Another benefit is the opportunity to establish connections, either official or personal, with upper level governments, which may turn out to be valuable assets either for political upward mobility and/or business-related activities. It is very likely that the relationship between money and the probability of getting elected is one as shown below:

That is, before a threshold, money exercises a significant impact on the likelihood of winning an election but after that its effect will level off. The threshold is expectedly the amount needed to employ a campaign team and invest in establishing a good relationship with the voters. This explains why the threshold keeps increasing on the one hand[12] but villagers denounce the effect of money on their voting behaviours on the other; some even saw such 'vote-buying' behaviour as an insult (He, 2007: 59). But this demands further explanation. Why do the candidates need to have a campaign team and/or invest in winning the support of fellow villagers? Village elections are democratic in the sense that village residents can exercise their rights to choose their leaders as there are more candidates than the number of positions, which forces candidates to compete for the positions. One way of winning the competition is to let the residents feel the benefits of supporting a particular candidate, which requires a team of people to help the residents see the benefits. The value of the immediate benefits varies from the price of several packs of cigarettes to banquet meals or even to a sizeable amount of cash. The long-term benefits could be reduction of tax, construction of public infrastructures, such as schools, roads, or care centres, or the prospect of increasing the villagers' income by introducing new employment and business opportunities.

These benefits have their own pros and cons in terms of their attractiveness to village residents, depending on both the village residents' quality of life and the level of economic development at the time of the election. In general, the immediate benefits should be more attractive to the residents whose quality of life is relatively low; even they are naïve enough to trust the candidates' promises of producing those long-term benefits, the short-term benefits are better than nothing. However, if short-term benefits are attractive, then very likely the level of economic development is low, which further means that it would not be very attractive to the candidate to become the village head because there is less collective resources under their control after they are elected. It is possible that some candidates are noble enough to compete to become the village head purely for the purpose of helping their fellow residents even though they may suffer financial loss. While we don't have evidence for assessing the number of such candidates, in the principle of protecting and increasing one's own interests, it is reasonable to expect that the number would be very small. In contrast, the long-term benefits are more attractive to village residents, but they are more uncertain as well. This is particularly so for relatively wealthy villages: short-term benefits are relatively less attractive as their quality of life is already satisfactory. Competitions in such villages are expected to be much fiercer because these villages tend to possess a large amount of collective assets.

In short, if we assume that candidates participate in village elections for the purpose of gaining control over village assets, then we would expect to see a higher percentage of capitalist candidates in economically developed villages[13] because these villages, by definition, have more assets. Being the village head means that the capitalist could have more collective resources at their disposal for investment and other businesses in the name of collective welfare. To what extent they do this for the village or for their own interest is a question we may not ever have a completely reliable answer for. A deputy-director of Civil Affairs in the city of Yi Wu (Zhejiang) did not think most of 'the capable candidates' competed in the elections for their own interest; rather, most of them aimed for a good reputation among their fellow residents and only a small proportion wanted to reap any monetary benefits from the tenure (Fang and Dong, 方柏华，董明, 2009: 62). However, this could not explain why some village residents were not happy with the performance of their capitalist village heads and having learnt the lesson demanded a contract to be signed by the candidates specifying how they would be penalized if they turned out to be selfish after election[14]. The fact that many social scientists and journalists in China call for 'democratic governance' instead of mere 'democratic election' seems to suggest that there are a large number of new capitalists who have benefited personally from being a village head at the expense of collective welfare.

This does not mean, however, that capitalists will not become village heads in economically underdeveloped areas; it is just that when they do participate in village elections, they will find it more competitive if they happen to live in relatively wealthy villages. In relatively poor areas, it is a different mechanism that brings the capitalists to the position of village leader. In these areas, the upper level CCP leaders realize that it would be unattractive for the capable business owners to be village leaders, so they set up policies with an explicit aim of promoting these business owners to village leaders. For example, in the relatively underdeveloped Gansu province in northwest China, there was a campaign of making CCP members into 'the firstly wealthy people' and making 'the first wealthy people' into CCP members (Tan, Fei et al., 谭飞, 2004). A county in Jiangsu province went as far as setting up ten thousand yuan as the threshold of assets required for becoming a village leader (Zheng and Xie, 郑燕峰 and 射阳, 2003). Clearly, in such cases, the capitalists were selected rather than elected to be the village head. These cases may not represent the will of the top leaders of the CCP, but they do indicate just how desperate local officials in relatively poor areas could be in making their places rich, which consequently increases the political significance of the new capitalists.

## How democratic are the local elections?

Regardless of the CCP top leaders' original intention, local elections have provided Chinese citizens with the first opportunity to choose their own leaders directly. While the elections may be the immediate objective, it is the hope of most observers that the experience of participating in the whole process itself will nurture the spirit of democracy. If this is the humble start of China's process of democratization, then we must firmly keep Charles Tilly's words in mind: democratization is full of setbacks, turnarounds and other forms of de-democratization (2007). We may not see these historical turns in the case of China as the time span is extremely short if we count from the beginning of village elections in the late 1980s. The key point, however, should apply: we would be historically naïve if we were to think that democratization will follow a straight-line path. In the context of contemporary China, democratization will not be a linear development for at least two reasons: how seriously the candidates and the voters take democratic principles and procedures in practice and how far the humble start in villages will go in the current political system. We shall discuss the first reason in this section and the second in the next.

Political scientists refer to the first issue as a matter of political culture: a critical criterion for assessing the existence of democracy is to check whether those competing for political office would make political compromises, whether they have the willingness to agree to disagree, and most importantly, the readiness to accept defeat without resorting to undemocratic and unconstitutional behaviours (Diamond, 1999: 165–74). This is not the kind of culture in which the CCP came to power; as shown in Chapter 2, it is rather the opposite. When Mao Zedong claimed that 'Who are our friends? Who are our enemies? That's the first question of our revolution', the idea of competing with political opponents peacefully and being ready to accept political failure was alien to both him and to his enemies (the Nationalists). Most importantly, even today there are no signs that the CCP is trying to nurture the democratic political culture: at least for its top leaders, political competition is a matter of life or death, compromise means defeat, and defeat is completely unacceptable; procedures are always created by and for the winner, so there are no such democratic procedures that all competitors would follow.

Given such tradition, it would be interesting to observe how the new capitalists would behave in local political competitions. A question of particular importance in relation to this group of wealthy candidates is the use of money in their participation in local elections. This important question is also a tricky one: on the one hand, local officials would like to see the new capitalists take up leading positions in villages because the capitalists would help develop the local economies – many local governments have called for private business owners working outside their hometown to return and become village leaders. On the other hand, it is often unclear where the limits of using money lie in competing for the position of village leaders; more specifically, where to draw the line between bribery and legitimate use of money in winning votes? While no state regulations specify the legal ways of winning votes, these usually include promises made before the final voting day: constructing public infrastructure projects, such as roads, schools, water and electricity, a nursing home, and so on. The new capitalists would either do these things by either donating to charities or contributing a large share of these projects. This is why township governments would be more than happy to encourage such candidates to become village leaders because the capitalists would effectively take over some of the duties from the towns. Finally, almost all capitalist candidates would declare that they would do the job without pay.

The sense of fair competition and democracy is nowhere to be seen in these 'positive contributions' to local economies. Government officials welcome these contributions because they improve local conditions on the one hand and they are not direct bribery for local residents' votes. To village residents, the tangible improvements of living standards are much more desirable than creating a fair, transparent, and democratic institutional system; the system can never be the end in itself; rather, it is only a means of achieving the end of obtaining a better material life. According to a small survey (n=216) in the City of Yiwu (Zhejiang, Fang and Dong, 方柏华，董明, 2009: 53), a region with a dominating private sector, in March 2008, when local residents were asked: 'Would you like to vote for a village resident who has a lot of money to be village leader?', nearly half said yes (49 per cent), 11 per cent no, and the rest 40 per cent were indifferent. I have never encountered a media report or an academic study that reports local residents' resistance to the new capitalists' money in pursuit of a fair political competition. Local residents think such competitions are fair because it is all about who can give them what they want; as what they want is better material life, it is fair for those who could deliver material benefits to win. According to such logic, a political competition is always a financial competition, and there would be nothing wrong if the richest man became the President of the nation.

The above observation is reinforced when we examine the illegal uses of money in village elections. Due to its secretive nature, it is obviously very difficult to estimate the prevalence of using money to bribe local residents for votes. There are two types of targets of such tactics: the most common is of course the voters; wealthy candidates would give out valuable goods, such as brand cigarettes, dinners at extravagant restaurants, electrical appliances, or even cash. The less common behaviour is to bribe the competitors; that is, to pay the competitors to withdraw from the elections and instead persuade supporters to vote for the candidate doing the bribing. The Draft of Amendments to *The Law of Organizing Village Committees* (《村组法修订草案》) did not define what should count as 'bribing voters' (贿选) and the legal procedures for dealing with such cases in case they take place. While examining the draft, some deputies of the National People's Congress pointed out that the number of bribing incidents has increased significantly.[15] There is a difficulty of definition here: as it is well known even outside China, exchanging gifts is party of the Chinese culture (Yang, 1994), how could such exchanges be distinguished from bribing behaviour without much dispute? Officials at China's Ministry of Civil Affairs were clearly aware of this challenge – in an official document released in 2005,[16] they required local officials to distinguish personal exchange and donations to charities and public projects from vote-buying behaviours. In practice, except for the most obvious cases, such as paying hundreds or even thousands RMB with a hint to vote a particular candidate, it is impossible to collect clear evidence for bribing voters. In other words, there is substantial room for 'implicit bribing behaviours', such as sending gifts to voters by a relative or a close friend of a candidate.

My concern here is with a more fundamental problem: the villagers do not seem to have any objections to the bribe; again, I am not aware of any incidents where local residents refused to take the bribes. This does not necessarily mean that they think it is appropriate to buy their votes. My fieldwork suggests that they do think it is not right to do so, but they would not refuse such bribery individually and no one would stand out to organize a collective reaction; in addition, they are very reluctant to damage their relationships with the candidates by declining the bribery. According to a study of a village in Qingdao, the province of Shangdong, 93 per cent of the surveyed 200 residents thought that bribing in elections was acceptable.[17] In principle, the voters would not like to take the bribe from any candidate if they realize that their future interests would be compromised after the candidate is elected. The vast majority of the residents believed that it was a great deal to become a village head because the rate of return would be very high. There must be a certain element of truth in this because otherwise it is very difficult to comprehend why the competition could be so ruthless given the elected head would not be paid for doing the job; some even resort to violence because it seems to be the only way either to get elected or to stop your competitor from getting elected. Once elected, the village head, for example, could earn a lot more by selling or renting out land or selling of village enterprises, in which attractive kick-backs are usually involved. For example, in the well-known City of Wenzhou, a close relative and campaign organizer for a candidate was stabbed to death on 21 March 2005 (Zhang, 章敬平, 2005: 59). In a similar incident, a private business owner in the City of Wuhan was knifed to death the day before the election day.[18] In the end, it is of no use for the village voters to refuse to take any bribes if all candidates would do the same thing – abusing their power to increase their own interests. If a village resident's vote cannot make any difference to the quality of the village head, then it would be actually rational to take the bribe – a bribe is better than no bribe if the consequence (future compromise of collective interests) remains the same.

## Relations among local elites

Similar to the issue of controlling the growth of private enterprises by setting up party cells that we discussed in Chapter 4, the CCP must also deal with the increasing number of capitalist village heads who were elected by their fellow residents.[19] This is an issue obviously due to the very fact that the authority of the new village heads is legitimized by public support rather than ascribed by upper level officials, which somehow may change the local power structure and distribution. One potential problem is the village heads' relationship with township leaders, which is never clearly defined. Village heads are responsible to those who elected them and they are not government officials because village committees are not government institutions (the lowest level of government is township); therefore, they do not have to report to town leaders. However, all villages are within the jurisdictions of a township, so village heads are only responsible for matters that are 'purely' for their villages; in practice, it can be very difficult to draw a line between 'village matters' and 'town matters'. The dual functions of the village residents' committee include, on the one hand, although officially they are not part of the government, they are expected by the township government to fulfil all governmental functions, especially providing public services (primary schools, nursing homes, infrastructures, and so on). Although often they carry out these tasks in connection with the township, they must take a considerable amount of responsibility alone. On the other hand and by definition, the village residents' committee must also represent the interests of the residents, but the relationship between the elected village residents' committee and the township government remains unspecified. The key question is at what point does the village have to depend on the township and at what point they do not?

Town leaders have motivations both for and against village elections: they would support village elections because the elected village heads would alleviate the township's financial and administrative burdens, but on the other hand they do not want to see their power shifting away from townships to villages. While the institutional ambiguities may trigger future confrontations between the two sides, this does not appear to be a serious issue because the elected village heads have strong motivation to establish and maintain a good working relationship between town leaders not only because they must rely on the township for completing many of the tasks they promised but also they expect help from township leaders, such as landing a better job, *after* their term is over.

A potentially more unstable relationship is between the elected village head and the village CCP secretary; it is particularly unstable when the elected head is a wealthy capitalist entrepreneur who is in a stronger position to challenge the Party secretary's authority. Previously, the two committees were (in many places still are) consistent in terms of policies and actions because the chairman of the CCP committee is the actual decision-maker (yi ba shou) while the head of the residents' committee is the second hand, which reflects the authoritarian ruling of the CCP at the lowest level. In such a system, the village head is not elected but appointed by the township leaders usually in consultation with the village CCP chairman. The introduction of the new local elections has changed the foundation of the relationship between the two committees: village leaders no longer, at least not completely, obtain their position from the CCP or township but from their fellow residents, providing them with a legitimate basis for becoming politically independent.

So far researchers in and outside China have inconsistent observations on the relationship between the Party secretary and the elected village heads. Some researchers working inside China reported several cases of the conflicts between the two village heads or the two committees (village residents' committee, led by the village head, and the CCP committee led by its secretary, Xiang and Zhou, 项辉，周威锋, 2001; Wan, 万慧进, 2007). Similarly, Baogang He, a Chinese researcher based in Australia, concluded that the new rich 'might be interested in opposing the domination of village party secretaries' (2007: 216); furthermore:

> They are able to resist the domination of and manipulation by village party secretaries by drawing on their economic wealth and resource. Village democracy provides a mechanism whereby the new rich can compete for village power and influence political decision making.... Local power-holders have to soften their coercion tactics when they face the resistance from the new rich because they have to rely on the rich for their revenue. (ibid.: 217) Village democracy if it exists in some villages is largely for the benefit of the new rich who enjoy the fruits of village democracy.... In the context of an increasingly depoliticized, powerless, and poor majority, the actual meaning of village democracy is largely reserved for the new rich....infant village democracy is largely pushed by the old class of villager cadre and new class of the new rich of rural enterprises.
>
> (Ibid.: 221)

Oi and Rozelle seem to agree in general on such characterization: 'entrepreneurs [the self-employed] show more interest in local politics, particularly in elections ... the number of self-employed is highly correlated to the number of contested elections ... because private entrepreneurs, many of whom lack Party affiliation, see election to the villagers' committee as a viable way of countering the power of the Party – an organization that up until recently has shunned private entrepreneurs' (2001: 171).

However, based on his fieldwork in two counties of drastically different political cultures, Jianjun Zhang has constructed a theory of 'collusion' among the capitalists and the Party secretaries: while the business owners develop the local economy, which the local leaders take as their political credit (cadre evaluation system and regional competitions, 2008: 127); in return, the local leaders help the private business owners by providing resources (land, credit, licences), dealing with upper level government agencies, and keeping local residents quiet in case of any conflicts between the business owners and local residents. This is largely due to the privatization of TVEs. However, later he pointed out that how local officials treat businesses depends on inter-personal relations; business owners may threaten local officials by claiming to invest somewhere else; local officials may retaliate if business owners defy their authority (ibid.: 129). Therefore, it is not a complete 'collusion'; the relationship is much more subtle and fragile as it is contingent on many factors. It is difficult to predict who will gain the upper hand.

According to Qingshan Tan's interview of the officials at the Ministry of Civil Affairs (2006: 295–6), when Jiang Zemin visited Gaozhou in Guangdong in 2000, '[t]he vice party head of Gaozhou made an abrupt comment on village election destroying the Party authority ... how elected village officials were achieving power at the expense of village Party cadres. Many village Party secretaries lost election and newly enriched villagers got elected'. The loss of power on the part of the Party secretary could be so devastating that some would kill the elected village head (Bai and Zhao, 白钢, 赵寿星, 2001: 290). In a widely reported case (Cui, 崔士鑫, 2001), 57 elected village heads in Shangdong province resigned because their corresponding Party secretary refused to hand over power to their hands, including the official seal and finance. Those who complained to the township government and Party committee were warned or even penalized, some were even removed from their post by the township officials.

To minimize the potential conflicts between the elected village heads, a large proportion of whom are the new capitalists, and more importantly to exercise better control of the Party over local organizations, the CCP has adopted the strategy of merging the two committees together by increasing the number of Party secretaries elected as village heads. In the trial version of *The Law of Organising Village Residents'*

*Committees*, there were no statements with regard to the role of local CCP committees in the elections. However, ten years later in its passed version an article on the leading role of the CCP committees was added to Article 3: 'The CCP's local organizations in rural areas should work according to the Party's Constitution, and should play a central role in the leadership'. CCP Central Committee Document No. 14 (2002) called for the Party committee to 'play a core leadership role in village self-government'. While the attempt to allow local Party committees to nominate candidates was defeated, Document No. 14 required Party committees 'to be in charge of organizing election works'. In addition, 'it sought to promote elected committee Party members to take up positions in village Party committees ... village Party secretary candidates should run and get elected as villagers' committee chair first, or their candidacy should be removed if failed to win villagers' committee election' (Tan, 2006: 298). It should be very clear that the CCP wants the village Party secretary to become the village head, and this could be done either by helping the Party secretary get elected, or if the elected head is not a Party member, he or she would be invited to join the Party and may even become the Party secretary. A solution, which was praised as 'an institutional innovation' was to let one person take the two posts (village head and Party secretary); some places call it a 'two-ballot' system (Hequ of Shanxi). Even when the Party secretary was not elected as the village head, according to Robert Pastor and Qingshan Tan (2001), the secretaries usually served on (or chaired) the village election committee that supervised village elections. Over the years of the 2000s, the percentage of CCP members working as members of village residents' committees increased to about 60–70 per cent and the percentage of village heads simultaneously working as Party secretaries is even as high as 88 per cent (Shi et al, 史卫民, 2008: 86). However, while this strategy may increase the CCP's control over village politics and reduce the likelihood of conflicts between two separate leaders, it increases the risk of abusing power by the single leader.[20] If such practice continues, the nascent democratic progress in local areas will take a big step backwards; democracy remains as a simple matter of voting for the village head rather than a procedure of checking those in power.

## Concluding remarks

Democracy is not just about elections; it is more about the public control over the abuse of power by the elected. Elections could exercise some control over the abuse of power by changing those in power, but they only take place when they are called for and could be manipulated. There are already some examples that the elected started to abuse their power without checking mechanisms: Shenzhen Pinghu village experienced admirable development from the early 1980s under the leadership of the Party Secretary and Chairman of the Village Committee Liu Zhaohong (刘照洪), who was selected to be a national model of work and other honours, and the village was nominated as one of the Hundred Best Villages in China. Then he became a 'local emperor', spending twenty millions RMB building a luxurious office building, another twenty million for a holiday compound, importing several luxurious cars, and travelling overseas with public money. He wasted millions by investing in a so-called high technology project. With his permission a large amount of money was spent without official receipts; most of the times the receipt was only a handwritten piece of paper. Some village residents reported to upper level governments but most of the times their petition was declined. It was only until their report reached the CCP's Central Committee of Disciplines that the case was established.[21] This is a relatively minor case compared with the more extreme case of Yu Zuomin (禹作敏) that was reported some years ago (Gilley, 2001). There are positive examples, of course, one of which is Cai Bogao (蔡伯高),[22] who was reported to take no money from the village and never even claimed any expense. He is not a member of the CCP. His eligibility was in question because he bought an apartment in Shenzhen. However, as so many fellow villagers wanted him to be the village head, they voted for his eligibility, which was then approved by the local Civil Affairs officers. In November 1999, 2965 out of 3003 residents voted for him. Good or bad, it seems that how well the current system works largely depends on the person in power rather than the system itself. If this is true, then not much progress has been made in the direction of democratization because one of the objectives of democracy is to minimize the effect of personal effects on politics.

How far will the current system go in the future? If the current practice is to be applied at higher levels, such as county, provincial, and national levels, then it is clear that this entrepreneurial and wealthy group of people should be in an advantageous position in higher level political elections. It is difficult to imagine that the CCP would allow this to happen for two reasons. First, it is not ideologically acceptable to allow the rich to occupy powerful political positions; even in Western democratic societies, this is not a desirable system, let alone in a Communist regime. Second, although the CCP has been quite successful of incorporating some members of this wealthy group into the political system, there is no guarantee that these newly developed capitalists would still firmly stand on their side once they are elected to become regional or even national politicians thanks to their economic power. On the other hand, however, if the CCP would not allow the current practice to expand to higher levels, they must find a legitimate and convincing reason, which will not be an easy task, because the basic principles implied in the current practice, including democracy, fair competition, and so on, are all valid and legitimate.

# 7
## Weapons of the Wealthy

There is an irony in the position of the new capitalists in Chinese society: although they are economically the most active, the most entrepreneurial, and later financially among the wealthiest, they often find themselves subject to a variety of constraints, discrimination, distrust, suppression, and even exploitation by the mighty state and its agents. After more than 30 years of liberalization of economic policies and the sanction of their economic and political roles in the nation's institutional system, the improvement of the new capitalists' economic and political statuses still cannot catch up with the increasing importance and contribution of the private sector as a whole. In an interview I conducted with a medium-sized private business owner in the summer of 2010, he told me that many business owners like him felt like they were 'working under several mountains'. Sarcastically making use of Mao Zedong's reference to 'feudalism, imperialism, and bureaucratic capitalism' as 'the three mountains on the heads of the Chinese people', this new capitalist was talking about unreasonable state regulations such as market entry and access to financial credit, constant harassment by local officials, and increasing costs of raw materials and labour, which can be somewhat confirmed by reports and commentaries in *China Business Times* (中华工商时报), the official newspaper of the All-China Federation of Business and Commerce (ACFBC).[1]

The questions I would like to answer in this chapter are the following: What strategies and actions would the new capitalists employ when they deal with these difficult situations? How would they use the money and wealth in their hands in confronting the authoritarian state? I must say at the beginning that these questions are not meant to imply that I sympathize with them; I would try to be as impartial as possible because my objective is to produce a sensible analysis, not to defend or criticize the business owners or the state officials. I shall examine several situations in which the capitalists have few alternatives but to confront government officials. The first will be the situation in which private entrepreneurs have to deal with unreasonable charges and fees requested by local or government officials. If the private business owners perceived these requests as unjustified, as some of them argued publicly, how did they stand up to the almighty political machine? We could learn a lot from their stories about how the first generation of the new capitalists perceive their political role in China's political system and how they evaluate the justice of government policies and behaviours. I offered a case study of such confrontation in a chapter of *Entrepreneurship in China* (Yang, 2007); here, I shall examine this issue at the national level. This is tightly associated to the problem of corruption among government officials with business connections to some influential business owners; history seems to repeat itself here if the reader could refresh their memory of the situation in the early 1950s (Chapter 2).

Then we shall examine how they behaved politically in a much more unusual situation – the political protests in the spring and the summer of 1989. It is unusual because it is one of the two rare occasions on which the Chinese people openly protested against the Communist regime.[2] Taking the event as a litmus test of political stance and strength, we can see whether private business owners had a common voice, how they saw themselves politically, and how they understood their relations with the Chinese state and with other social groups.

Finally, I turn to the extent to which the new capitalists defend their interests and images collectively. The most recent confrontation, albeit not directly and openly, is the Chinese state's release of a series of policies that aim to promote large state-owned enterprises as part of the stimulating package for bringing China out of the financial crisis of 2008. The significance of these policies is that they seem to signal the limits imposed on the growth of the private sector. It is interesting to see what owners of private businesses would do when their collective interests are jeopardized. The confrontational situations may be still rare, but it is very likely that they will become more frequent in the coming years.

## The costs of being private in a Communist regime

The emergence and growth of 'the underground economy' or 'second economy' have been widely identified and studied in transitional economies, including former Soviet Union nations, Eastern Europe, and China (Ernst and Alexeev, 1995; Geber and Hout, 1998; Stark and Bruszt, 1998; Szelenyi, 1988; Woodruff, 1999). Particularly in the early stages of economic transformation, entrepreneurs in these countries invented new organizational forms, mostly hybrid in terms of ownership (percentage systems, VGM, TVE, and other types of joint ventures) in order to be economically profitable as well as politically acceptable in the new and highly changeable environment. A common feature of these new organizational forms is the exchange of economic earnings for administrative protection and favours between the organizations and their supervising state agents.

Researchers of private enterprises in China have long reported the costs for cultivating a good relationship with local governments (Ho, 1994: 196–200; Kraus, 1991: 142–65; Rocca, 1992: 40; Wank, 1999: 166–72; Young, 1995: 67–92). For example, Kraus (1991: 157–59) found that during 1985 to 1988, there were up to 43 types of administration fees, many of them unreasonably imposed on individual and private businesses and therefore dubbed 'three rampancies' (三乱, fees, fines, and requests for donations). Liu (1992) also reported that in exchange for administrative facilitation and political protection, 'voluntary donations' and locally imposed fees became the major sources of local revenues not only for constructing public projects but also for increasing local leaders' personal income. Leading social scientists on this issue in China were not hesitant to point out this problem either; according to them, regardless of the campaigns launched by the national government to fight against these predatory actions, the average amount of fees and charges for a private enterprise went up from about RMB 22,000 in 1993 to 35,000 in 1995 and 39,000 in 1997 (Zhang and Ming, 1999: 140). Data from the NSPBO for the years after 1997 suggest that the figures were fluctuating from 30,000 to 45,000 between 2000 and 2006, although the fees and charges vary much more dramatically and the fees and charges as percentages of total profit were declining. More recent studies have confirmed the findings. For example, Zhang Jianjun, a social scientist trained in the US and now teaching at Beijing University, found in his fieldwork that '[a]lmost all entrepreneurs mentioned their unpleasant experiences with the government, either in the process of applying for licenses and permits or getting necessary resources controlled by the government' (2008: 154).

But few have openly voiced their resentment, let alone taken action to change the political relationship with the government. To obtain a sense of how prevalent the difficult relationship between private business owners and local officials is, let's take a look at the results from the National Survey of Private Business Owners (NSPBO), as the business owners might take the participation in the survey as an opportunity to express their resentment. As the related items in the surveys changed over the years,[3] I present the results in two parts. Firstly, for the surveys in 1993 and 1995, the private business owners were asked whether they had encountered any difficulties in a series of business activities, and if they had, what the main reason was. Here, I focus on four important activities: purchasing raw materials, marketing, obtaining electricity and business premises. The results are highly consistent over the two years: around 85 per cent of private business owners had difficulties (a little, some, or a lot) in obtaining business premises (space), about 78 per cent reported different levels of difficulties in obtaining raw materials and electricity, and about 75 per cent had difficulties in marketing. The main source of these difficulties, however, was not always 'having a difficult time with government agents'. Among those who reported difficulties in those four business operations, private business owners were more likely to encounter discriminatory (at least in their eyes) treatment from government agents when they tried to obtain electricity and space (about one-fourth), while for the two more market-determined activities (raw materials and marketing), government agents did not seem to create much difficulty for private businesses.

What did the private business owners do when they had disputes with government agents? The surveys from 2000 to 2006 asked this question, although the options provided were not always the same. In 2000, the actions were presented together, which allows us to see the distribution of respondents across all these actions. For this year, 71 per cent of those who reported disputes with government agents (n = 244) chose to negotiate privately through personal connections, about 27 per cent chose more confrontational actions, including reporting to upper level government (17 per cent) and appealing to court (10 per cent). From 2002, these options were presented separately, thus making it impossible to examine the distribution of choices of private business owners having disputes with government officials. However, the responses from these separate questions tell roughly the same story: private business owners normally try to resolve their disputes with local officials privately (around 60 per cent). The additional information we learn from these more recent surveys is that there have been an increasing number (50 per cent to 65 per cent) of private business owners who would resort to their business associations, including All China Federation of Business and Commerce, to resolve disputes with governments. Clearly, many of them would employ more than one tactic – very likely attempting to find personal and organizational resolutions at the same time, and resorting to more confrontational actions only after they have run out of more peaceful options.

The new capitalists hold some mixed feelings towards state officials. At the political level, they know that their private businesses and assets are not completely secure despite the Communist state's repeated assurance. The state is simply so powerful that there is still a long way from constitutional endorsement to actual protection of private properties. The solution is to move their families and at least part of their assets overseas, mostly the US, Canada, and Australia. In daily business operations, they must abhor the state officials who constantly squeeze some money from their profits. Nevertheless, there are no other choices than to buy a relatively 'collegial' working relationship with state officials. I have discussed such 'double entrepreneurship', which demands both tactics and skills, in a previous book with specific reference to a few cases.

In dealing with government officials, those private business owners who become delegates of the People's Congress or Political Consultative Assembly would benefit from their memberships. As one of them said in an interview, 'administrative agents would not likely to investigate your firms if you are members [of any of the two institutions]; if they do investigate and find some problems, they would be more lenient than they are to other firms'. The agents know that they may make some trouble for themselves if they investigate 'the delegate business owners', because these private business owners normally have close connections to the local leaders. Clearly, only a small number of business owners would be able to enjoy such special treatment.

For the majority of private business owners in China, when facing an exploitative government official, here are the options: (1) to comply, that is, simply giving away what the official requests; (2) to resist, which further could come in two general forms: (2a) 'hard protest' against the official by obtaining help and support from higher-level officials, the media, or even legal procedures; (2b) 'soft protest', that is, attempting to reduce the amount of extraction by resorting to personal connections or giving away a smaller amount to the official in exchange for a smaller extraction, a form of bribery, obviously. A case study in my previous book (Yang, 2007, Chapter 6) shows how a female entrepreneur dealt with unreasonable extractions imposed by an official of a department of the national government. The strategy that the business owner took was 'hard protest' by revealing the experience to journalists and writing to upper level state officials; it is difficult to see who won in that case because the public seemed to be more interested in the dark sides of each party than the damage to their reputation that both sides suffered. Such 'hard protest' is rare; for most private business owners, 'soft protest' would be the most popular strategy, not only because it is the most cost-efficient but also because it explains another widely adopted practice, that is, the construction and maintenance of a net of personal connections. Almost all relatively large business owners that I have interviewed rely on this net of personal connections for their survival and success, which could also explain the increasing number of cases of corruption involving both private business owners and local officials. Mr Hou, a new capitalist from Chongqing, described his experience as follows (Chan and Unger, 1991: 112 and 113):

> The Foundation for the Disabled ([Deng Pufang, the elder son of Deng Xiaoping, is the president of this Foundation] once again came asking for a 'donation'. You have to 'donate'; you simply can't refuse. The amount of 'donation' depends on the size of your business. If you don't give, they'll make you wear 'small shoes' [bring all kinds of inconveniences to you]. Because my business was quite big, I had to 'donate' up to a thousand yuan each time, several times in one year. Apart from Deng Pufang's institution, many others came around. I was even told that I'd better provide a donation towards the construction of the Asian Games Village. We feel our lives are under pressure from all sides.
>
> To be a successful *ge ti hu* you have to build up your connections. We have to get to know people from the public security organs. It's necessary for our business. The people in the public security bureau have very low salaries, so they like to make friends with *ge ti hus* who have money. We help each other out in a way. We feast them, buy them cigarettes, entertain them. In a way we're friends – wine-and-dine friends.

It is almost universally believed among private business owners that it is impossible to survive or win the market competition by strictly complying to state regulations, including taxation, safety measures, welfare for employees, and so on. They claim that they would all go bankrupt if they comply, a justification that we may call 'the understandable violation of law'. Many of them set up two books, one for tax agents and one for their own use. In the first book, most of them lose money, therefore having little tax to pay. The only thing they must do is to establish good relations with tax officers, which means bribing them. 'If you sort out the relations, everything should be fine' indicates a toleration of transforming state assets (taxes) into personal gain (reduction of tax). One business owner told me: 'If the leader thinks it is important, it will get done; if the leader thinks it is not important, no matter how hard you try, nobody will do it'. A social scientist in China shared with me a case study of a female entrepreneur who was selected to meet a female minister, where the city major and Party secretary were all present. The female minister asked the major and the secretary to support the female entrepreneur's business, who reported: 'Later on I found it became so easy to deal with the government. For example, in 2004, all enterprises under government ownership must be transformed (sold), and there is one estate company next to mine. I learnt that the estate company was worth more than eight million, but I got it for about six million; without my connection with the leaders, that was impossible! That's a turning point for my business'. Two years before, she also enjoyed an opportunity to meet President Hu Jintao. More importantly, she got a photo of her shaking hands with President Hu, which helped her win many clients – some of her clients told her later, 'I would do business with you completely due to the photo'.

## The return of 'sugar-coated bullets': rent seeking and corruption

On the surface, all the above costs are charged in the names of tax, fees, or any other legitimate terms. There is however a more profound ideological reason for charging them; that is, they are to make up the lower ideological status of the new capitalists, which explains why local officials were so unscrupulous in showing contempt to private business owners before Deng Xiaoping dismissed the ideological issue. Since the tax reform in 1994, which happened to be the time the status of private businesses was firmly established, local governments can retain a proportion of taxes collected in their jurisdictions; therefore, local officials have strong motivation to help and support private enterprises, especially those who made a substantial contribution to local governments' revenue. The increased amount of financial income under the control of local officials is not only an indicator of the success of their political career but also a source of the improvement of their personal wellbeing, including luxurious cars, offices, overseas travels, and even bribes made by anyone who must let the officials benefit from the transactions they aim to achieve. In other words, corruption of local state officials is a necessary consequence of the decentralization of the financial system without any political mechanisms for checking their power (Sands,

1990). Extraction of financial contributions from private enterprises remains a practice widely adopted by local officials, but this time they try to increase financial income through officially legitimate mechanisms and in the name of developing local economies. Consequently, the amount of fees and charges has declined since then, at least relative to the profits.

In dealing with the extractions, most of private business owners do not have such privilege of being protected by top leaders through official connections. Therefore, informal opportunities must be either employed, if they already exist, or created through all forms of 'sugar-coated bullets'. As it becomes riskier to directly offer the bribes to the officials in power, most bribes are offered to the family members of the officials, such as helping and financing their children to go abroad to study, allocating a high-paying job to a family member of the official, giving away shares or dividends to family members, and so on. According the CCP's official newspaper, *People's Daily* (7 August 2002), in the two years of 2000 and 2001, 4,081 officials, including ten former ministers, vice ministers, and key state firm executives were audited; about 1500 of them were found to have problems, 500 were removed from their posts, and 1000 were forwarded to judicial departments. Furthermore (3 March 2003), from 1998 to March 2003, a total of 207,103 cases of corruption were handed over to the procurator for investigation. Corruption is particularly rampant in the industry of real estate because it requires the direct collusion of government officials who are in charge of land and the estate developers in order to produce enormous amount of profit, which they would share at the expense of the state and local residents. The percentage of estate developers among the top wealthiest list has been on the rise over the years. Cases of such collusion include some of the top local officials, for example, one of the Deputy Mayors of Beijing Liu Zhihua (刘志华), a Deputy Minister of Department of Finance Zhu Zhigang (朱志刚), a Vice Chairman of People's Consultative Assembly of Guangdong province Chen Shaoji (陈绍基), Deputy Mayor of the City of Suzhou Jian Renjie (姜人杰), and the Mayor of the City of Shenzhen Xu Zongheng (许宗衡).

How do private business owners see the corrupted officials? Who would stand up and say 'I would rather lose my business than bribe a corrupted official'? It seems that this group of wealthy people care more about money-making than moral integrity. Bribery or collusion with government officials in general is a weapon of the wealthy; it was when the old capitalists dealt with the coming Communists at the end of the 1940s and the early 1950s, and still is in the twentieth and the twenty-first century.

How many of the new capitalists feel ashamed of their immoral behaviour and undisciplined pursuit of financial wealth is an interesting question for future research. On the other hand, the fact that they could be so immoral and undisciplined indicates just how corrupt the Communist government officials are as well and how undemocratic China's political system is. The leaders of the CCP would rather allow their powerful members to keep being corrupt than give up their political dominance so that another political party and an independent judicial system could curb corruption in a more effective way. In this sense, the immoral capitalists are less responsible for their immoral behaviour – in most situations they have no choice but to bribe the government officials in order to set up or expand their businesses.

## Private business owners in political protests

If the new and petty capitalists experienced discrimination and contempt from state officials in the decade or so from the start of economic reforms at the end of the 1970s to the end of the 1980s, we would expect at least some of them to stand up to defend their interests and to take the rare opportunity to join the students' protests in the summer of 1989. The main protestors were the students and intellectuals (university academics, academy researchers, journalists, and so on); in most studies of this incident, except for a few sporadic cases (see below), private business owners were almost invisible in media and academic reports. One reason is likely to be the fact that at the time when students started to mobilize themselves for protests, the private sector had only for a short time been recognized by the Chinese state. In early 1987, the Central Committee of the CCP announced, for the first time, that the private economy could become a complement to the national economy that had been dominated by state plan and state-owned enterprises. Accordingly, the National People's Congress sanctioned such policy by modifying an amendment to the Constitution in April 1988. Note that, although this may appear to be a breakthrough with reference to the CCP's previous policies, it was more a cautious experiment than whole-hearted support and recognition. Despising and discriminating against private business owners remained common among state officials and even ordinary people. At the end of 1989, there were little more than 90,000 registered private enterprises in China, most of which were extremely small and operating in the rural areas. This meant that private business owners, unlike the students, did not feel that they could mobilize a collective action at the national level.

In addition, despite the fact that many private business owners suffered from constraints and even discrimination, most of them, including those individual businesses (*ge ti hu*), were the beneficiaries of the new economic policies – they were economically better off than university academics, and at least some of their losses in paying off rampant fees and charges were compensated by evading taxes, taking advantage of dual prices, faking big brands, and other business misbehaviours. A survey conducted right before the protests at Tiananmen Square showed that most people would go to the streets to protest for three major reasons: corruption among top leaders (28 per cent), unbearable increase of prices (26 per cent) and major mistakes in decision-making by the state (19 per cent); a substantial percentage of people (16 per cent) would not protest at all.[4] Many students saw private businesses as a source of at least some of these problems and consequently did not see them as their allies, at least not at the beginning. An enemy of your enemy may not be your friend.

In such context, it is no surprise that private business owners did not exercise much influence on the protests. The most notable case is The Stone Group, led by Wan Runnan, Cao Siyuan, and Zhou Duo. Another group of private business owners that drew some attention from the state media were the 'Flying Tigers' – a group of 'mostly small-time entrepreneurs' (Barmé, 1991: 55) – who seemed to have done nothing more than passing some food, drinks, and messages around the students. Although their support was much appreciated – some students even shouted 'Long live Beijing's getihu!' at Tiananmen Square – the major characters remained the students,[5] the intellectuals, the journalists, and to a lesser extent some workers and government agents, who all normally distained the petty entrepreneurs either because the businesses were too small to be respectable or because the business owners were always suspected of illegitimate transactions.[6] It was therefore an overreaction on the part of Jiang Zemin, who took over from Zhao Ziyang as the CCP's General Secretary, and announced soon after the crackdown on the protests that private business owners were prohibited to join the Party, obviously a form of punishment.

Jiang's announcement was an overreaction also because it was unclear – perhaps we shall never be able to know – what was in the mind of most private enterprise owners at that time. While it is nearly impossible to have a sense of the percentage, it is certain that not all private business owners were supporting the students. Indeed, many of them would think that they were one of the targets of student protests since many of them were earning much more than university professors at that time – 'scientists producing rockets are earning less than those selling eggs on the street'. It is safe to say that Wan Runnan's direct involvement in the protests seems to be exceptional rather than representing the general stance of private business owners at that time. A co-founder of Stone, Shen Guojun, opposed the Stone's involvement in the protests (Kennedy, 1997: 764). In addition, a small number of private business owners such as Mou Qizhong, the founder and one of the owners of Nande Group (Yang, 2007, chapter 7), openly denounced the protests as 'dong luan' (turmoil), a derogative label given the protests by the state media. Indeed, Mou might represent the private business owners who desperately needed a peaceful political environment, albeit an authoritarian one, to complete their business transactions.

That Wan Runnan played a leading role in the protests seems to be undisputable. According to an article published in *People's Daily*,[7] Wan said at an illegal radio station that: 'The government has stood at the opposite to the people, so it is not a government of the people anymore. People of all sectors should mobilize themselves, crash the curfew and overthrow the government'. Clearly representing the view of the Communist state, the author of the article accused not only Wan and his Stone Group but private business owners in general: 'Private and individual businesses like Stone were the most active in supporting this movement!' because they provided food, drinks, medicine, wireless telephones, loudspeakers, and other equipments.[8] At the end of the article, the author pointed out that Wan's ultimate objective was 'to implement privatization, to let the so-called middle-class take the leading position, to abolish the Four Fundamental Principles, and to establish the so-called "Congress Democracy"'. On 24 June 1989, the Public Security Ministry issued a warrant for the arrests of Yan Jiaqi and six others, including Wan Rennan: 'These seven took part in the behind-the-scenes planning and direction of the counterrevolutionary riots in Beijing' (Liang, Nathan and Link, 2001: 591). One example of such 'planning and direction' was a meeting with AFS [Autonomous Federation of Students] leaders at the International Hotel, in which Wan 'raised six conditions for withdrawal from Tiananmen square: "(1) Pull back the army, (2) abolish martial law, (3) dismiss Li Peng, (4) retire Deng Xiaoping, (5) retire Yang Shangkun, and (6) restore Zhao Ziyang"' (Liang, Nathan and Link, 2001: 439). It was also claimed that Wan donated large sums of money to the students.

Nevertheless, it remains unclear in what capacity Wan was playing such a significant role in the protests. Was he speaking on behalf of private business owners, in other words, was he seeing the movement as a political process to enhance the interests of the new capitalists, or was he taking those actions and speaking those words as a person – who just happened to be a private business owner – enthusiastic about turning China into a democracy? The state media would definitely claim it was the former although there is no supporting evidence for this claim. An editorial of *People's Daily* on the 22 of February 1990 ('On Fighting against Capitalist Liberalization') asked the following questions: 'Is there an economic source behind those promoting capitalist liberalization? Is there an economic force that supported them?' The article made a very affirmative answer, and this economic force was the middle class, private enterprises, and *ge ti hu* – 'they are the economic source of capitalist liberalization'. Even the Communists themselves would not believe such confusing logic; otherwise, we would not have seen the rapid growth of the private sector since the early 1990s. After the crackdown, the Stone Group continued to exist, perhaps as a symbol of the leniency of the CCP. As Kennedy argued, actually '4 June saved Stone' because it ended the in-fights among the top managers (1997: 762).

It is inappropriate to evaluate the role of the new capitalists based on what they did in the spring and summer of 1989, because the whole private sector was still at the margin economically and many local officials were very much doubtful of the political legitimacy of private enterprises in practice. Private enterprises were so weak at that time that the Stone Group was one of the largest and most influential. Perhaps fortunately for the CCP, at that time there were very few private companies as financially and politically influential as Stone. It is difficult to speculate on how they would behave if a similar event broke out today. Would they follow the lead of students and young radical intellectuals, given there are politically radical university students and intellectuals in today's China? Or would they stand in defence of the Communist state for the sake of maintaining a peaceful environment for their businesses? Given the diversity of the new capitalists, the most probable scenario would be that they would break up into different political groups, with those seeing their interests aligned with the Communist state protecting the current system while those having bad memories of state officials offering support to the students and intellectuals.

The political turmoil in the summer of 1989 must have reminded top leaders of the CCP that it is not to the interest of their political dominance to alienate the newly emerged group of private business owners. A wiser strategy is to incorporate them into the current political system. Although this strategy did not come easily with many voices in and outside the Party against it, eventually the pragmatic policy of strengthening the Party's ruling status prevailed. Jiang Zemin's speech at the CCP's 80th anniversary in 2001 accomplished this turning point. It is true that there were already CCP members working inside private enterprises, but it has been since his speech that the CCP has formally opened its door to the newly emerging capitalists and started a process of establishing organizational infrastructure within private businesses at the same time. Furthermore, the most successful private business owners that the CCP finds politically loyal and reliable are rewarded with the memberships of People's Representatives or Political Consultation Assembly Members. There are no ideological and organizational barriers anymore for the capitalists to join the sole ruling party. In return, the capitalists yield some control of their businesses to the Party and agree to behave within the boundaries of the current political system. Business associations, with the All-China Federation of Industry and Commerce (*quan guo gong shang lian*) being the most prominent, serve as the channels of communication between the state and private businesses, resolving most of the issues within the institutional structure rather than contentiously in public. In short, better access to political power is provided without letting the business associations develop into a part of a genuine civil society. In the last chapter, I shall conceptualize these institutional arrangements as expressions of 'elite corporatism' as they represent corporative exchanges between the political and the business elites in today's China.

The Chinese people have learnt a great lesson from the 1989 incident: the Communist state will employ whatever is at its disposal to punish those who would dare to attempt to make political demands by organizing mass protests, even though the demand targets a particular person, such as Li Peng or Deng Xiaoping, without calling for a fundamental change to the current political system. In the following years, all protests are ad hoc and of much less significance with an aim to voice grievances of social injustice or deteriorating economic situations. The impact of such a suppressive system on people's political behaviour can only yield one of the following two results: either giving up any legitimate ways of expressing one's views as they are all ineffective, or waiting for the opportunity to use the illegitimate ways to overthrow the whole system. At the moment, it is the former strategy that most people have followed.

How should we explain the increasing number of corruption cases and, more importantly, the difficulty of eliminating them? As Mao Zedong clearly realized right before the Communists came to rule China at the end of the 1940s, the capitalists might use 'sugar-coated bullets' (money, favours, sex, and so on) to corrode his fellow Communists who were so anxious to enjoy the fruits of victory after many years of sacrifices and hardships. That did not happen on a large scale thanks to the constant external threats (Korean War, Taiwan), harsh discipline within the CCP and the quick demise of the old generation of capitalists. It is somehow ironical to find that although today's 'sugar-coated bullets' are far more fierce than they were 60 years ago, the CCP leaders seem to be running out of tactics for tackling the rising number of corruption cases. To say that the CCP has become complacent after being in power for 60 years is not completely true – it may be the case for many local officials, but those at the very top have reiterated many times the potential threat of corruption to their ruling power. The fundamental difference between now and then is that the CCP does not treat the new capitalists as their potential 'class enemy' anymore although there is still some distrust. The CCP has learnt to be less contentious and to employ more friendly tactics. Instead, by making economic growth the central task for the whole nation, the CCP has effectively and perhaps inadvertently encouraged, if not directly formed, an alliance between state officials and business owners. This alliance, with one side monopolizing key resources and the other organizing the production process, is the root source of corruption in today's China. Therefore, the most effective solution to eliminating corruption is to break such alliance by substantially reducing state officials' power in business affairs. Clearly, this is not what the CCP would like to do, which is why corruption is going to stay in China as long as current state policy continues.

The following case illustrates the above points very well. Wang Wenqi was the CCP secretary of Hengjing town, Taicang county, Suzhou. He asked CCP members and cadres in his town to become rich first and then help others get rich by setting up their own private firms; those who couldn't set up their own businesses were dismissed. He justified his view as the following (Zhang Jianjun, 2008: 134–5):

Why cannot party members and cadres engage in private business? ... we have enough reasons to encourage party members and cadres to get rich first. First, Deng Xiaoping called for letting a few get rich first. Who are these "few"? Of course it should be us – party members and cadres. ... Second, the Communist Party is a party of the proletariat. But we have been in power for over 50 years. It is nonsense if we are still the proletariat. So I think we should transfer ourselves from a propertyless class to a propertied class. ... Third, how can we realize General Secretary Jiang's "three representatives"? If you set up a private business and pay taxes to the state, then you represent the essential interests of the people; if you have a factory, machines, and technology, you then represent advanced productive forces; industrial culture and factory culture are advanced cultures in the countryside, so you naturally represent advanced culture if you have a factory. Fourth, if cadres engage in private business, the masses can be assured that they can develop private business. You serve the people within working hours. But outside those eight hours, you are the boss in your factory. This can increase your contact with the masses. Fifth, only if cadres have businesses can we speed up the change of government functions. The key work for the party is to develop the economy. How can you develop the economy without establishing firms? ... If the rich are neither party members nor cadres, where do our authority and reputation come from? It is easier for me, a party secretary, to have a lot of rich people working in the government. If we have only poor people working here, how can we do our job well?

Here is the challenge for the CCP top leaders: on the one hand, local officials will not be motivated to develop their local economies without seeing the benefits of doing so, but this would mean the exchange of power with money; on the other hand, to prevent the local officials from directly getting involved in business transactions would mean to deprive them of their ruling power. The political system does not permit them to stand outside the economy while developing it.

## Emerging collective identity and actions

As pointed out above, a fundamental difference between today's corruption and those in the early 1950s lies in how the CCP defines their nature. In the 1950s, those cases involving old capitalists were seen as the attack of the capitalists as a class on the new regime. After the start of economic reforms, such perception of the new capitalists only returned, in much less confrontational terms, during the protests in the summer of 1989, and was soon dismissed quietly after Deng Xiaoping's call to terminate the debate over how capitalist or socialist the reforms were. To the interest of the CCP, terminating the debate would not only eradicate the ideological barriers to economic growth but also minimize the chance of developing a collective identity among the new capitalists.

It is very much true that the new capitalists in China have not developed a strong sense of belonging to the same and distinctive social group – as we have seen in the previous chapters; this is an enormously diverse group in almost all aspects: financial assets, political status, social reputation, education, and so on. A large number of labels exist, such as 'the new rich' (Goodman, 2008), 'the middle class' (Cheng, 2010), 'private entrepreneurs', 'non-state personnel' (widely use in China), and so on, most of which are loosely defined at best, but they are created for the convenience of referring to these people rather than recognizing a collective identity. Social scientists in China have made their contribution to the CCP's call for building a 'harmonious society' by purposely keeping away from contentious terms, such as class, while in the meantime promoting the use of more ambivalent but seemingly more universal terms, such as strata (Guo, 2008).

However, we would be either ignorant or deceitful if we deny a slowly growing sense of collective identity among the new capitalists. Under the current circumstance, there are not many opportunities for this sense of collective identity to express itself, particularly not through collective and open actions, but that does not mean that the identity does not exist. It is indeed very difficult to define the scope of the identity (how many among private business owners would think they belong to this social group), its distinctive features (how this group is different from others such as 'the middle class', 'the economic elite', and so on), and its stability (how changeable it is over time). Nevertheless, we do know some situations in which they are separated from other social groups, and such categorization or labelling process itself reinforces the formation of a shared identity among the new capitalists. Here are a few examples.

In defending and protecting their interests, one weapon that the new capitalists have learnt to pick up recently is their business associations. Starting as a political underdog, the new capitalists, especially the leading figures at the national level, know more than anybody else that they must fight harder to obtain a respectable place in China's Communist system, which is only achievable through organized actions. The fact that the CCP has set up a distinctive sector (jie bie, 界别) for the All-China Federation of Business and Commerce (ACFBC) effectively sanctioned private businesses owners as a legitimate political group, a recognition that nurtures and strengthens a sense of shared identity among them. Perhaps the most daring and the most successful expression of this shared identity is ACFBC's repeated requests (three times in 1998, 2002, and 2004) made to the National People's Congress to add an article in the nation's Constitution to protect private properties. Indeed, perhaps the most distinctive identity indisputably shared among the new capitalists is the wealth and assets in their hands, and they would do their best to justify the legality, the legitimacy, and the morality of their assets. The ACFBC has set this as one of its key missions, and its official newspaper (*China Business Times, zhonghua gongshang shibao*) has assigned itself as 'the guardian of the non-state economy'. For example, in the most recent confrontation with the Communist state, this newspaper published a series of reports voicing the new capitalists' resentment against the state's discriminatory policies in allocating resources differently to the state and the private sectors, respectively, calling for the breaking up the monopolies of state enterprises and the retreat of private businesses (guo jin min tui). Compared with the other political organization that also represents the interests of the new capitalists, the Democratic Construction Association (min jian), the ACFBC is politically more active and visible thanks to its business nature (therefore politically less threatening).

The new capitalists are clearly aware that wealth could also play against their interests when it sets themselves apart from the ordinary Chinese people, particularly the working class. A strong sense of resentment ('hatred of the rich', chou fu) is reported to have fermented across the whole Chinese society, although we do not know the precise scale of such sentiment. Zang has identified three reasons why 'the new rich' (private business owners, state-enterprise managers who bought up their enterprises[9], and so on) have aroused so much negative feeling among the ordinary people: 'original sin' (illegal ways of making money), 'inequality', and 'unkindness' (2008: 59). While it might be a stereotypical misconception on the part of the general public to believe that most of the new capitalists have committed 'the original sin' (violating state regulations, laws, moral codes, and social norms when earning the initial capital or 'the first barrel of gold' in Chinese), the generalization itself reinforces a shared identity of the new capitalists, that they are all in the same boat in earning 'dirty' or even 'cold-hearted' money in the process of becoming rich. Some of the most influential private business owners, such as Liu Yonghao (刘永好) and Yin Minshan (尹明善), have urged their fellow capitalists to keep a low profile in public to avoid further resentment. On a more positive note but with the same objective, other members of the new capitalists have employed influential intellectuals and academics to glorify their public image by emphasizing the economic contributions, the hard working and competitive ethos, and the donations to charities.

While these strategies and actions are employed for the whole group of the new capitalist at the national level, they are also adopted at the local levels. When members of a local private business association are in trouble, particularly with local government officials, they would resort to their association and see if the association could help them out. Almost all leaders of Wenzhou Business Associations outside Wenzhou have personal connections with local officials (ibid.: 250–1); for example, in Shenyang, the capital of Lianing Province, government agents pledged that they would solve all requests and demands by Wenzhou businessmen without delaying to the next day. The advantage cannot be clearer: any medium-sized or small private business does not have the bargaining power to defend itself in front of the powerful government, so the association offers a form of collective power. In one example reported by some social scientists in China (Chen et al., 陈剩勇, 汪锦军, 马斌, 2004: 237), in April 1997, 20 trucks with goods from Wenzhou were confiscated by officials from the local Court of Inspection (jian cha yuan) on their way to a city in Anhui Province. It was clear to the business owners of the trucks that the local officials wanted money in the name of prosecuting fake products. The Association of Transportations immediately sent a team of representatives to negotiate with local officials. In a sense, they were very lucky because the State Council was in the process of launching a campaign against rampant fee collections by government agents – the so-called san luan (three unreasonable actions: charges, fees, and fines) discussed earlier in this chapter. The case was thus brought to the attention of Leaders of Anhui Province, who brought the case further to a meeting of the State Council, who eventually revolved the dispute (they didn't say exactly how).

In another case (ibid.: 248–9) during the SARS endemic in 2003, the Bureau of Environment Protection launched an unannounced inspection of synthetic leather producers. There are more than ninety such producers who had formed their own business association. During this inspection, 20 manufacturers received fines by the Bureau for pollution. On behalf of the members, the Secretary of the association voiced his resentment: 'The industry of synthetic leather has had a thirteen year history in Wenzhou. The government's attitude towards pollution has always been ambivalent, and there has never been an inspection. Now due to SARS, many enterprises have to either close down or stop production; they are in crisis. At this moment, government agents do not give a hand to the enterprises; on the contrary, they put salt on the wounds!' Such confrontation was resolved in the end with the intervention of a deputy-major of Wenzhou, who ordered the Bureau to reduce the fine by 10 per cent and postpone the payment.

# 8
# The Capitalists, the Workers, and the Communist State

## China's changing social structure in the past three decades

With China's economic reforms has come a fundamental change of the nation's social structure. Broadly speaking, we can say that China has followed two paths of privatizing the national economy. The first path is to allow and later encourage people to set up their own private businesses. Previously living in perhaps one of the most egalitarian societies in the world and calling each other 'comrade', the Chinese population has diversified: many of them have started their own businesses by employing their former 'comrades', subsequently forming a new generation of capitalists.[1] The second is to transform small and medium sized state enterprises into private companies by selling off their assets to either foreign investors or former managers of these enterprises, or other business owners (Ma, 2010; Yusuf, Nabeshima and Perkins, 2006).

These processes of privatization have profound social implications. These new capitalists, except those from overseas, have become bosses of their former comrades. In the meantime, previously 'the masters of the new society', millions of industrial workers find themselves becoming a 'new crowd of the dispossessed' (Solinger, 2004), most of whom have to turn to these new capitalists for re-employment. Merely three decades ago, the Chinese state was almost the only employer of the urban labour force, providing the workers with not only life-long employment but cradle-to-grave welfare as well (for a review of the role of the workers in Mao's era and in state and collective enterprises, see Whyte, 1999). Today, tens of millions are employed by the new capitalists and have to bear a variety of exploitations. Indeed, even the National Bureau of Statistics has started to publish statistics with the newly created categories of 'employer' and 'employee', a perfect example of how statistics represent social change. This is not to deny the emergence of the new middle class (professionals, government agents, and so on), who are contributing to China's changing social structure as well. However, it is the polarizing structure of the new capitalists and the 'new' workers that has radically shaped the social structure of today's China.

While the new social structure requires corresponding state policies and regulations on employment relations, the implications of China's changing social structure go well beyond the employers and their employees. One fundamental consequence of the above transformation is the respective relationship of the new capitalists and the workers with the Communist state. The first half of the People's Republic's history was in a sense a process of eliminating the capitalist class from China's social and political landscapes alongside with the nationalization of all capitalist enterprises. Industrial workers were 'the leading class' and the elite of the social basis on which the Communist regime was established; the capitalists were their common enemy. After a short period of seemingly collegial relationship between the workers and their bosses in the first few years of the new regime, the workers soon overturned their relationship with the capitalists in a series of political campaigns organized by the Communist state, most notably the Five-Antis described in Chapter 2. The capitalists were deprived of their assets, removed from their managerial positions, and even humiliated publicly during political campaigns lasting to the end of the Great Proletariat Cultural Revolution (Yang, Kuisong, 2009). In contrast, the workers enjoyed a comprehensive package of welfare, although this meant 'organized dependency' (Walder, 1992) and 'paternalistic surveillance' (Solinger, 2004).

It is too much an exaggeration to say that the second half of the PRC's history has been a reversing process to its first 30 years. Nevertheless, that the Communist state's policies and practices have shifted mostly in favour of the new capitalists is undeniable, even though nascent capitalist entrepreneurs suffered from various hostile treatments and institutional discriminations, particularly before Deng Xiaoping's 'Southern Tour' in 1992. Researchers including myself have documented and analysed this process (see, for example, Kraus, 1991; Yang, 2004, 2007).[2] Besides the increasingly favourable state policies, in the meantime the new capitalists have enjoyed much closer relationships with the Chinese state, especially at the local levels and both formally and informally, as presented and discussed in the previous chapters.[3] Soon after the suspension of ideological debates under the order of Deng Xiaoping, the Communist states (national and local) and the new capitalists discovered each other as close

allies: the states want to enhance their political legitimacy and state officials' personal wealth by developing the economy, while the capitalists
need political and administrative support – sometimes even collusion –
from state officials in order to satisfy their desire to make profits rapidly.
Formally, the number of capitalist representatives in political organizations (People's Congress and People's Political Consultative Assembly)
has increased from zero to hundreds at the national level and thousands
at local levels. Informally, the new capitalists, especially the influential
ones, often have state officials as their close friends or enjoy direct and
easy access to resources under the control of government officials.

Parallel to the ascent of the new capitalists' economic and political statuses has been the descent of the workers', at least in economic
terms. Researchers, both in and outside China, have documented the
deteriorating conditions under which the workers have been suffering,
and this is the case not only for domestic firms but for foreign and international firms as well (for example, Chan, 2001). For domestic private
enterprises, as we shall see in this chapter, the main problems include
rate of payment lower than the official threshold, no written employment contract, prolonged working hours, no or poor safety provisions,
and lack of welfare insurance.

To summarize, I use the following diagram (Figure 8.1) to represent
the historical change of the relations between the Chinese Communist
state, the capitalists, and the industrial workers:

Which side, that is, the workers' or the capitalists', is the Chinese
Communist state on? How does the state justify its changing policies towards the capitalists and the workers? Where do state officials
stand when there are disputes between the workers and their bosses?
In theory, there are three possibilities: (1) on the workers' side, (2) on
the capitalists' side, and (3) keeping itself impartial. As indicated above,

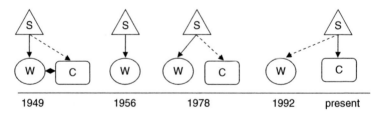

*Figure 8.1*  Changing relations between the Chinese state, the workers, and the
capitalists
*Note:* S = the Chinese State; W = Workers; C = Capitalists; Solid line = support; brokenline =
weakened relationship.

there are many signs that the state is drifting away from the workers' side. However, I believe it would go too far to claim that the Chinese state has abandoned the workers and does not care about their welfare anymore. Even for the sake of maintaining its own ruling status, the Communist state would not see itself alienating its former basis of political support, albeit it is a challenge to convince the massive working class that all of the policies in favour of the capitalists might sooner or later be beneficial to the workers as well.

In relation to that, it would be extremely unwise – and therefore extremely unlikely – that the Chinese state will stand on the side of the capitalists either, at least not publicly. Had it been on the capitalists' side, even merely perceived to be so, the Chinese state would have brought ridicule upon itself and found it enormously difficult to legitimize its rule. In the end, the third possibility is the most probable and sensible; that is, the Chinese state would at least present itself as being independent of the interest of any particular class. It may sound ironical but that is what the CCP seems to aspire to be, a non-partisan political party. The top leaders of the Chinese Communist Party (CCP) are clearly aware of the increasingly diverse interests of difference classes as a result of their reform policies, although obviously they would not want to admit the necessity that these interests would be in conflict.

To prevent this from developing into a source of political contention, they have tried to invent new political principles that aim to reconcile the potentially incompatible interests, including Jiang Zemin's theory of 'Three Represents' and Hu Jintao's call for establishing a 'Harmonious Society'. But what do these terms really mean in practice? In light of the growing contention between the workers and the capitalists, how could the Chinese state keep independent of each side? How could they justify their independence, if this is indeed what the state takes as its overall political strategy in this new era of diverse interests? In the rest of this chapter I shall attempt to answer these questions by firstly addressing the ideological challenges to the CCP. Then I shall give a brief account of how the Chinese state has tried to strike the delicate balance by examining the political processes through which the state enhances the political status of the capitalists on the one hand but without entailing too much resentment from the workers on the other. Next and more specifically I shall study how the Chinese state deals with labour disputes, whose number has been on the rise during the past decade. I finish the chapter by making some observations on the implications of these issues for China's political development.

## Ideology and regime survival

Recall an important point that I made in Chapter 3: all states must find ways for resolving the tension between ideological principles and pragmatic tactics, but ideology is particularly important for authoritarian and totalitarian regimes as it could lend an extra boost to the shaky foundation of their legitimacy. How how long an authoritarian regime could survive therefore largely depends on its capacities to deal with such tension.

The CCP came to power in 1949 with two credits in hand, but neither can escape some serious questions. First, the CCP made a critical contribution to winning the Anti-Japanese War and later won the civil war against the Nationalists. It would be incorrect to say that the Chinese people did not support the CCP when it came into power; they did. However, the CCP gained the support through military victory rather than through institutional procedures. It should be understandable that the special circumstance around 1949 would not permit the reconstruction of institutional procedures, let alone strict compliance with them. In this sense, the CCP's ruling status was legitimate at the time it became the ruling party. But this has become a fundamental problem that has not been properly resolved and therefore has troubled the CCP since then and will trouble it again in the future. That is, how does the initial legitimacy turn into a permanent status? The CCP does not seem to have a widely-accepted answer, only asserting that history and the Chinese people chose it to be the leading (dominant) party. Given that the people did make that choice around 1949, whether they would make the same choice again at another time should be an open question rather than a permanent certainty. Obviously, this is a much more general issue, so I will stop with these comments.

The CCP's second credit was an ideological vision of a new society that won the hearts and minds of the largest social group, that is, the peasants. Here, there is a question as well. While the CCP has always claimed that it is the vanguard of the workers' class, the workers have always been the minority among its members. That the CCP claims itself to be the vanguard of workers is not because most of its members were workers but because the orthodox Marxism dictates it so. When the CCP came to power in 1949, most leaders of the Party were intellectuals or army generals. More importantly, the Party had much less contact with China's industrial workers than it did with the peasants, obviously due to the fact that it was the Nationalists who were controlling most of the cities, where most workers resided. Although some CCP leaders, such as

Liu Shaoqi and Zhou Enlai, led some protests and campaigns in those cities, the Party as a whole did not have much experience of leading the workers' class until they won the civil war. In 1953, about 10.5 per cent of 6.37 million CCP members were workers (CASS, 2011). By the end of 2010, this figure declined to 8.8 per cent while the total number of the CCP exceeded 80 million (Xinhua, 24 June 2010). Even adding the peasants to the calculation, which was 24 million in 2010, the percentage of both workers and peasants in the CCP was about 38.7 per cent.[4] In contrast, nearly 4 per cent of CCP members in 2010 were working in the private sector. While it is difficult to know what these members do in private enterprises, at least some of them would be private business owners or managers. Given that private business owners were prohibited from joining the Party before 2003, the changing percentage of the two classes in the CCP is remarkable. When their victory was in sight, despite their ideological commandment, the Communist leaders realized that their ideological enthusiasm must yield to the reality that they would not be able to run the new regime smoothly by relying on the workers alone. They spent a lot of time trying to convince some of the biggest capitalists, especially those with little connections with the Nationalist government, to stay in the mainland. To stay, or to leave, was the question in many capitalists' mind in the years around 1948 to 1950. Either because they ran out of alternative options, or were finally convinced by the Communists, eventually many did stay. The confusion or scepticism existed on the Communists' side as well – many cadres followed different rules in dealing with the capitalists; for example, some encouraged soldiers and workers to take valuables from the capitalist, only to be reprimanded later on. Even Liu Shaoqi was not immune from such ideological and practical confusion, as his friendly attitude towards the capitalists entailed some critiques in the Party. In short, the sceptical attitudes towards each other remained.

Soon it became clear that the main reason that the Communist regime did not deprive the capitalists of their assets immediately was because it needed time to consolidate its power. When CCP leaders believed that the economy was under their control, that is, when it became clear that the capitalist enterprises were largely dependent on the new state, the Communists were then in a rush to show they were on the side of the workers. During the Five-Antis, workers, backed by the army and the new administration, would go as far as humiliating or even torturing their employers to show *they* were the new masters. All this was justified by the Communist ideology and the evils of capitalism. It was in this campaign that the capitalists realized that the only option for them was to give up all their assets in exchange for a chance to survive.

It turned out that the 20 years without capitalists (approximately 1958 to 1978) happened to be the most difficult time for the People's Republic. The good days for the workers, even as 'the masters of the new society', did not last long as they were demoralized when not being rewarded for hard work – rewarding hard work would lead to inequality and materialism, which in turn would weaken the legitimacy of Communism. Together with a series of political campaigns, the egalitarianism eventually brought the economy to the brink of collapse. Ironically, the only solution appeared to be to bring back the capitalists, firstly from overseas and then by creating a new generation from within.

The vicissitudes of capitalists in Communist China suggest that, the Chinese state as whole did not have a coherent strategy to square their ideological commitments with the immediate challenge of recovering the economy. I did not know where the Communist state would stand in the opposing relationship between the capitalist and the workers. Deng Xiaoping said 'no debate' was one of his inventions, which amounts to suspending the CCP's ideological commitment. Soon most of the Party leaders accepted that tangible improvements of quality of material life would lend a much stronger support to the legitimacy of the Communist state than its orthodox ideology.

The CCP leaders are clearly aware of the changing social structures and their political significance, of course. While the new ideological inventions, such as 'Three-Represents' or 'Harmonious Society' sound attractive, the underlying ideological logic remains very obscure. Again, the key question is: how could a political party represent conflicting interests, such as those of the workers and their private employers? It would be outlandish to argue that the interests of the two sides *are* consistent or harmonious – it would be ideal if they are, of course – but the fact is that they are not. Besides other motivations, a possible explanation for these new slogans is that it would require different political parties to represent different interest groups, respectively, but this would mean opening up China's political system to political competition, which the CCP has persistently refused to do. The CCP's strategy so far is to let the voices of conflicting interests be heard and to keep all of the negotiations behind the doors. Nevertheless, it should not be completely impossible when one day a social group accuses the CCP for failing to represent their interest and request that their own political party be legally established. Given the weakness of social groups and the strong hands of the Chinese state, this scenario remains very remote. But perhaps it is just a matter of timing and triggering it up – when the economy starts to slow down or a disastrous event broke out, it is not so incredible that new requests for political change will be voiced out again.

## Employment disputes between the new capitalists and the workers

But before discussing the role of the Communist states in employment disputes, it is necessary to firstly give an account of the overall situation. Here, I focus on the domestic private enterprises; that is, the following numbers and figures exclude state-owned enterprises (SOEs), collective enterprises, foreign firms and joint ventures, although I will use figures for state-owned enterprises for the purposes of making comparisons. The number of labour disputes has increased across all sectors, but the following figure (Figure 8.2) shows that during the years from 1997 to 2003, the number of labour disputes increased at its fastest rate for those privatized from state enterprises (in Chinese, *gai zhi*) and eventually overtook those for the SOEs and originally private enterprises in 2003. It becomes clear that the privatization of state-owned enterprises has been the major source of labour disputes as the workers feel unfairly treated during the process.[5]

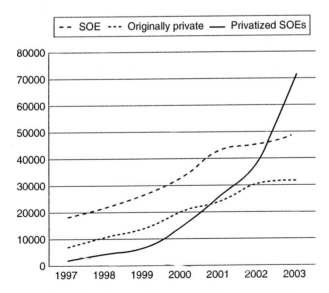

*Figure 8.2*　Number of employment disputes in China, 1997–2003
*Source*: China Yearbook of Labour Statistics (2004).

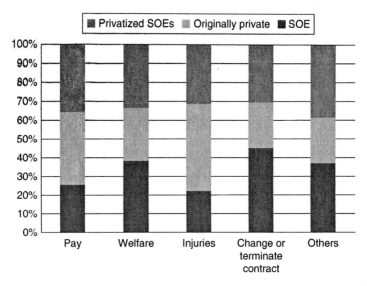

*Figure 8.3*   Sources of employment disputes by ownership in China, 2003
Source: National Survey of Private Business Owners, 2004.

Now we take a step further by examining the distribution of different types of employment disputes across the three types of enterprises in 2003 (Figure 8.3). For the SOEs, the main issue was with changing or terminating employment contracts. Without going into the details of the privatizing process of SOEs, we should not be surprised to find that the workers have become more contentious when their job security is under threat. This is also the case for those SOEs that were privatized in the past decade or so, but on top of the disputes over contracts, pay is another major category of disputes. For these type of enterprises, the pay usually refers to the severance pay when an SOE was transformed into share-holding company. Pay is also an issue for those originally private firms but the meaning is quite different; here, the problem is with no pay, low pay, delayed pay, or unfair pay rate.

As this represents a major problem with regards to the concern of this chapter, let's take a closer look at these disputes in the case of private enterprises. The Department of Labour of China's national government conducted a survey on 18,310 private enterprises in 2003 and found that 15 per cent (or 3,056 firms) did not pay their employees with the full amount or not on the scheduled dates; in one of the places, only half of the studied firms paid their employees monthly, the rest paid either quarterly, biannually, or even annually (Wang, Zeqiang, 2007: 51).

Another problem is that many new capitalists paid their workers by the number of completed pieces rather than the number of working hours. As the minimum wage is based on the latter, paying by pieces is a disguised way of paying less. Here is the trick: suppose a worker has worked H hours and produced P pieces of a product. Also, suppose the minimum hourly wage is W. If she is paid at the minimum wage, then she should get HW. Now, suppose she is paid by P, and the capitalist sets the piece rate at X, so the worker will be paid PX. The question is: what is the relationship between HW and PX? Put in another way, which is bigger, HW/P (the piece rate based on minimum hourly rate) or X (the piece rate set up by the capitalist)? The answer is all up to the capitalist who has the right to set up the pay rate. For example, if a worker produced 100 pieces in 8 hours, and the minimum wage is 5 yuan, then the worker should receive 40 yuan, and the actual piece rate is therefore 0.4 yuan. Now, if the capitalist sets the piece rate at 0.3 yuan, then the worker only receives 30 yuan, making the hourly rate 3.75 yuan, which is actually below the minimum wage. More generally, the capitalist can set the value of X so low that PX is smaller than HW, regardless of the value of P, even though P will soon reach its maximum – how many pieces can a worker make during a day? This means that, for the workers to make the same amount of money they will have to work longer, and this explains why what the piece should be has been a major source of conflict. Nationally, out of all the employment-related cases of disputes in 2002, 70 per cent were about unfair or delayed pay, and 80 per cent involved private businesses (Xia, 2004; for an example in Wenzhou, see the report 15 November 2004, Xinwen Dongtai).

A substantial percentage of private enterprises do not have written employment contracts with their employees. And the absence of written contract would allow the capitalist to make any demand on the worker without taking the risk of getting caught. The exact figures differ depending on the sample used in each empirical study. According to the All China Federation of Trade Unions, which is supposed to represent the interest of the workers, only 30 per cent of private enterprises signed employment contracts with their employees, and the figure increased to 47 per cent in 2006. The percentages are much higher based on a survey conducted by the All China Federation of Business and Commerce, the national body representing private employers: around 73 per cent in 2005 and 2006. Some journalists estimated that in 2003 in the province of Zhejiang alone there were about 1.8 million such 'underground workers' (meaning, workers without signed employment contracts, Shen and Yu, 2003).

Given the sensitive nature of these disputes and their complexities, it is extremely difficult to gather reliable statistics of how many disputes were eventually resolved and how. Incidents reported in the media including the internet indicate that there are various forms of resolution, including private negotiations, mediation by government officials, and collective negotiations between representatives from both sides. One thing is certain, however, that employment disputes in China have become more and more contentious, including individual complaints, group petitions, collective sabotage, and even physical attacks on the business owners. This trend is even reflected in official statistics; for example, Figure 8.4 clearly shows that since the turn of this century, the number of employment disputes resolved by adjudication has been higher than those by mediation.

### Employee welfare

In Western developed economies, it is a well established policy and practice that employers provide at least the basic welfare coverage

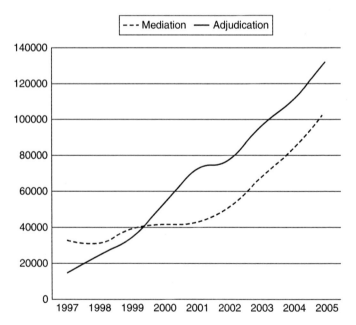

*Figure 8.4*  Resolution of employment disputes in China, 1997–2005
*Source*: China Yearbook of Labour Statistics (2006).

(safety, pension, compensation in case of injury on the job, and so on) for their employees. Therefore, it may be difficult for readers in the West to understand the disconnection between business ownership and the responsibility of providing employees with welfare benefits. It is however perfectly reasonable to the Chinese people not to expect private business owners to take on such burden, either because private businesses, by their very nature of being 'capitalist', are only interested in the exchange of labour and salary, or because most of them have suffered from unfavourable policies and thus feel no obligation to take up the responsibility of welfare provision. In contrast, employees of SOEs enjoy a whole range of benefits, even when the situation in many SOEs has been deteriorating. The situation in collective enterprises varies, depending on a particular enterprise's economic performance. Operating 'outside the system' (*ti zhi wai*), private enterprises do not have the privileges that SOEs enjoy, such as bank loans, access to valuable raw materials, administrative support, and so on, but on the other hand employee welfare is not an essential part of their production cost. Such discrepancy in status means that the employees may even think it is not sensible to require or even to expect a level of welfare provision in private enterprises similar to that in SOEs. Indeed, it is only in some exceptional cases that employees of private enterprises have the benefits of housing, childcare, pension, or any other benefits. Welfare provision is largely outside the contractual relations between the employers and the employees.

China's economic reforms, albeit appearing gradual on appearance, actually have proceeded so swiftly that the exact institutional relationship between private business owners and their employees has been left an institutional lacuna. Although the Chinese government has been experimenting with the idea of providing a universal welfare system by severing the connection of welfare provision to ownership, the process has been very difficult, to say the least. A more general question is: what rights and responsibilities does each side – the employer and the employees – have? As the answer has remained largely unclear for a long period of time, it is very hard to pin down the following question: what could one side do if the other side violates the rules, given the existence of clear rules? The problem, at least partly, is with the rules. It is only for a limited number of matters, such as minimum wage, that both sides know what to expect from the other side. For many other employment matters, including working hours, working conditions, medical coverage and insurance, redundancy and compensation, there are no rules or no clear rules.

The lack of clear state regulations means that although we will be able to measure the prevalence of welfare provision in the private sector, we are not in a position to evaluate the statistics against any legislative requirements or policy guidelines because they simply do not exist or only exist in very vague terms. Ironically, that makes the statistics presented below even more interesting, because they point to the following question: given the absence or the ambiguity of guidelines, how many private business owners would still provide welfare benefits to their employees?

Based on the results from the NSPBO, Table 8.1 shows the percentage of private enterprises that provided five types of welfare to their employees from 1994 to 2005 (no questions on welfare were included in the 1993 survey). First of all, the reader may have noticed that the figures for 1994 (from the 1995 survey) were much higher than those in the other years. As the questions in the 1995 survey were formulated in a format different from those in the rest of the surveys and it was the first time these questions were included, the numbers for this year are particularly questionable. For the years from 1996 to 2005, it is clear that the most widely provided welfare (about 70 per cent) is labour insurance in 2003 and 2005, which is a type of insurance for serious work-related injuries. This should be understandable due to the humanitarian nature of the welfare. The proportions of medical insurance and retirement insurance (or pension) are lower although they both have been on the rise. The welfare offered the least widely is unemployment insurance, with only 30–40 per cent private companies claiming to provide such coverage. These figures are not surprising either because the provision of these insurance policies is a traditional responsibility

*Table 8.1* Welfare provision for employees in China's private enterprises, 1994–2005

| Welfare | % of enterprises with provision | | | | | |
|---|---|---|---|---|---|---|
| | 1994 | 1996 | 1999 | 2001 | 2003 | 2005 |
| Labour insurance | 93.6 | 54.3 | 61.1 | 68.6 | 70.1 | 73.3 |
| Pension | 88.1 | 31.1 | 49.0 | 49.4 | 59.8 | 62.3 |
| Medical insurance | 92.3 | 47.2 | 56.2 | 42.4 | 54.3 | 55.8 |
| Life insurance | 89.1 | 37.5 | 45.9 | NA | NA | 49.1 |
| Unemployment insurance | NA | NA | NA | 28.5 | 40.4 | 43.9 |

*Source:* National Survey of Private Business Owners, 1995–2006.

of SOEs. In SOEs, these percentages are expected to be 100 per cent, although these firms have found it increasingly difficult to provide the promised financial support. Again, we need to keep in mind that for a long time private enterprises did not have institutionalized obligations to offer these benefits; therefore, it is groundless to make any judgements based on these figures. Today, the Chinese government does require the provision of labour and medical insurance to employees of all types of enterprises, but in practice the policy is poorly enforced. Many private business owners argue that if they comply fully with state regulations, they would all go bankrupt. This may be an exaggeration to justify their non-compliance with state policies, but there seems to be an element of truth in it as the state does not appear to be keen on implementing the policies strictly.

## Trade union

Results in the above section indicate that, while the percentage of private enterprises that provided medical insurance and other welfare was on the rise till the middle of this century, only about half of them provided the benefits to their employees. More importantly, the figures do not show whether most employees or only a small number of employees enjoy the benefits, and even if most employees receive the benefits exactly how much their employers actually paid. The figures are likely to have been over-reported due to political or moral correctness and the fact that they are reported by employers themselves rather than by the employees or an independent agent; even if they are not, the actual amount does not appear to be big: the mean of the average payment for any insurance for an employee was around 125 yuan, and the median was mostly zero. Finally, even if the provision is claimed to have been provided on paper, disputes will arise when employees claim that their employers have failed to honour the promised benefits.

What could employees do in such situations? It is very likely that they will take one of the following options: filing a complaint to the local government agency, bringing a law suit to court, or negotiating informally with the business owner through personal connections. Our knowledge remains highly sketchy with regards to the distribution of these options taken among employees and the circumstances under which they are adopted.

One organization has an inescapable responsibility of helping out the employees, namely, the trade union. In reality, however, it is widely believed that under China's Communist regime trade unions in SOEs do not enjoy a respectable level of autonomy and independence. While they are responsible for the administration of employee welfare, they are almost completely dependent on the CCP Committee inside each enterprise for having access to resources and making decisions (Lee, 1986; Ng and Warner, 1998). A more recent study, however, has voiced a caution against such over-generalization of the relative weakness of the unions (Ding, Goodall, and Warner, 2002), because whether a trade union leader could do anything in protecting employees' welfare is largely contingent on the leader's relative position in the power structure of the enterprise.

If the extent to which a trade union in SOEs could stand up for employees' rights remains unclear, then we know even less about its role in private enterprises. For example, it was claimed that trade unions 'were almost entirely absent' in the private sector (Clarke 2005: 11), but according to Xia (2004), the first trade union in China's private sector was established as early as in 1984, and 20 years later (that is, in 2004) 87 per cent of private enterprises in the province of Zhejiang established a trade union. Fortunately, all waves of the NSPBO included a question on whether there was a trade union in the private enterprise under study, which enables us to take a closer look.

Table 8.2 shows that the percentage of private firms with a trade union increased quite rapidly from only 8 per cent in 1993 to more than 53 per cent 13 years later in 2006. What might be behind this temporal upward trend? We know that in his well-known 1992 South China tour Deng Xiaoping urged local officials to create a more liberal institutional environment for all type of enterprises in order to speed up China's economic growth, but how could his general policy, no matter how powerful it was, have any direct impact on the establishment of trade unions in private enterprises? We also know that the People's Congress – China's legislative body – systematically revised *Law of Trade Union* in 1992 (first passed in 1950) and made even further amendments in 2002. It is nevertheless presumptive to attribute the trend represented in Table 8.2 to these legislative actions; as a matter of fact, one is left puzzled

*Table 8.2*   Percentage of private enterprises with trade unions in China, 1993–2006

|         | 1993 | 1995 | 1997 | 2000 | 2002 | 2004 | 2006 |
|---------|------|------|------|------|------|------|------|
| %       | 8.0  | 12.7 | NA   | 34.4 | 49.7 | 48.8 | 53.3 |
| Valid n | 1440 | 2866 |      | 3026 | 3255 | 2460 | 3240 |

*Source:* National Survey of Private Business Owners, 1993–2006

after reading the articles of the Law, because none of them is written specifically for the establishment or the operation of trade unions in the private sector. Therefore, there is nothing else we can do now but leave this issue to future studies.

What we can do here, by analysing the data collected in the NSPBO, is to test the effect of the establishment of trade unions on the provision of a particular welfare to employees in a private enterprise. This part of the analysis involves two steps, both using the data for the year 2006, the most recent year that relevant data are available. First, the association between the presence of trade unions and the provision of a number of welfare benefits is tested with an odds ratio for each pair of relation (for an explanation of odds ratio, see the discussion of the model below).

In Table 8.3 we can see that trade unions do seem to have a positive effect on welfare provision – all the lower ends of 95 per cent confidence intervals of odds ratios are above the value of 1 (a value of 1 would indicate no association). For example, private enterprises with an internal trade union are at least twice as likely to provide labour insurance as those without. Even for unemployment insurance, those with a trade union are at least 70 per cent more likely to provide such benefit than those without. These results do not necessarily mean that a trade union is a cause of welfare provision, because we do not have direct evidence to show that trade unions in private firms have taken actions to obtain and protect welfare benefits for their members.

In the next step, I aim to test the robustness of such relations with a slightly more sophisticated statistical model. It would take too big a space to present results for all benefit provisions. Here I take the provision of labour insurance as an example because this is usually seen as the most basic welfare that employees deserve, even in private enterprises. More specifically, I construct the following binary logistic

*Table 8.3* Odds ratios for trade union and welfare provision, 2006

| Welfare | Odds ratio | 95% confidence interval |
|---|---|---|
| Labour insurance | 3.1 | (2.6, 3.7) |
| Medical insurance | 2.0 | (1.7, 2.3) |
| Pension | 2.8 | (2.4, 3.3) |
| Unemployment insurance | 1.7 | (1.5, 2.0) |
| Injury insurance | 2.0 | (1.7, 2.3) |

*Source:* National Survey of Private Business Owners, 2006.

regression model to assess the effect of the presence of a trade union on the provision of labour insurance.

$$\ln\left(\frac{p}{1-p}\right) = X\beta$$

On the left hand side of the model, $p$ is the probability of providing labour insurance to employees. On the right hand side, $\beta$ is the vector of coefficients and $X$ is a matrix of explanatory variables with cases. Besides the presence of a trade union, three other explanatory variables are included for testing the robustness of the trade union effect. The first one indicates the business owner's political status, that is, membership of the CCP. At least in theory, CCP members are expected to stand up for the employees' rights and interests. I then included two business indicators of a private enterprise, hypothesizing both bigger profit (after tax at the end of 2005) and larger number of employees to be associated with a higher chance of providing labour insurance. Natural logarithm is taken for these two variables in order to normalize their distributions.

The statistical model presented in Table 8.4 shows that the effect of the existence of a trade union inside a private enterprise remains robust after taking into account the effects of the other explanatory variables. That is, the presence of a trade union makes it more than 50 per cent more likely for the private enterprise owner to provide labour insurance for the employees. Another statistically significant explanatory variable is the number of employees – the larger the number, the more likely that a private enterprise would offer labour insurance. More precisely, the odds of providing employees with labour insurance increase multiplicatively by 1.55 when the natural logarithm increases by one unit. The underlying mechanism might be that the capitalist employer must take his or

*Table 8.4*   Binary logistic regression on provision of labour insurance, 2006

| Explanatory variable | Coefficient | p-value |
| --- | --- | --- |
| Trade union | 1.52 | 0.000 |
| Membership of CCP | 5.43 | 0.112 |
| ln(number of employees) | 0.44 | 0.000 |
| ln(after tax profit) | 0.06 | 0.117 |

n=2177, Nagelkerke R-square = 0.183
*Source:* National Survey of Private Business Owners, 1993–2006.

her employees' welfare seriously when the total number of employees reaches a certain point, even though the cost of doing so is much higher than smaller firms. The effect of a trade union could also be closely associated with the number of employees as the former would easily become stronger and more resourceful when there are a large number of employees. In contrast, membership of the CCP does not and profits do not appear to have statistically significant impact on the likelihood of offering labour insurance. Private business owners in China do not seem to feel obliged to offer labour insurance to their employees even if they are members of the Communist party and earning a large amount of profit.

These findings, however, should be taken with some caveats. First, as mentioned before, the survey was conducted by interviewing the business owners, not their employees, so the provision of welfare may have been over-reported. For the same reason, other forms of exploitation, such as delay or deduction of pay, could not be included in the survey instruments. Second, even if a particular welfare is provided, the survey results do not reveal which employees have received it. Was it all employees or just a handful of 'key employees', such as managers, technicians, and sales representatives? Finally, the provision of welfare obviously varies from industry to industry and from one region to another; such variations will be the focus of a future study.

Wang Zuqiang (王祖强, 2007) organized a survey in Zhejiang province, covering 114 private enterprises and 826 employees. There was a strong correlation between the size of a private enterprise and the likelihood of signing an employment contract: more than 90 per cent of large enterprises (500+) had contracts, 60–70 per cent for medium sized enterprises and he didn't report the percentage for small firms (p. 45). Out of 82 valid responses, 62.6 per cent gave a notice to employees before firing them (p. 47), and only 11 per cent offered any payment to employees when the private business owner violated the employment contract (p. 47). Consequently, only 25.6 per cent of all employees worked till their employment contracts expired (p. 47). The average annual income for the studied employees was 13,898 yuan. In contrast, in 2003 the average annual income in enterprises, cooperatives (shi ye) and governments was 18,232, 25,831, and 29,326 yuan, respectively (p. 50). According to an investigation conducted by the Department of Labour of Wenzhou, only half of all private enterprises paid their employees monthly, the other half paid either quarterly, half a year or even annually (p. 51).

Some private business owners do not want to set up a labour union inside their firms. Local governments do not want to force them to do this because the local revenues depend on these private firms. How independent are the labour unions? Where do their running budgets come from? How are the leaders chosen? According to Wang Zuqiang's survey, out of 826 employees, only 56 per cent believed that the labour unions represented their interests.

## The Chinese Communist State in between the Capitalists and the Workers

How has China's Communist state dealt with the increasing number of employment conflicts between the capitalists and the workers? In reacting to the growing number of labour conflicts, the Chinese state has called both sides to reach a 'win-win' solution. For example, the CCP issued a call for establishing 'a new type of labour relations' that safeguards the interests of both the businesses and the workers.[6] As Robert Solow (1990) pointed out more than 20 years ago, even in mature market economies, the state plays a central role in resolving employment disputes (Figure 8.5).

While this is a helpful framework for analysing the relationships between workers, employers, trade unions, and the state, the actual meanings of the relations between the parties must be interpreted in China's particular context. First of all, in almost all nations the state is expected to provide an institutional and legal infrastructure in which the employers and the employees work out their specific relations. This is done normally through legislations and policies but may include direct interference as well, especially when cases that may disrupt the

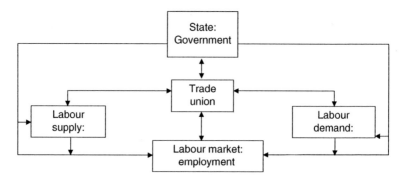

*Figure 8.5* Robert Solow's conceptualization of labour markets and trade unions

economy arise, such as large-scale strikes. The Chinese state has done its share on this front, apparently through the legislation of a series of labour-related laws. While there is room for further improvement, the major weakness is not the lack of legal regulations but the weak reinforcement of these regulations on resolving employment conflicts. As far as I am aware, so far there are few systematic studies, if any, on how many employees and employers are aware of these laws and whether they use them when a conflict occurs. Anecdotal evidence, including my conversations with some employers and employees[7], indicate that the answer is largely negative. I have gathered a strong sense that most people either did not know the laws, or even if they did, they simply did not pay much attention to them, either because they would have to pay a big price to follow the legal procedures – this is particularly true for the employees – or because they believe it would be much more straightforward to use their own resources such as personal connections to resolve the issue.[8] Most employees are very suspicious of whether the state will stand on their side, even though the national figures show that the percentage of cases in which the employees won (from 47 per cent to 60 per cent) has been much higher than those the employers won (10 per cent to 21 per cent) through from 1997 to 2005 (Huang, Mengfu, 2008: 124). These perceptions are confirmed by research conducted in Zhejiang, where it was found that local government tended to make decisions favourable for the employers (Wang, Zuqiang, 2007: 79). In a case study of a town in Wenling (Zhejiang province, ibid.: 211–7), the trade unions and the employer associations created a set of procedures for negotiating pay rates collectively without realizing that all procedures were already clearly laid out in the legal documents published by the Department of Labour as far back as 1995! In short, the lack of knowledge of labour laws, the distrust of the judicial system, and the inertia of employing personal connections rather than formal legal institutions add up to explain the weak role of the Chinese state in resolving labour disputes. Therefore, what the Chinese state must do more of is to make effective, fair, and affordable legal services available to employees for resolving the increasingly difficult and large-scale employment conflicts.

Besides legal services, the Chinese state must provide more institutional support as well. More specifically, there is a great shortage of supply of labour inspection officers, who are struggling to cope with the increasing number of cases. As a way of improving the situation, in 2001 China established the 'trilateral negation mechanism' (三方协调机制), following the International Labour Organization's practice. The three parties are: the All China Federation of Trade Unions, China's Federation of Enterprises (中国企业联合会), and the Department of Labour and Social Welfare. This seems to have effectively increased the number of formal employment contracts between the employers and the employees, but there is much evidence to show that they have dealt with the cases effectively and fairly.

Finally, with extensive organizational networks penetrating the Chinese society, the Chinese state is supposed to ease employment conflicts through organizational mechanisms. At least, two types of organizations are at its disposal: trade unions and CCP party committees. However, the role of the Chinese state remains obscure in these organizations. First of all, since 1998, the All China Federation of Trade Unions (ACFTU) has launched a campaign to maximize its members, particularly targeting non-state enterprises. By the end of 2006, there were 884,000 trade unions, of which 81 per cent are in non-state enterprises, with 81.61 million members (Huang, Mengfu, 2008: 167). However, the percentage of private enterprises with a trade union is still low, about 32 per cent in 2007 (ibid.: 6). More importantly, a large proportion of union heads were appointed either with the permission of the employer or by the local government, so they may not actually represent the interests of the workers. Clearly, the capitalists are making good use of their advantageous position in the local state-employer-employee trilateral relationships. Local state officials would not put much pressure on the capitalists for making the trade unions represent the interests of the workers because in many places private enterprises have become the major source of local revenues. In addition, the remaining oversupply of labour and the floating nature of many industrial workers put the workers in a disadvantageous position, thereby weakening the power of trade unions. Despite the demand of stronger trade unions by the workers, the Chinese state has provided little help because it does not want to stand up against the new capitalists on the one hand and it wants to keep trade unions under control on the other. Independent trade unions cannot satisfy such demand as they are illegal (the CCP learnt the lesson from the June 1989 incident). However, when the workers' petitions are ignored by trade unions, labour agents, and local governments, the situation could reach such an unbearable point that the workers have no alternative other than organizing protests among themselves. Usually, top leaders of local government had an emergent meeting and yielded to the workers' demand. The workers seem to have learnt the trick of organizing such activities: there are normally no leaders so that no one will get targeted by the security officers, they will try to keep violence out of the process so as to leave no excuse for the government to label the event a criminal act. Such a case-by-case approach again illustrates that the Chinese state has not come up with a clear and effective set of principles and strategies for dealing with the conflicting interests between the new capitalists and the workers.

Another type of organization that China's Communist state could use for easing the increasing employment conflicts are the CCP party committees established within capitalist (privately owned) firms. Indeed, that's exactly one of the functions that the CCP top leaders hope these committees could fulfil.[9] However, one cannot help but wonder whether these committees are established truly for resolving employment conflicts or for enhancing the CCP's control over these private firms. Despite the urge and the campaigns organized by the CCP's Department of Organizations for increasing the rate of party committees in private enterprises, the whole process has encountered some difficulties (the capitalists' apathy towards such policy, the floating nature of party members, and the difficulty of recruiting new members). On the other hand, even if a party committee is set up in a private firm, it is sometimes used as a channel for the capitalist to establish or improve connections with the local CCP Party Secretary or government. Those private firms with a CCP committee in them enjoy more chances of meeting local officials, having early access to important information, and being selected to enjoy a favourable policy. That is, the whole business of setting up CCP committees becomes truly a business in the commercial sense. Cases in which such committees mediate between the workers and their capitalist bosses – let alone standing up and protecting the interests of the workers – are almost unheard of.

The Chinese state is still in the process of discovering or creating a coherent ideology that could go beyond the interest of any particular social group. It is one of the greatest challenges for the CCP to explain how it could still represent the majority of the people and the most advanced elements of everything when the whole social structure is transforming into a variety of social groups with dramatically different, if not necessarily conflicting, interests. This is even more difficult given that the CCP refuses to let different political parties represent different social groups. This social-political structure conundrum will test the robustness of the CCP ruling capabilities in the next decades.

More importantly, Martin King Whyte asked the following questions after giving a brief account of the rising numbers of conflicts between the capitalists and the workers: 'Should this growing contentiousness be taken as an indication that China's workers may at some future point pose a serious political challenge for the regime? Does the combination of declining worker status and increasing convergence of conditions across enterprise types mean that China may yet have a Solidarity movement in its future?' (1999: 194). His answer is basically negative. Even ten years after the publication of his chapter, it remains true that the scale and the scope of conflicts remain within the managerial capacity of the Chinese state – there is 'widespread unhappiness but general compliance' (ibid.: 195). His explanations include the oversupply of labours, that the diversity of the employees' working experience and conditions makes it very difficult for them to mobilize effectively, and most importantly, that few workers aim their protesting actions at the Chinese state itself.

# 9
# Elite Corporatism

Readers who have patiently reached this point must have the following question in mind: what is your point after showing so many details about the capitalists in China? Here is the short answer in three sentences, while the remaining chapter will be the long one:

(1) Conditions for the capitalists in China to develop into an independent social and political force have never been ripe, although we cannot rule out the possibility that they will be in the future;

(2) Their dependence on the Chinese state makes a corporatist relationship between the Chinese state and the most powerful capitalists the most desirable for both sides, which was the case under the Nationalist government as well as under today's Communist rule;

(3) While this relationship somehow fits the conception of 'corporatism', it takes a flavour of elitism as well, because the capitalists have not been economically strong enough to confront the mighty state collectively.

Therefore, the dependence becomes a matter for 'the selected favourites'; that is, only those most influential capitalists (or the elite capitalists) would have the chance of enjoying the dependence on the state. They know they have to pay the price of the loss of their independence and autonomy, but they are too weak to care and consequently become indifferent and learn to focus their attention on the favours they obtain from the state. Hence my pessimistic conclusion: the capitalists in China will make little contribution to the nation's transition to a liberal and multi-party democracy. By elaborating on these points, I summarize and connect the findings presented in the previous chapters and extend them to some larger questions such as the difficulties of achieving liberal democracy and the scenarios of political development in China.

## Why are the capitalists so dependent on the Chinese state?

In an ideal-typical market system, the operation of capitalist enterprises expectedly has little to do with the state: all elements needed for the production of goods and services are obtained from the market via rules of exchange that are accepted by the parties in the transactions. Therefore, the state plays no role in the process and the enterprise owners have no need to interact with the state. Obviously, this is only a hypothetical situation; in reality, the state has many reasons for stepping into the process. At the very least, the state, itself not producing anything directly, must find ways of collecting financial capital to run its administrative machines; hence the cliché 'there is nothing certain in life but death and taxes'. The capitalists would still have little to do with the state if the relationship were purely about tax, which is only a matter of taking into account an additional type of cost. But there are many situations in which they will find it almost impossible to stay away from the state: the raw materials (cotton, metals, and so on) may be part of the resources under the state's control, the capitalist enterprises must use public spaces – land, roads, rivers, and so on – for completing productions and transactions, the state is obliged to protect its citizens who happen to be employees of the capitalists, business relations between capitalists enterprises in different nations may become international affairs, and the state may find some rules in the market in conflict with the principles that the state holds dear, and so on. Given these possibilities, it is no surprise that even in the most liberal capitalist system, business enterprises must in one or another way rely on the state in order to keep their businesses functioning smoothly.

The balance between the state's coercive power and the business's financial power may tilt in either direction, which leads to the following important but difficult question: what do we need to know in order to have a reasonable idea which way the relationship will shift? Because many intermediary factors may be in play between the two sides and the relationship is so contingent on historical contexts and even personal idiosyncrasies, it is perhaps hopeless to give a generic answer to this question. It is possible, however, to produce a brief but hopefully sensible and coherent answer for the case of the Chinese capitalists based on what we have learnt in the previous chapters. Like many other questions in the social sciences, we have to rely on our intuitive and logical thinking without any access to hard and clear procedures. Such thinking is not without foundation – knowledge, experience, common sense, and so on – although we must admit that the connection between the foundation and the conclusions may appear to be, to a certain extent, mythical.

When reading the history of the capitalists in China, which is extremely short in comparison with the entire history of the nation, we do not have to work very hard to find out the following fact: there were very few periods when they were not at war, the Opium War, several civil wars between the feudalist state and the rebellious or revolutionary armies, and two World Wars. Notwithstanding the interruptions and the damage to businesses, the wars put these normal economic activities in the background and consequently lent the state an absolutely legitimate claim, in the name of national security, for extracting resources from every sector of the society. The old generation of capitalists in China never had a sustained period to develop their businesses, and the state never offered useful support to their businesses, on the contrary, either the state was busy struggling to survive, or it was broken into several warring states, or all it was interested in was demanding contributions from businesses. The idea that the state is expected to provide an institutional infrastructure to the market and business transactions was alien to the Chinese state before the Second World War. Correspondingly, business owners were quick to learn all sorts of strategies and tactics, many of which are either immoral or illegal in today's or those days' standards. In those turbulent times, to be able to depend upon the state was a good luck; independence was not something they would hope to enjoy.

Wars or security crises in general obviously are not the only situations in which the capitalists must succumb to the demands of the state. It is very likely that today's capitalists will enjoy the longest time of peace in China's history. Nevertheless, in many aspects they have become dependent on the state more heavily than their predecessors. Ironically, this comes when the Chinese state would like to concentrate its attention and resources on economic development rather than be distracted by other more urgent matters. It is even more ironical given that the state has initiated the process of introducing market mechanisms into economic activities: private properties are not only recognized but also protected by the new amendments of the Constitution, prices are to be decided by the negotiations between the sellers and the buyers rather than by state agents, labourers can move almost freely, and so on. The subsequent enviable high rates of economic growth are widely perceived as a natural outcome of these economic liberties that Communist China has adapted itself to accept and make use of.

So why do the new capitalists become more dependent on the Chinese state after the state has set up economic growth as its top priority? The solution to this irony is that economic growth can be – and actually has been – achieved *without economic liberty*. Today, the most prominent case is the People's Republic of China, but several other cases already existed before the PRC started economic reforms, including Singapore, South Korea, the Republic of China (Taiwan), and some South American countries. The intensive involvement of the state in economic development – some social scientists call it 'embeddedness of the state' – does not leave much room for all capitalist enterprises to freely grow; rather, high speed economic growth is achieved via heavy investment by the state in selected economic sectors and state-owned enterprises. The state is far more than a rule-setter, a regulator, or a service provider; it becomes an investor – just think about Singapore's Temaseck Holdings and China's state investments in many parts of the globe, from building a hospital in Tanzania to Thames Water in England – and it becomes an entrepreneur. It is very difficult to find any Party secretary or local governor who has not personally been involved in setting up a business; even *People's Daily*, the Chinese Communist Party's official newspaper, would sell its shares on the stock market. Adam Smith would be extremely amazed by how the hand of the Chinese state could be so visible in the workings of the supposedly invisible market and could still achieve such economic growth.

In such context, the new capitalists in China do have a much bigger institutional space than what they had under the previous Socialist system – today, nobody would argue about that anymore. But China observers seem to have stopped pointing out just how constraining the institutional environment still is – the high rates of growth have heavily overshadowed the problems in institutional structures and daily business transaction; as long as growth is achieved, all the rest becomes insignificant or even ignorable. It is indeed true that the Chinese state has withdrawn from small scale and daily management of most of the enterprises, but this should not make us miss the fact that it can exercise great influence on private enterprises *whenever it would like to* and therefore private enterprises in China could develop but only within the remit set up by the Chinese state. To the newly rich capitalists, the state remains an intimidating giant. It controls all the essential resources (land, financial credit, key public infrastructure, all government positions, and so on), it can produce or change policies, either legal or administrative, without much consultation of the public, it constantly monitors and supervises some key aspects of every business (permit, tax, quality control, employment relations, financial transactions, and so on), anyone of which could cause a business serious difficulties. This is why the new capitalists pay so much attention to state policies, spend so much time creating and maintaining close relations with local state officials but still worry about whether someday the state could take away their properties or profits, to which there is little they can do. In short, the fate of the new capitalists is still in the hands of the Communist state. This lack of economic liberty well explains the co-existence of fast economic growth and the survival of the authoritarian regime.

Due to their indispensable nature, we may call the above forms of reliance of the new capitalists on the Communist state 'hard dependence'. There are at least two relatively 'soft' forms of dependence, one ideological and the other organizational. They are soft not only because the capitalists can still run their businesses without having to deal with them but also because the state has not been able to find a clear-cut solution. The Communist state still has the upper hand – there should be no illusion about that, but this upper hand is not as harsh as that of the hard dependence.

Ideologically, some key questions regarding the identity of the capitalists that the Communists, the capitalists themselves, and the general public in China all must answer are: Who are the capitalists? Are they the enemy of the Communist state and the working classes, or should they enjoy the same status as other members of the society do? How should their assets and managerial work be evaluated in the process of production? Is it legitimate or morally correct for them to keep some of the profits produced? These questions are of different nature, therefore, the answers may not be consistent with each other. However, in the process of establishing and maintaining their power in the new People's Republic, the Communists lumped all these questions together either due to their immaturity, or the over-enthusiasm after the military success, or the intention of removing all non-Communist groups from China's new social structure. Whatever the reason, no distinctions were made in answering these questions. In practice, this means that some legal issues were resolved politically, or some moral issues led to economic consequences. For example, tax evasions, production fraud using fake materials, or even bribing state officials are all legal matters and should be resolved legally through legal institutions. Nevertheless, they were interpreted politically as 'attacks by the political enemies' on the new regime, exemplified in the Five-Anti campaigns in the early

1950s and later in the Anti-Capitalist Liberalism campaign in the 1980s, which led to persecution without legal procedures. Again, there is an irony here: the capitalists 'attacked' the Communist regime exactly because they are so dependent on it! They would try every trick to avoid tax, such as keeping two books, one for the tax agents and the other for themselves, because they have no say in how much they must pay; they take short-cuts in producing popular goods partly because they do not have access to valuable resources that are under the control of state officials or state-owned enterprises; they find a great variety of ways of establishing and maintaining close personal relations with state officials to a large extent because there is no other more transparent way of obtaining valuable resources. The Communist would never find the reasons for these 'attacks' in their own system, of course, at least not publicly.

Once the Communist state cannot deny the growing importance of private enterprises anymore, it cannot shy away from the political identity of these enterprise owners – all in all, it is the state that allowed and even encouraged them to become rich, so it would not make sense to still treat them as potential class enemies or second-class citizens. Nevertheless, eventually it is up to the state to show its generosity by granting these new capitalists a legitimate place in the Communist structure, although it is questionable whether this is done wholeheartedly. Again, the political question is mixed up with legal and moral ones: the new capitalists should be treated fairly and deserve their status in the nation's political system, but what about their illegal or immoral behaviour? Many of these issues have been sidelined or excessively downplayed for the purpose of justifying the correctness of the changing tone towards the new capitalists. The switch from one set of ideological principles to an almost opposite one is completed conveniently as a matter of delivering a speech or producing an official document. Why does it suddenly become legitimate for business owners to take profits from the products produced by their employees, which previously was claimed to be morally wrong and economically inefficient? The capitalist mode of production was criticized as incompatible with the modern industrial production and exploitation a moral sin committed by the capitalists. Why are these issues not problems anymore? Deng's decision to brush them aside in order to let the nation concentrate on production may help promote economic growth in the short run, but suspending the task of solving these ideological issues will only create more serious problems in the long run. As the Communist state has given up its responsibility to invent a new ideology (or perhaps they have not been able to) from which people could find solutions to fundamental questions in their economic and political life, the new capitalists have no choice but to keep depending on the state to justify their business transactions and behaviour. It is in this sense that they are 'softly' dependent on the Communist state ideologically.

Another form of 'soft dependence' of the capitalists on the Communist state is organizational. Before discussing the case of the capitalists in China, a general note is needed here. Since coming to power in 1949, top leaders of the Communist regime have always put the sustainability of their ruling as the top priority. This is a fundamental difference between a democracy and an authoritarian regime: in a democratic state, it is understandable and even acceptable for the ruling party to lose power; however, for the rulers of an authoritarian regime, to lose power is much more than disappointing – it is shameful and unacceptable; it is the end of their world. This absolutely unyielding and uncompromising grasp of ruling power is the origin of all strategies, politics and actions taken by the Communist state in particular and perhaps by all authoritarian regimes in general. One of the strategies is to set up an organizational infrastructure that penetrates to every corner of the society, thus leaving no room for any organizations that plan to operate outside such a system. There is no natural ecology, and consequently there is no demography of organizations, as their birth and death are not an outcome of competing for external resources but of their relations with the state.

When the new capitalists started to emerge as a legitimate and indispensable social and economic group (there is no need to talk about the old capitalists here as their organizations were in crisis when the Communists came and soon disappeared), it was the winter for new organizations. Retrospectively, it is difficult to believe that the millions of nascent business owners did little in organizing themselves, which on the other hand is unsurprising if we understand how the Communist organizational infrastructure works. Under the direct surveillance of the Bureau of Business Administration, the associations of individual business owners and private business owners are not far from being nominal. The All China Federation of Business and Commerce (ACFBC) was revived under the direct instruction of the CCP's Department of United Front (DUF), and a deputy head of DUF is appointed to be its Party Secretary. At the national level, the Democratic Construction Association (DCA, or min jian) is the only political organization left that could at least on paper represent the interests and the voices of the new capitalists and the only political party that the CCP would allow them to join. It is nevertheless clear that the CCP has put a cap on the number of new recruits that DCA could take as its total membership has remained extremely stable over the years. While the elite capitalists have been gradually absorbed into the ACFBC, most of the rank and file are left unorganized. All in all, we would not miss much by making the following two observations: (1) the new capitalists must rely on the Communist state and accept its 'leadership' if they want to organize themselves; (2) at least at the national level, the organizations are for the elite members only, thereby demonstrating the practice of elite cor-poratism as a special example.

Local associations of private businesses have mushroomed in the past few years. It is not sensible to categorize them, however, as part of 'an emerging civil society', because civil society is meaningless if it is not tested in confronting the state. Many observers and social scientists call them 'civil society' simply because they are initiated, organized, and administered by their members, and indeed there have been thousands of such associations established and running as such in recent years. Nevertheless, how many of them can truly protect their members' interests in an open manner? How many of them would refuse to set up a Communist committee within them? How many would stand up to the state should a local state official order to shut them down? In fact, it is the opposite that has been happening: protecting their members' interests is only a small part of these associations' functions and in the rare situation when they are required to do so, they rely on close con-nections to state officials.

## Why is politics in China always about the elites?

Almost all discussions of any aspect of China's politics sooner or later comes to the following question: when might China become a democracy? In this context democracy is used in the sense of multiple political parties competing for the ruling power equally and fairly, that is. I would give my views of why it has been so difficult to achieve this in the next section. Here, I would address the other side of the same coin: why has authoritarianism been so robust in China? Obviously, to do justice to this enormous question would require an analytical history of China, but I cannot skip this question since it is so tightly connected to the core concept that I have been trying to arrive at: elite corporat-ism. But the complexity of this issue means that I can only briefly lay out the core argument in the context of the changing status of China's capitalists.

In general terms, elite corporatism is the necessary and pragmatic solution to easing the tension between totalitarianism and liberal democracy. For the ruler's perspective, it is easier to rule with a totalitarian regime, but as the resentment to such rule would soon build up, it is however not sustainable. On the other hand, the conditions for ruling with a democracy are extremely difficult to satisfy: among those competing for political power, few would play by the rules, and even if they wanted to do so initially, the violation of the rules by other parties would teach them the lesson that the only rule to follow is to win without following any rules. Coercive power (armies and the police) becomes the ultimate basis of power. As Mao Zedong acutely realized: the ruling power comes from gun barrels. Eventually, the challenge becomes to obtain the ruling power by coercive power but to rule cautiously so as to avoid the irreversible momentum of slipping into a totalitarian regime. Elite corporatism comes as a convenient model of ruling somewhere in between these two extremes: on the one hand, it keeps all potential competitors under control, while on the other hand, managed properly, it would maximize the level of acceptance of the regime among the ruled. The elites are the leading or the influential figures in each section of the society, who exercise significant clout over the ordinary members of that section often informally by persuasion and behaviour rather than threats and punishments. However, they remain as non-ruling elites forever because they are not allowed the ambition of becoming a political competitor. They subject themselves to the 'leadership' of the ruling party in exchange for all sorts of benefits (protection, access to resources, recognition, and so on).

Now, there are several assumptions embedded in the above conceptualization: (1) the authoritarian regime would not give up the use of force against any political opponent and more fundamentally would not change itself into a liberal democracy; (2) the newly emerging elites or the elites working outside the state system either are too weak to confront the state or would not take their political independence seriously, or both; (3) the general public (or 'the masses', to use the Chinese terminology) would not stand up against the state without the elites' leadership. All of these largely fit the reality in China. What happened in the summer of 1989 confirms part of the first assumption, but the internal power struggles among the top leaders of the CCP also suggests that this may happen again at some moment in the future when a leader would repeat what Zhao Ziyang did or even follow what Mikhail Gorbachev did to his own Communist Party. We shall come back to this question in the next section.

As for the second assumption, even the most successful capitalists in China are not powerful enough to challenge the Communist state, although they are financially much more powerful than those who did challenge the state in 1989. Given the state's control over all essential resources (land, financial credits, raw materials, international trade, taxation, and so on) and the key industries (aviation, telecommunication, media, energy, and so on), the new capitalist enterprises do no have much hope of becoming competitive enough economically, let alone politically. It is the second part of the assumption that matters: how seriously do the new capitalists take their political independence? In other words, how much does political independence mean to them? If we expect them to become politically independent simply because they possess more assets and therefore would request political protection of their assets, as some social scientists of China have hoped, then we will be disappointed, because this could be achieved under the current system. The new capitalists may not completely trust the Constitution, but they do not have evidence challenging the Communist state's sincerity either. To incorporate the new capitalists' economic interests is part of the deal of elite corporatism. As we learnt from the previous chapter, the Communist state has even somehow sacrificed the interests of the working class in dealing with employment disputes. Furthermore, the Communist state has kept silent on the illegal and immoral behaviour of many new capitalists; in the meantime, it actually has promoted the status of most of the elite capitalists. All in all, the Communist state has minimized the number of complaints that the new capitalists may make about how the state has treated them. We must stop attempting to derive political implications from the new capitalists' economic gains. Financial gain from their businesses is a double-edged sword – it could promote the capitalists to an independent force but it can also make them realize just how valuable their symbiotic relationship with the state is. So far, it is the second possibility that is developing. In the end, it is the new capitalists' political conscience that matters. Are they the kind of people who would hold on to their financial assets without caring much about some fundamental values, such as liberty and democracy? It is possible that some day one of them would become a figure like Russia's Mikhail Khodorkovsky, but it depends on what lesson the Chinese capitalists learn from this case – they may be inspired by Khodorkovsky's courage in pursuing a democracy, or he may be perceived as a negative example of standing up to the authoritarian state. Currently, the politics that most capitalists in China care about is specific state policies, not what kind of political system China should have.

I am pessimistic because I find it an extremely daunting task to instil the values of liberty and democracy in the minds of the new capitalists.

Finally, let's turn to the assumption about the ordinary people. To say China's politics is always elite politics does not necessary exclude the role of 'the masses'. However, the clear and almost-taken-for-granted distinction between 'the leaders' (the elite) and 'the masses' (the ordinary people) in China's political vocabulary is highly suggestive: the masses are politically significant only when they follow the elites. As the innovator of 'the mass line', Mao Zedong was also the master of mobilizing the masses in fighting against his military and political enemies. His philosophy, which is still one of the core ideas of the CCP's political philosophy, is that political success will be achieved if the political elite could gain the support of the masses by giving them what they want. We can make two important observations on the underlying processes in China's politics. First, this philosophy represents a special variety of corporatism: the corporatist relationship between the state and masses, in which the state offers what the masses desire to have and in return the state receives political support and loyalty from the masses. Note that, here, what the masses want is assumed to be a better material life – before it was sufficient supply of food, clothes, housing, medical care, and so on, and now it is housing, children's education, car, luxury items, and so on. In other words, the masses have no political requests or ambitions, they would not care very much if they are deprived of freedom, liberty, election of their own political party, or any other political rights, and they would not find it too big a problem to live under an authoritarian regime as long as the regime is doing a good job of improving their material life. Sometimes I wonder whether the Chinese people are the most obsessed with the quality of material life in the world. You don't necessarily need a democracy to achieve a better material life; actually, an authoritarian regime could do an even better job. Another observation we can make is the neglect of the political rights of the minority. Given the corporatist relationship between the state and the masses, democracy is defined as the process of finding out who are the majority as the majority will be the masses. It is simple arithmetic: the peasants, the workers, and soldiers constitute the largest percentage of the population; therefore, they are the masses and should play a major political role. This 'tyranny of the majority' was what J. S. Mill was most concerned about when writing his *On Liberty*, which was vividly but horribly displayed in the Great Proletarian Cultural Revolution, but I am certain that the Chinese have learnt the lesson: a society or a political system must clearly identify and protect the basic human and political rights of each individual citizen, and these rights are no less important than material life; otherwise, there must be something wrong with the people and the society as a whole. It is for these reasons that I believe China's politics has been an elite politics and will remain as such for a very long time.

## Why is democracy so remote from China's political development?

As I see it, the elite corporatism presented above is one of the largest obstacles to establishing a genuinely democratic political system in China. Over thousands of years of political struggles the Chinese political elites and the ordinary people have the following ideas ingrained in their mentality: politics is a matter for a small number of elites. Such political inequality is a fact of life that everyone must learn to live with. It even becomes desirable to leave politics to the elites as otherwise there will be political disorder. This is a fundamental reason why, once in power, the political elites will enjoy unconstrained power, and it is legitimate to use any means in dealing with any potential threat. The options for the masses are either to be associated with the elites and therefore gaining benefits from them, or to keep away from them; there is no third situation in which the masses would be monitoring the elites without any associated interests. Political confrontation will only lead to suppression; peaceful competition is impossible because no basic political rights will be respected and protected. The winners will take all and will use all resources to maintain their status at all costs. On the surface, the difficulty of achieving democracy in China is the enormous difficulty of transforming the Communist Party's political dominance. This is part of the problem, but more fundamentally it is a problem of achieving political order by peaceful political competition, it is a problem for the Chinese, particularly the elites, to learn how to obtain and maintain political power without resorting to coercive power, to learn to accept political defeat and still respect the opponent's success. It all sounds simply a change of mind, but it will be a gigantic transformation for the nation's political future.

Another big obstacle to democratizing China's political system is the unavoidable potential limitations of democracy and similarly unavoidable relative advantages of an authoritarian regime. Even for its most enthusiastic advocates, democracy is not a perfect system – we are not short of cases of countries where a democratic political system coexists with many political, economic, or social problems. Democracy is a metrical variable that could take many different values, not a binary one with two clear-cut values. When its value approaches the lower end, its disadvantages will be revealed: stagnation of decision making, manipulation of the election process either by money or by violence, alienation of social groups so much so that it becomes impossible to reach agreement, and the potential risk of slipping into the tyranny of the majority, and so on. The authoritarian regime is well aware of these problems and would quote them to justify their grip on power. On the other hand, there are things that an authoritarian regime could do a much better job of than a democratic one – China is only one of the cases where enviable economic development is achieved under an authoritarian regime, and this is not the only benefit the regime could deliver. Think about building up a powerful military force – it would be very difficult to imagine that a democracy would do a better job in Russia or China. Think about curbing the growth of the population: many people in India might wish they had an authoritarian regime to control the population. For these reasons, one cannot help but wonder why China or any other authoritarian regime would have to take democracy so seriously given the limitations of democracy and the advantages of authoritarianism.

If we want to know the unconditional value of democracy, we must go beyond the 'tangible' functions that a state is expected to perform, such as developing the economy, national security, provision of a variety of cares, and so on. A key function that a democratic state can provide while an authoritarian one is not willing to is to protect its citizens' political rights to freely sett up their own political parties, freely and peacefully express their political views, and freely participate in political actions without being at all threatened. Indeed, when these rights are not deemed divine, sacred, inviolable, and un-exchangeable with 'tangible benefits', democracy will lose much of its appeal and authoritarianism may appear to be a more attractive option.

This intentional emphasis on the costs of democratization and the benefits of authoritarianism while in the meantime focusing on the 'hard' performance as the basis of legitimacy and sidelining political rights is behind the whole idea of 'piecemeal (jian jin, 渐进) or incremental (zeng liang, 增量) democracy'. One version of the idea runs as follows:

China's political reforms, the transition of political institutions in particular, have fallen behind many other countries, which is an undisputable fact. Nevertheless, the underdevelopment of China's democratization is mainly due to the immaturity of a variety of basic conditions for achieving democratization. From the perspective of realizing 'the soft landing' of institutional transitions, piecemeal democratization would be the realistic route on China's way toward democratic politics because it emphasizes gradually creating the conditions for steady political reforms.

(Tang Liang, 唐亮, 2001: 336, my translation from Chinese)

Another version of almost the same argument comes from Dr Yu Keping, a Deputy Director of the CCP's high-profile think tank Central Bureau of Translation and Compilation:

The most important development in China's politics after reforms and opening the door is that China has been on her way to incremental democracy, which is the only way to good governance under China's current circumstance.

(Yu Keping, 俞可平, 2003: 155).

More specifically, there must be some accumulation of economic and political conditions, such as economic development and political legitimacy, it is piecemeal, incremental or gradualist; there will be some breakthroughs but there will be no abrupt (read revolutionary) changes, as all changes are path-dependent. It pays special attention to procedures, particularly legal procedures. It recognizes the role of civil societies and the role of governments, encouraging governments to be innovative in developing partnerships with the ordinary citizens.

At the core of the piecemeal/incremental democracy is to ask people to give up any attempt of asking the Communist state to open up political competition, because such fundamental change is too revolutionary, too abrupt, too costly, too risky, and therefore not preferable. To keep the costs and the risks to the minimum, all political changes must be achieved incrementally within the current political framework. In their words, we shall pursue democracy and do whatever we can to make the governmental agents more responsible and accountable, but we shall do that without challenging the authoritarian status of the CCP. Both Tang and Yu made a long list of evidence for the progress that the CCP has accomplished in making China 'more and more democratic', such as rule of law, civil society, the monitoring function of the media, local elections, 'service-type of governments', and so on. What they have tried to shy away from is whether the CCP would like to return basic political rights to the Chinese people and subject itself to open and fair political competition. As Andrew Nathan put it sharply, 'The issue, rather, is whether China should have, wants to have, or is going to be forced by history to have a political system in which positions of top power are obtained through open, competitive, periodic elections' (2008: 27). Within China, it is understandable that one cannot be as blunt as Nathan, but Professor Cai Dingjian (蔡定剑), who unfortunately passed away in 2010, made the same point (but his words would be much less blunt, understandably):

> China will not have a system of multiple political parties. That is an important principle of the CCP. But many experts who advocate political reforms over the years have suggested it be opened up slightly, and if the Party opens it up, it may not necessarily lose its ruling power.... I personally think that if the Communist Party wants to change the way of ruling and to solve social conflicts, an important point is to acknowledge the demands of different interest groups. But different interest groups should have their own representatives [political parties].
>
> (2010: 87, my translation from Chinese)

But why can China's Communist state still hold on to its political dominance? When, as Nathan said, will history force the CCP to open up political competitions? History is an abstraction. More concretely, we must think about the Chinese people, including the new capitalists who I have introduced, described and analysed in this book. From this perspective, an explanation for the long-term ruling of the Communist state is that the Chinese state's pursuit of power and the Chinese people's pursuit of high quality material life are largely consistent with each other. The nation can become very powerful – it has become much more powerful than it was 40 years ago, and the Chinese people can become very wealthy as well – at least a large number of them have even though the proportion remains tiny. However, the Chinese people must understand that power and wealth will not necessarily make the country respectable and attractive. To be respectable and attractive, you must offer a set of values that people of other countries recognize, accept, and even welcome, and you must show that you live for those values, and that the material life is only a natural outcome in pursuing those values.

# Notes

## 1 The Political Significance of Capitalists in Communist China

1. It is difficult to know whether these people shared any political identity, but they were usually labelled as 'conservative' within the CCP. They openly call today's private business owners 'capitalists' or 'members of the emerging capitalist class'. Most of their views were published in the magazine *In Pursuit of Truth* (真理的追求), which was shut down in 2001. See, for example, 葛丁, 2001, '中国的私营企业主是否形成了一个资产阶级?' (Have the Private Business Owners in China Formed a Capitalist Class? No. 4) and 林炎志, 2001, '共产党要领导和驾驭新资产阶级' (The Communist Party Must Lead and Control the New Capitalist Class, No. 5).
2. 张厚义, '私营企业主阶层在我国社会结构中的地位', 《中国社会科学》1994 年6期.
3. 朱光磊等, '当代中国私营企业主阶层社会属性问题研究', 《教学与研究》, 1994 年4期。
4. I must point out that such usage is misleading because the corresponding Chinese phrase to 'red capitalists', 红色资本家, has a very different meaning. The person who coined this phrase was Marshal Chen Yi (陈毅), the first Mayor of Shanghai in the People's Republic, who assigned this title to Rong Yiren (荣毅仁) because Rong, with his father, decided to stay at the mainland and work with the new Communist Regime rather than to move to Taiwan or Hong Kong.
5. Zhang Houyi (张厚义), one of the leading researchers on private enterprises in China, defined 'private entrepreneur' (siying qiye zhu) as 'a person who has managed to possess property either through capitalization of personal income or through the private operation of a collective, public, or joint-venture enterprise' (1995: 33).
6. The belated and weak development of capitalism in China is an important question not only academically but politically as well. It is by the instruction of Zhou Enlai (周恩来), the first Premier of the PRC that a three-volume history of Chinese capitalism was produced (Xu and Wu, 1985, 1988, 2003).
7. Obviously, how much of China's economy is a market economy is highly controversial, with China's full market economy status not yet being fully recognized. Without going into the economic details, the very existence of 130 or so giant enterprises under the direct control of the state would make the recognition difficult. It is not merely that they are state-controlled but more importantly they monopolize the most important industries. This issue is greatly relevant to the economic wellbeing of private enterprises in China, which we shall discus with more details in Chapter 7.
8. Here is an anecdotal illustration: I once had a conversation with a researcher of Indian origin. As my origin is China, we naturally started to compare the two countries. I doubt she knew who Andrew Walder was, but she definitely shared his point: 'You see, as a democracy, India cannot do anything about this population! China is authoritarian, but that's exactly why it can do anything the government wants!'

9. There was a survey in 2008, but it seems that the University Service Centre at the Chinese University of Hong Kong, from which I obtained the datasets, couldn't get hold of the data anymore since 2006.

10. Documents about the surveys (questionnaires, codebooks, and interviewer's manuals) do not contain any information about who actually completed the questionnaire. This is particularly ambiguous if there are two or more owners. In addition, it requires detailed knowledge about the enterprise in order to answer some of the questions related to, for example, finance and personnel.

## 2   The Demise of the Old Capitalists in the New Society

1. I am aware that some China specialists have argued for some continuities of the transition from the Republic era to the PRC, such as the way in which the economy was planned (William Kirby, 1990), the function of danwei (单位, work unit, Xiabo Lü and Elizabeth Perry, 1997), and the family (Susan Glosser, 2003). While I appreciate the Tocquevillian point that a revolution can never get away from the shadows of the previous regime, we should avoid going as far as arguing that revolutions bring no changes at all. I would find it very difficult to accept that the changes identified here were not real or significant.

2. This is not to say that the capitalists have always *wanted* to depend on the state. Clearly, the situation varies from one historical era to another and from place to place. While this might be true for some capitalists, others had tried to keep independent. Indeed, there has been a debate over the relationship between the capitalists and the Chinese state, at least for the era under the rule of Guomindang (the Nationalists); see, for example, Wrigt (1988), Fewsmith (1985), Coble (1986), and Henriot (1993).

3. Edmund S. K. Fung asserted that 'With small membership and no political clout, they [the democratic parties] were insignificant in post-war politics and more ineffectual than the MPGs of the war period' (2000: 302). I have found this comment somehow subjective and controversial. Size alone should not be the sole or the most important criterion for measuring a political party's significance; these parties were actually in control of education (especially higher education), science and technology, and a significant portion of the national economy. These parties simply represented the social groups that were proportionally small in the 1940s.

4. For example, an editorial of the New China Daily stated that 'Without democratic rights, the necessary condition for mass mobilization for fighting the war is lost, as are the enormous strengths of an all-out national and racial war of resistance' (Fung, 2000: 188).

5. Source: September the 3rd Society: http://www.93.gov.cn/history/library/51046980271987791110.shtml, accessed 14 March 2011).

6. This section does not mean to be a comprehensive historical coverage of the Five-Antis campaign. For such studies in English, please see Barnett (1968), Gardner (1969, Shanghai), and Lieberthal (1980, Tianjin). I have also relied on some recent studies by Chinese historians in writing about this section.

7. In Shanghai, the Three-Antis were expanded to the commercial industries through the Four-Antis (Zhang, Xule, 2006, but he didn't explain how this

happened): corruption, fraud, unreasonable profits, and tax evasions, which targeted capitalists. Later, Mao instructed that 'anti-unreasonable profits' would cause a lot of confusion and consequently resentment because it was very difficult to define what they were. Therefore, this item was eliminated in the following Five-Antis.

8. 《中共中央关于首先在大城市开展"五反"斗争的指示》,《建国以来重要文献选编》第三册，中央文献出版社，1992，第53页。

9. Many capitalists thought this accusation was unfair (Lieberthal, 1980, chapter 8). This is understandable because they had behaved in the same way under the Nationalist regime. They had no chance, of course, to protest against imposing such motivation behind their behaviours.

10. In Chapter 7 of his book Revolution and Transition in Tientsin, 1949–1952, Lieberthal (1980) presented a case study of how the campaign worked at a particular factory.

11. As part of the campaign, a team of writers at the CCP's Department of Propaganda and the Chinese Academy of Social Sciences, such as Yu Guangyuan and Ai Siqi, published a series of articles attacking the capitalists' behaviours in the Party-run newspapers and magazines.

12. It is very likely that the Chinese name is 吴中一, so the pinyin should be Wu Zhongyi.

13. The state determined the value of each enterprise, which then was transferred into a certain number of shares. The capitalists received an interest of about 5 per cent from 1 January 1956 for seven years, but it was extended for another three years. The state stopped paying the interest in September 1966, the year when the Cultural Revolution was launched.

14. For example, in his memoir, 《若干重大决策与事件的回顾》(Reflections on Some Important Decisions and Events), 薄一波 suggested that it would have been more desirable if the Chinese state had made a longer use of the beneficial functions of capitalist enterprises (1991: 477).

## 3   The Growth of the New Capitalists

1. One of the first things that Deng Xiaoping did in kicking off the economic reforms was to talk to some of the most prominent members of the old generation of capitalists, including Rong Yiren and Hu Juewen, encouraging them to work as a businessman again.

2. Please see the first few chapters of my *Entrepreneurship in China* (2007) for an analytical introduction to the institutional environment in which private enterprises started to emerge.

3. Different indicators exist for measuring inequality. Even for the same indicator, such as the Gini coefficient, there are different calculations (for the case of China, see Chen et al., 2010). One thing is certain, however, that inequality has increased in China from year to year since the economic reforms started in 1978.

4. This is what a government official in Shanghai said to Yasheng Huang when Huang told him his intention of talking to private entrepreneurs: 'As a Harvard professor, why are you interested in those people selling watermelons, tea, and rotten apples on the street?' (Huang, 2008: ix).

5. This is what Deng Xiaoping said during a conversation with several prominent capitalists of the old generation, including Rong Yiren and Hu Juewen; see 'We should make use of foreign funds and let former capitalist industrialists and businessmen play their role in developing the economy', Collected Works of Deng Xiaoping, volume 2 (http://english.peopledaily.com.cn/dengxp/vol2/text/b1280.html).
6. 'The United Front and the Tasks of the Chinese People's Political Consultative Conference in the New Period', Collected Works of Deng Xiaoping, volume 2 (http://english.peopledaily.com.cn/dengxp/vol2/text/b1300.html).
7. In 1988, the National People's Congress passed an amendment to the Constitution for protecting private properties, based on which the national government published corresponding detailed regulations. Since then, official statistics have been collected separately for 'private enterprises' and 'individual household businesses'.
8. In the survey, business owners were asked to report the total number of employees by the end of the previous year, hence the discrepancy between the years in this table and the survey years.
9. In plain English, inter-quartile range is a measurement of a quantitative variable's variation without being affected by the influence of extreme values.
10. As I shall discuss the political identities of the new capitalists in the following chapters, this aspect of their profile is omitted here. Also, most of the surveyed private business owners were married and had no religion, which very likely is why the survey organizers stopped including such questions in the survey questionnaire.
11. Here, my presentation is not meant to be comprehensive for two reasons related to the contents of the questionnaires used in the surveys. First, some of the questions, although included in some years or even all survey years, are not relevant to my concerns. For example, the place where the interviewed business owner studied or how many people were initially involved in setting up the business. Second, some questions, although relevant to my study, were not used in all surveys, making it impossible to present a temporary tend. For example, marital status and religion were included only in 1993 and removed in the following surveys, and ethnicity was included only in 2002. The removal of these items is very likely because these are quite sensitive topics to private business owners and also because there is not much variation (92 per cent married, 85 per cent having no religion in 1993, and only less than 4 per cent being ethnic minority in 2002).
12. The educational levels used in the surveys were not consistent, particularly before and after 2000. I have combined some categories together and recalculated the corresponding percentages.
13. The survey questionnaire also included questions with regard to the respondent's closest relative and friend's occupation, ownership of work unit, position, and professional title. As these are very vague – what if the respondent could not choose or did not have such as 'the closest' relative or friend – I shall not present the results here. I have done some editing and re-organization when I found the original values either too complicated or redundant.
14. These data come from the surveys of 1993 and 1995 only as since 1997 these questions were not included anymore.

15. Here, the private business owner's occupation refers to the occupation *right before* they started their own businesses, not any occupation before that. Also in the surveys, their father's occupation refers to the 'major' occupation, assuming that their fathers did not often change jobs.

16. Since 1997, the survey organizers of NSPBO changed the questions, making it impossible to derive reliable and precise information on the respondents' occupation – either the questions were omitted (1997) or multiple choices could be taken. In constructing the graphs for 1993 and 1995, I have recoded the categories for two reasons: to make the results simpler and to avoid some sparse cells (less than five cases).

17. Indeed, statistics measuring the correlations between these two variables, including chi-square, Phi and contingency coefficient, are all statistically significant. As the samples were not amenable to statistical inference, I have not presented them here.

18. The data for this part of the analysis come from the surveys conducted in 1993 and 1995; the survey organizers stopped including such information from 1997.

19. Strictly speaking, what was solicited in the survey was the year and month in which a responding business was registered as a private enterprise. This might not be the same year as the business was actually starting to operate in practice, of course, but the discrepancy should not be substantial.

20. The 1993 survey did include a question on the industry of the respondent's business; however, the categories are very different from those used in the following surveys, therefore the data from this survey were not included in producing this table. Categories used in the 2006 survey are different as well but to a minor extent.

# 4  Wealth and Power, Business and Politics

1. This could explain the different views on the relative positions of government agents during China's economic reform, although such controversy seems to have become something of the past. With his 'market transition theory', Victor Nee (1989, 1991, 1996) has argued that economic reforms have redistributed important resources from the hands of government agents to other newly emerging social groups, including the private business owners, which has entailed a number of counter-arguments. I think Nee's point still makes some sense, but what he observed was a temporary phenomenon in the 1980s, when government officials were still trying to keep themselves away from private business. However, such situation quickly changed once the restriction was lifted, which renders his observations not consistent with the reality anymore.

2. In Chapter 3 of her book *Power and Wealth in Rural China: The Political Economy of Institutional Change*, Susan Whiting (2001) illustrates this situation in China's rural areas.

3. In the surveys before 2000, the question on economic status was actually formulated in terms of income rather than economic status itself. While income may not be able to completely represent one's economic status, I would expect a very high correlation between the two; therefore, we should not worry much

about the comparability of the data across the years. Also, in the original questions, 1 was the highest score while 10 the lowest. To correct the inconsistence between the position and the size of the number, I have transformed the scores so that a bigger mean score represents a higher position.

4. Here I use Pearson correlation coefficient rather than statistics for ordinal variables (such as Gamma) because I think the variables should be treated as scale (quantitative) rather than ordinal variables although there are only ten possible values. Distance between any two scores is meaningful and the distributions are approximately normal.

5. In 2006, there were about two hundred private business owners out of nearly three thousand members of the People's Congress. But the figure may not be very accurate as some people may be selected as a member not as private business owner but for other identities, such as women, intellectuals, model workers, and so on.

6. http://www.newsgd.com/news/china1/200610310045.htm (accessed on 6 July 2011).

7. The CCP's Central Committee issued an official document in February 2007 requiring regional and local party committees to make an effort in recruiting some qualified private business owners into legislative as well as party organizations.

8. More precisely, there were 4.98 million domestic private businesses in 2006 (www.china.com.cn, 22 April 2008, accessed on 25 November 2010). The numbers of People's representatives and members of political assemblies were reported in *Report on the Development of Private Economies in China*, which was edited and published by All China Federation of Businesses and Commerce (quan guo gong shang lian).

9. An official document issued by the CCP's Department of United Front in December 1955 clearly indicated that the small number of 'representative capitalists' should be 'promoted to deputy governors of province or deputy mayors'.

10. For example, Zhu Guanglei, a professor of government at Nankai University, made the argument in 1994.

11. On 25 November 2008, the CCP Committee and the Government of Guangdong published *The Decision by the Government of Guangdong on Speeding up the Development of Private Businesses*, http://scitech.people.com.cn/GB/126054/139079/8405656.html, accessed on 16 April 2011.

12. Such incidents happened in some counties in Hebei, Jilin, Gansu, and Beijing. See Zhao Minwang (赵民望, 公然鼓励老板投资'买官',《中华工商时报》2005年7月14日。).

13. 'Three-no' members refer to CCP members who have no party certificate, no belonging branch, and no activities. 'Invisible members' are those who would not like to reveal their identity as party members. 'Pocket members' are members of the CCP who keep their membership certificate in their pocket without submitting it to the party committee of their new workplace.

14. The original Chinese title of the document is 关于在个体和私营等非公有制经济组织中加强党的建设工作的意见(试行) (Instructions on Strengthening the Work of the Party within Individual, Private and Other Non-Public Economic Organizations), accessible at http://cpc.people.com.cn/GB/64162/71380/71382/71383/4844924.html.

15. Reported in http://www.chinanews.net on 23 August 2003.
16. This question was not included in the 1997 survey for an unknown reason.
17. The survey questions used in the surveys were not consistent: in 1995, 1997, and 2000, the respondents were asked whether they were members of the PC or the PPCA before being asked which level, if they were a member, it was. From 2002 to 2006, the filtering question was omitted, taking any missing value as 'not a member'. To make the results comparable, I think it is sensible to treat the missing values in 1995, 1997, and 2000 as 'not a member' as well; otherwise, the percentages for these years would be much higher.
18. In a study with the same objective in the city in South Anhui Province, Tao Qing (陶庆, 2004) included similar variables.

# 5  Between the Communist State and Private Enterprises: Private Business Associations

1. The website of the Ministry of Civil Affairs (http://www.mca.gov.cn) constantly publishes the number of a variety of 'civil organizations' (charities, foundations, professional associations, leisure and sport organizations, and so on). Currently, there are more than 150,000 such organizations registered at the Ministry.
2. As far as I am aware, the most recent document was issued on 13 May 2007, which emphasized the importance of separating governments from business associations without specifying any specific measures.
3. Some historians in China have conducted excellent research on business associations during the Republic era, see the articles by Zhang Kaiyuan, Xu Dingxin, Hu Guangming and Yu Heping in Huang (2005).
4. Note all members of the ACFIC are non-state enterprises. Some SOEs, town-and-village enterprises (TVEs) and joint ventures have joined the ACFIC as 'enterprise members' although they are a minority.
5. The statistics about business associations in China are sparse at best. A team of researchers at Qinghua University found that of all business associations 69 per cent were set up by sponsoring government agents and only 14 per cent were established by their members (cited from Huang 2005: 8).
6. It is illegal not in the sense of breaking any state law but in violating an order issued by the State Council's Department of Civil Affairs (2001), which states that 'any activities with an aim of establishing social organizations without permission will be deemed as illegal'. In fact, the legal status of such orders remains ambivalent.
7. Note that many associations of Wenzhou businesses are not located in Wenzhou but in the city or region in which they operate. These are called 'yi di shang hui' (business associations in other places). The first one was officially approved in 1995 in the city of Kung Ming in Yunnan Province, and the total number of such associations has reached more than a hundred.
8. The Wenzhou model has attracted some attention from researchers in the West. Nevertheless, as far as I am aware, there have been few publications in English on the development of business associations in Wenzhou (Zhang (2009) used some findings from Chinese researchers in Chapter 8 of his book). Some Chinese academics, such as Shengyong Chen and Jianxing Yu,

have published some reports based on their fieldwork. As this paper focuses on the state-business association relationship for the whole of China, I shall not present details of studies on Wenzhou.

9. There was a survey in 2008, but the survey organizers had not released the data for public use at the time of writing.

10. See Jonathan Unger's study on business associations at a district in Beijing in 1996 and Chen Jiaxi's more recent study in Jiangsu (2007). During my own fieldwork in a large city in northern China, some owners of small businesses thought that the associations were government agents and they had no contact with them other than paying the membership fee every year when renewing their licenses. Results from the most recent survey on private business owners in 2008 show that one of the most widely reported issues (49%) was that business associations were too much like government agents.

11. Zhang Jing has launched a fierce attack on the lower status of 'shang hui' (in contrast to 'xie hui', which has enjoyed a higher status due to their connections with the government); see his article in Huang (2008).

12. For example, the governments of Wuxi and Wenzhou have made such a breakthrough in 2006, see reports about these two cities in Huang (2008).

13. Clearly, this is a hypothesis that is very hard to test fully due to its implicit nature.

14. For example, Yu Jianxing (郁建兴) and his colleagues (2004: 222) have argued that the civil society in the sense of confronting the state would be not only difficult but also full of conflict, which may eventually lead to divisions of the whole society; in today's China, such confrontation between the state and the society would only make the state even more suppressive and social forces would shrink.

# 6  Capitalist Candidates in Local Elections

1. For an assessment of the influence of these organizations on village elections in China, see Chapter 5 of Tan Qingshan (2006), *Village Elections in China: Democratizing the Countryside.*

2. I have been very puzzled why zu zhi fa (组织法) has been translated into 'Organic Law' in the English literature. I checked several English dictionaries, including *Oxford English Dictionary*, but couldn't find any meaning of 'organic' that is somehow related to organizations.

3. Some researchers in China, for example, Lang (郎友兴), have reported some internal debates among top leaders over the potential political consequences of passing the legislature of village elections. According to them, leaders of the Ministry of Civil Affairs, such as Cui Naifu (崔乃夫), made a great effort in passing The Law of Organizing Village Committees at the National People's Congress. They didn't specify, however, who within the top circles of the CCP were 'The Conservative', that is, those who argued that The Law would undermine the leadership of the CCP in rural areas.

4. In this sense, Kevin O'Brien's (1994) assessment of the significance of village elections is more realistic, who saw the encouragement (or at least permission) of village elections by the CCP's leadership as a tactic of increasing the peasants' compliance with state policies.

5. A document issued by the Central Committee of the CCP acknowledged the problems, pointing out that many local governments were not functioning and unable to tackle the emerging crimes such as theft, robberies, and even killings (中共中央文献研究中心:《十一届三中全会以来重要文献导读》, 北京人民出版社, 1982 年, 第1061页). Very likely this was based on the information collected and reported by the Ministry of Civil Affairs (Tan, 2006: 271).

6. Nevertheless, Bai did not explain why Peng Zhen was so enthusiastic. In his article, 郎友兴 (2007) listed some explanations by some China specialists, including that Peng had rich experience in elections back to the war years, his strong belief in letting the masses become true masters of their country, his intention to strengthen the CCP's leadership, and his desire to consolidate his power in the CCP leadership. Most of these, however, are speculations without convincing evidence.

7. Yang (2006: 97–8) reported that the target population was rural adults (18+), a multi-stage sampling procedure was followed, and the response rate was 91 per cent (1162 out of 1270).

8. This may not actually be surprising because there is no reason to believe that Beijing residents would be much more supportive to democratic values than people living in rural areas with far less political control.

9. As far as I know, the most systematic study was conducted by Shi Weimin (史卫民) and his colleagues (2008). Surprisingly, however, they claimed that the wealthy village leaders were not significant enough to deserve serious attention. Researchers outside China have reported inconsistent results: Susan Lawrence (1996) argued that poor villages had a stronger desire to implement village democracy, Kevin O'Brien (1994) and Amy Epstein (1996) argued that it was in the middle-level income villages that elections were greatly promoted, and finally Jean Oi (1996) found a reverse relationship between economic development and the competitiveness of elections, which is in contradiction to what was reported in China.

10. In the Chinese literature, there are a few terms for describing the wealthy village leaders, such as 'xianfu nenren' (先富能人), 'jingji jingying' (经济精英). It is difficult to know whether they are 'the capitalists' as defined in this book (business owners pursuing profits with investment in production), although it is very likely that most of these wealthy elites fit the definition here.

11. These figures come from Lu Fuying (卢福营, 2008).

12. The very nature of such investment means that it is difficult to know the exact figure of the threshold and it must vary from place to place. The estimation by He Zengke (何增科, 2002: 29) was ten thousand yuan, which was close to figures reported by other Chinese researchers (章敬平, 2005). A case study of a village by刘燕舞 (2010) suggested that every candidate paid over 5000.

13. Such expectation is consistent with Baogang He's study (2007: 60). However, Jianjun Zhang's (2008) comparative study on South Jiangsu and Wenzhou shows the important effects of the previous economic situation (more specifically, the weight of private enterprises in the local economy) and the strength of local government.

14. I am not aware of any systematic study that provides reliable information on the village residents' reactions to the performance of capitalist village heads. Fong and Dong (方柏华, 董明) reported the results from a small survey (n = 164) in the City of Wuxi in Zhejiang, where 70% of the respondents

were happy or very happy with their elected wealthy village head. However, they didn't say how the sample was drawn. In Chapter 3 of this book, Zhang (章敬平, 2005) reported a case of signing contracts between the elected head and village residents, which would allow the residents to sue the head if the head violated any pre-drafted articles.

15. Xiong Wei (熊伟), '遏制村委会贿选' (Preventing Bribed Elections of Village Committees), 南风窗, 28 April 2011.
   《关于做好2005年村民委员会换届选举工作的通知》(Note regarding ensuring the quality of our work during the transition and elections of village committees in 2005).

16. Xin Ming (辛明), 一名大学生眼中的农村"贿选" (The Bribed Election Rural Areas in the Eyes of a University Student), 中国青年报 (*China Youth Daily*) 2 November, 2009.

17. This happened on 28 June 2006; see 徐云鹏 (2006).

18. I am not aware of any reliable statistics of the prevalence of elected capitalist village heads (heads who own private enterprises) for China as a whole. All we know is that there tend to be more capitalist village heads in economically developed regions than those relatively underdeveloped ones. Shi Weimin and his colleagues (史卫民 et al., 2008) presented the percentages of 'capable men' (neng ren) being elected as village heads for several provinces during 1998 to 2003: in Hebei, the percentage increased from 31 per cent in 1998–2000 to 64 per cent in 2000–3; in Guansu, the figures increased much mildly from 32 to 43 per cent, but increased much more in Shangdong from 44 to 86 per cent. They acknowledged that these statistics might be unreliable as the term 'capable men' could be defined very differently across regions. I think it is a much broader concept that definitely includes 'private business owners'.

19. A newspaper article reported several cases where 'the first-hand' (yi ba shou, or the person who carries both titles of village head and Party secretary) abused the power in hand ('8省村官违法违纪报告：一把手居多作案手法多样', 《中国青年报》*China Youth Daily*, 2 August 2005).

20. Sources of this case come from the report in The China Youth Daily (4 September 2000) and 《南方农村报》(*South Countryside Daily*, 24 February 2003).

21. This case is based on the report by Wang Jinhong (2003) and a report in http://www.sina.com.cn, 1 December, 2003).


# 7 Weapons of the Wealthy

1. The reader may want to go back to Chapter 4 for background information about ACFBC.

2. The other took place in 1976 when some people, mostly intellectuals, called for democratic transformation of China's political system.

3. The surveys in 1993 and 1995 used one set of questions, which were abolished in 1997, the 2000 survey used a different format, and the surveys of 2002, 2004, and 2006 employed a different set of questions.

4. The survey was reported inZhang Mingyi 张明澍 (1994). Targeting people of 15 to 75 year olds, the survey was conducted during the first five months

of 1989, with the valid sample size (1995) out of 2200 distributed question-naires, covering 13 cities.

5. Anita Chan and Jonathan Unger (1991) reported a rare case (in terms of the frequency of such cases) where two individual household owners in the city of Chongqing (Sichuan province) took the initiative of instigating local university students to copy their counterparts in Beijing. They were arrested, however, because they pretended to be students from a university in Beijing.

6. Such widely held negative attitudes towards private business owners in the 1980s were confirmed, although anecdotally, by Gold (1989) and Chan (1989).

7. 叶光 (Ye Guan), '万润南搬起"石头"要砸谁?' (Whom did Wan Runnan want to hit with the Stone?), 《人民日报》1989年8月17日 (*People's Daily*, 17 August, 1989).

8. According to Scott Kennedy (1997: 763), the total value amounted to RMB 200,000.

9. Similarly, in his study, Jianjun Zhang (2008) refers to the former managers of TVEs as 'managerial capitalists', who 'became business owners through managerial buy-outs during privatization', and he contrasts them with 'private entrepreneurs' (136), that is, those who started their own businesses. '[A]ll big capitalists in the region [Sunan] were managerial capitalists' and they 'had closer relations to local governments than private entrepreneurs'. But they face a legitimacy problem as they took advantage of collective assets, so they were less respected than private entrepreneurs (138). Zhang observed that managerial capitalists tend to be 'more conservative politically'.

## 8 The Capitalists, the Workers, and the Communist State

1. The use of the word 'capitalist' entailed some controversy in the 1990s, and after 2001, with the closure of magazines such as In Pursuit of Truth (zhen li de zhui qiu), the Communist state has banned its use. Apparently, this is because the state does not want to bring words such as 'class' or 'class con-flicts' back into the public discourse. The official titles of private business owners are 'private business owners' or 'the new wealthy class'.

2. In China, the literature on private enterprises and private business owners has grown rapidly, of which the most noteworthy are the annual reports published by researchers at the Chinese Academy of Social Sciences.

3. Such 'symbiotic relationship' or 'relational convenience' between private business owners and state officials has been documented and analyzed by researchers both in and outside China (for example, Wank, 1999; Dickson, 2008; there seems to be two authors (李宝梁, 杨清) of the same paper titled 从超经济强制到关系性合意——对私营企业主政治参与过程的一种分析).

4. Bruce Dickson reports some much higher percentages based on his own sur-vey: according to him, the percentage of peasant and worker members in the CCP dropped from 83 per cent in 1956 to 63 per cent in 1994 and 45 per cent in 2002 (2004: 145).

5. How the privatization occurred and why it brought up so many labour dis-pute cases are very important questions that are too complicated to be treated here. Interested readers may want to consult Green and Liu (2005) and Yusuf et al. (2006).

6. 《中共中央关于巩固和壮大新世纪新阶段统一战线的意见》(CCP Central Committee's instructions for strengthening and expanding the United Front in the new century and new phase', August 2006, cited in Huang (2008: 22–3).

7. My fieldwork was carried out in the summers of 2009 and 2010 in two large metropolitan cities in China, one in the north and the other in the south. I interviewed a total of 31 private business owners and about 55 employees, and the length of interviews varied from ten minutes to more than two hours, depending on how busy the interviewee was and the context of the interview (shorter at work and much longer at dinner).

8. A case study of construction workers by two Chinese social scientists (潘毅 and 卢晖临, 2009) provides confirming evidence, in which the workers never resorted to legal procedures when they could not get their pay or experience any other difficulties.

9. As Disckson (2004) points out, the CCP has adapted itself to sustain its ruling dominance, and one of the strategies is to co-opt the newly wealthy elites. These 'political capitalists' normally treat their workers much better than their fellow capitalists, either because their successful businesses make such treatments affordable, or because they are under the spotlight of the media, or because they have a stronger sense of their workers' rights and welfare, or some combinations of these.

# References

Ao, Daiya. 敖带芽, 2005,《私营企业主阶层的政治参与》[The Political Participation of Private Business Owners], Guangzhou: 中山大学出版社.

Bai, Gang and Zhao Shouxing. 白钢, 赵寿星, 2001,《选举与治理: 中国村民自治研究》[Elections and Governance: A study of self-governance among village residents in China], Beijing: 中国社会科学出版社.

Bai, Yihua. 白益华, 1995,《中国基层政权的改革与探索》[The Reforms and Explorations of Lower-Level Governments in China] (中国基层权利的改革与探索), 卷1, 北京: 中国社会出版社.

Barmé, Geremie. 1991, 'Beijing Days, Beijing Nights', Jonathan Unger, ed., *The Pro-Democracy Protests in China: Reports from the Provinces*, Armonk and London: M. E. Sharpe, Inc, pp. 35–58.

Barnett, A. Doak. 1968, *Communist China: the early years, 1949–1955*. London: Pall Mall Press.

Baum, R. 1996, 'China After Deng', *China Quarterly*, 145: 153–75.

Bergère, Marie-Claire. 1989, *The Golden Age of the Chinese Bourgeoisie, 1911–1937*, Translated by Janet Lloyd. Cambridge: Cambridge University Press.

Bernstein, Thomas and Xiaobo Lü. 2003, *Taxation without Representation in Contemporary Rural China*, New York and London: Cambridge University Press.

Bo, Yibo. 薄一波. 1991,《若干重大决策与事件的回顾》[Reflections on Some Important Decisions and Events], Beijing: 人民出版社.

Jeremy Brown and Paul Pickowicz (eds). 2007, *Dilemmas of Victory: The Early Years of the People's Republic of China*, Cambridge, Mass.: Harvard University Press.

Bruce Bueno de Mesquita and George W. Downs. 2005. 'Development and Democracy', *Foreign Affairs*, 84(5): 77–86.

Cai, Dingjian, 蔡定剑. 2010,《民主是一种现代生活》[Democracy is a Way of Modern Life], 北京, 社会科学文献出版社.

Chan, Anita and Jonathan Unger. 1991, 'Voices from the Protest Movement in Chongqing: Class Accents and Class Tensions', in Jonathan Unger (ed.), *The Pro-Democracy Protests in China: Reports from the Provinces*, Armonk, N.Y.: M. E. Sharpe, pp. 106–26

Chen, An. 2002, 'Capitalist Development, Entrepreneurial Class and Democratization in China', *Political Science Quarterly*, 117(3): 401–22.

Chen, Jiandong, Dai Dai, Ming Pu, Wenxuan Hou, Qiaobin Feng. 2010, 'The Trend of the Gini Coefficient of China', Brooks World Poverty Institute Working Paper No. 109, Manchester: University of Manchester.

Chen, Jiaxi. 陈家喜 2007,《改革时期中国民营企业家的政治影响》[The Political Influence of Private Business Owners in China's Reform Era], Chongqing: 重庆出版社.

Chen, Shengyong et al. 陈剩勇, 汪锦军, 马斌, 2004,《组织化, 自主治理与民主-浙江温州民间商会研究》[Organizations, Self-Regulation and Democracy: A study of civil business associations in Wenzhou, Zhejiang], Beijing: 中国社会科学出版社.

——. 陈剩勇, 2009, '村民自治何去何从--对中国农村基层民主发展现状的观察和思考' [Where Will Village Self-Government Go? Observations and Thoughts on the Current Situation of Democratic Development in Rural China], 中国政治, 6: 66–72.

Cheng, Li, ed. 2010, *China's Emerging Middle Class: Beyond Economic Transformation*, Washington, DC: Brookings Institution.

Cochran, Sherman. 2007, 'Capitalists Choosing Communist China: The Liu Family of Shanghai, 1948–56', in Jeremy Brown and Paul G Pickowicz (eds), *Dilemmas of Victory: The Early Years of the People's Republic of China*, Cambridge, Massachusetts and London: Harvard University Press, pp. 359–85.

Cui, Shixin. 2001, 崔士鑫, 这五十七名"村官"为何要辞职 [Why Did these Fifty-Seven "Village Officers" Want to Resign?), 乡镇论坛 2001–5 http://www.chinaelections. org/NewsInfo.asp?NewsID=49344

Deng, Xiaoping. 1993, 《邓小平文选》第三卷 [Selected Works of Deng Xiaoping, volume 3], Beijing: 人民出版社.

Diamond, Larry. 1999, *Developing Democracy: toward consolidation*. Baltimore: Johns Hopkins University Press.

Dickson, Bruce. 2003, *Red Capitalists in China: The party, private entrepreneurs, and progress for political change*, New York and London: Cambridge University Press.

——. 2004, 'Dilemmas of Party Adaptation: The CCP's strategies for survival', in Peter Hays Gries and Stanley Rose (eds), *State and Society in 21st Century China: Crisis, Contention, and Legitimation*, New York: Routledge, pp. 141–58.

——. 2007, 'Integrating Wealth and Power in China', *China Quarterly*, 192: 827–54.

——. 2008, *Wealth into Power: The Communist Party's Embrace of China's Private Sector*. New York and London: Cambridge University Press.

Dong, Furen. 董辅礽, 2001, 《中华人民共和国经济史》 [An Economic History of the People's Republic of China], Hong Kong: 三联书店 (香港) 有限公司.

Ernst, Maurice and Michael Alexeev. 2005, *Transforming the Core: state industrial enterprises in Russia, Central Europe and China*, Boulder, CO: Westview Press Inc.

Fang, Ning. 房宁等, '西方民主的起源及相关问题' [The Origin of Western Democracy and Related Issues], 《政治学研究》, 2006 年第 4 期.

Fewsmith, Joseph. 1985, *Party, State, and Local Elites in Republican China: merchant organizations and politics in Shanghai, 1890–1930*. Honolulu: University of Hawaii Press.

——. 1999, 'Elite Politics', in Merle Goldman and Roderick MacFarquhar (eds), *The Paradox of China's Post-Mao Reforms*. Cambridge, Mass.: Harvard University Press, pp. 47–75

Foster, Kenneth W. 2002, 'Embedded within the Bureaucracy: Business Associations in Yantai', *China Journal*, 47: 41–65.

Fung, Edmund S. K. 2000, *In Search of Chinese Democracy: civil opposition in nationalist China, 1929–1949*. New York and London: Cambridge University Press.

Gao, Chunyi and Yang, Xiaoping. 2003, 高春毅、杨晓平, '工商联三提修宪完善私营财产保护制度' [The ACFIC Made Three Requests to Amend the Constitution for Protecting Private Properties], 《中华工商时报》 [The ACFIC Proposed Three Times to Amend the Constitution for Protecting Private Properties], *China Business Times*, 3 March 2003.

Gardner, John. 1969, 'The Wu-fan Campaign in Shanghai: A Study in the Consolidation of Urban Control', in A Doak Barnett (ed.), *Chinese Communist Politics in Action*, Seattle: University of Washington Press, pp. 477–539.

Gerber, Theodore P. and Michael Hout. 1998, 'More Shock than Therapy: Market Transition, Employment, and Income in Russia, 1991–1995', *American Journal of Sociology*, 104: 1–50.

Gilley, Bruce. 2001, *Model Rebels: The Rise and Fall of China's Richest Village*, Berkeley, CA: University of California Press.

——. 2005, *China's Democratic Future: How it Will Happen and Where it Will Lead*, New York, NY: Columbia University Press.

Glosser, Susan. 2003, *Chinese Visions of Family and State, 1915–1953*. Berkeley: University of California Press.

Gold, Thomas. 1989, 'Guerrilla Interviewing among the Getihu', in Perry Link, Richard Madsen, and Paul Pickowicz (eds), *Unofficial China: Popular Culture and Thought in the People's Republic*, Boulder, Colorado, Westview Press, pp. 175–92.

Goodman, David. 1995, 'New Economic Elites', in Robert Benewick and Paul Wingrove (eds), *China in the 1990s*, New York and London: MacMillan, pp. 132–44.

——. ed. 2008, *The New Rich in China: Future Rulers, Present Lives*, Routledge.

Green, Stephen and Guy S. Liu. 2005, *Exit the Dragon?: privatization and state control in China*. New York, NY: Wiley-Blackwell.

Guan, X. F. 2007, 'Labour Disputes Threaten Stability', *China Daily*, 01/30/2007, p. 3.

Guo, Gaozhong. 郭高中, 2006, 河津富豪返乡竞选村官多数当选 [Wealthy Businessmen from HeJin Returned to Get Elected to be Village Heads], http://www.chinaelections.org/NewsInfo.asp?NewsID=46923, 16 March 2006.

Guo, Yingjie. 2008, 'Class, Stratum, and Group: The Politics of Description and Prescription', in David Goodman (ed.), *The New Rich in China: Future Rulers, Present Lives*, New York, NY: Routledge, pp. 38–52.

Goldman, Merle and Roderick Macfarquhar. 1999, *The Paradox of China's Post-Mao Reforms*, Cambridge, MA: Harvard University Press.

He, Baogang. 1997, *The Democratic Implications of Civil Society in China*. Basingstoke: Palgrave Macmillan.

——. 2007, *Rural Democracy in China: The Role of Village Elections*, Basingstoke: Palgrave Macmillan.

Henriot, Christian. 1993, *Shanghai, 1927–1937: Municipal Power, Locality, and Modernization*. Translated by Noël Castelino. Berkeley: University of California Press.

Hershatter, Gail. 1986, *The Workers of Tianjin, 1900–1949*. Stanford University Press, Stanford, California.

Ho, S. P. S. 1994, *Rural China in transition: Non-agricultural development in rural Jiangsu, 1978–1990*. Oxford: Clarendon Press.

Huang, Mengfu. 黄孟复, 2005, 《中国商会发展报告》No.1 [Report on the Development of Business Associations in China], 北京, 社会科学文献出版社.

——. 2008, 《中国商会发展报告》, No.2, 北京, 社会科学文献出版社.

Huang, Yasheng. 2008, *Capitalism with Chinese Characteristics: entrepreneurship and the state*, New York and London: Cambridge University Press.

Huntington, Samuel P. and Joan M. Nelson. 1976, *No Easy Choice: political participation in developing countries*, Cambridge, Mass : Harvard University Press.

Ji, Shengli, et al. 2005, 纪圣麟, 周炳泉, 陈平: '"先富群体" 竞选 "村官" 现象的调查与思考', [Investigations and Thoughts on the Phenomenon of the Wealthy Group Competing for Village Heads] 《浙江蓝皮书: 2004年浙江发展报告, 社会卷》, Hangzhou: 杭州出版社.

Jia, Xijin et al., 贾西津, 沈恒超, 胡文安等, 2004, 《转型时期的行业协会: 角色, 功能与管理体制》 [Business Associations in the Transformation Era: roles, functions, and management systems], 北京, 社会科学文献出版社.

Kennedy, Scott. 1997, 'The Stone Group: State Client or Market Pathbreaker?', *China Quarterly*, 152: 746–77.

——. 2005, *The Business of Lobbying in China*. Cambridge, Mass.: Harvard University Press.

Kirby, William. 1990. 'Continuity and Change in Modern China: Economic Planning on the Mainland and on Taiwan', *The Australian Journal of Chinese Affairs*, 24: 121–41.

Kraus, W. 1991, *Private Business in China: Revival between Ideology and Pragmatism*. New York, NY: Hurst and Company.

Lang, Youxing, 郎友兴, 2007, 政治精英与《村委会组织法》的起草、颁布和实施之过程：一个博弈的视角 [Political Elites and the Drafting of The Law of Organizing Village Committees, Its Publication and Implementation], 中国农村研究网 (http://www.ccrs.org.cn/).

Lee, L. T. 1986, *Trade Unions in China: 1949 to the present (the organization and leadership of the all-China federation of trade unions)*, Singapore: Singapore University Press.

Li, Zhancai. 2009, 李占才,《十字路口: 走还是留?民族资本家在1949》[At the Intersection: To Leave or To Stay? Domestic Capitalists in 1949], 山西人民出版社.

Liang, Zhang (compiled), Andrew Nathan, and Perry Link (eds). 2001, *The Tiananmen Papers*, London: Abacus.

Lieberthal, Kenneth G. 1980, *Revolution and Transition in Tientsin, 1949–1952*. Stanford, California: Stanford University Press.

Liu, Yaling. 1992, 'Reform from Below: The Private Economy and Local Politics in the Rural Industrialization of Wenzhou', *China Quarterly*, 130: 293–316.

Liu, Yanwu. 刘燕舞. 2010, 泡沫政治——观察村庄选举中的贿选现象 [Bubble Politics: observing bribes in village elections]. 三农中国, Jan 30 2010. http://www.chinaelections.org/NewsInfo.asp?NewsID=168004.

Lu, Fuying. 卢福营, 2008, '治理村庄: 农村新兴经济精英的社会责任--以浙江省永康市的私营企业主治村为例 [Governing Villages: the social responsibilities of the newly merging economic elites in rural areas],《社会科学》, 12.

Lü, Xiaobo and Elizabeth Perry. ed., 1997, *Danwei: the changing Chinese workplace in historical and comparative perspective*, Armonk, NY: M. E. Sharpe.

Ma, Shu Yun. 2010, *Shareholding System Reform in China: privatizing by groping for stones*, Cheltenham: Edward Elgar Publishing Ltd.

Marx, Karl. 1977, *Capital: a critique of political economy*, volume one, translated by Ben Fowkes, New York: Vintage Books.

McGregor, R. 2007, 'More Powerful than Ever', *Financial Times*, 12 October 2007.

Nathan, Andrew. 2008, 'China's Political Trajectory: What Are the Chinese Saying', in Cheng Li, ed., *China's Changing Political Landscape*, Washington, DC: Brookings Institution Press, pp. 25–43.

Nee, Victor. 1989, 'A Theory of Market Transition: From Redistribution to Markets in State Socialism', *American Sociological Review* 54: 663–681.

——. 1991, 'Social Inequalities in Reforming State Socialism: Between Redistribution and Markets in China', *American Sociological Review*, 56: 267–82.

—— and with Rebecca Matthews. 1996, 'Market Transition and Societal Transformation in Reforming State Socialism', *Annual Review of Sociology*, 22: 401–36.

Nevitt, Christopher Earle. 1996, 'Private Business Associations in China: Evidence of Civil Society or Local State Power?' *The China Journal*, 36: 25–43.

204 *References*

Ng, S. H. and Warner, M. 1998, *China's Trade Union and Management*. London: Macmillan; New York: St Martin's Press.

O'Brien, Kevin. 1994, 'Implementing Political Reform in China's Villages', *Australian Journal of Chinese Affairs*, 32: 33–60.

O'Brien, Kevin J., and Lianjiang Li. 2001, 'Accommodating "Democracy" in a One-Party State: Introducing Village Elections in China', in Larry Diamond and Ramon H. Myers (eds), *Elections and Democracy in Greater China*, New York and London: Oxford University Press, pp. 101–25.

Oi, Jean C. and Scott Rozelle. 2001, 'Elections and Power: The Locus of Decision-Making in Chinese Villages', in Larry Diamond and Ramon H. Myers (eds.), *Elections and Democracy in Greater China*, New York and London: Oxford University Press, pp.149–75.

Pan, Yi and Lu Huilin. 潘毅/卢晖临, 2009, '新世界中国' 地产公司工地调查——看建筑行业拖欠工资的根源' [An Investigation on the Construction Site of 'New World China' Estate Company: To look for the origin of delayed salaries in the construction industry], http://www.snzg.com.cn/ReadNews.asp?NewsID=2995.

Pastor, Robert A. and Qingshan Tan. 2001, 'The Meaning of China's Village Elections', in Larry Diamond and Ramon H. Myers (eds), *Elections and Democracy in Greater China*, New York and London: Oxford University Press, pp. 126–48.

Pearson, Margaret. 1994, 'The Janus Face of Business Association in China: Socialist Corporatism in Foreign Enterprises', *Australian Journal of Chinese Affairs*, 31: 25–46.

——. 1997, *China's New Business Elite: the political consequence of economic reform*. Berkeley: University of California Press.

Pei, Minxin. 1994, *From Reform to Revolution*, Cambridge: Harvard University Press.

——. 1998, 'Chinese Civic Associations: An Empirical Analysis', *Modern China*, 24(3): 285–318.

——. 2008, *China's Trapped Transition: The Limits of Developmental Autocracy*, Cambridge, Mass.: Harvard University Press.

Richman, Barry. 1969, *Industrial Society in Communist China*, New York, Vintage Books.

Rocca, Jean-Louis. 1992, 'Corruption and Its Shadow', *China Quarterly*, 130:402–16.

Russell, Bertrand. 1938, *Power: A new social analysis*. London: G. Allen & Unwin.

Saich, Tony. 2000, 'Negotiating the State: The Development of Social Organizations in China', *China Quarterly*, 161: 124–41.

Sands, Barbara N. 1990, 'Decentralizing an Economy: The Role of Bureaucratic Corruption in China's Economic Reforms', *Public Choice*, 65(1): 85–91.

Shen, Xiquan and Yu Qin. 沈锡权, 余勤, 2003, '180 万 "地下工人" 权益谁保护 浙江民企有隐忧' [Who Would Protect the Rights of the 1.8 Million 'Underground Workers': a worrying phenomenon among private businesses in Zhejiang], 经济参考报, 30 August, 2003.

Shi, Jinchuan et al. 史晋川, 汪炜, 钱滔等, 2008, 《转型与发展: 萧山民营经济研究》 [Transformation and Development: A study of the private economy in Xiaoshan], 浙江大学出版社.

Shi, Weimin et al., 史卫民, 潘小娟等著, 2008,《中国基层民主政治建设发展报告》[Report on the Development of Constructing Democratic Politics among Low-level Government in China], Beijing: 中国社会科学出版社.

Solinger, Dorothy. 1992, 'Urban Entrepreneurs and the State: The Merger of State and Society', in Arthur Rosenbaum (ed.), *State and Society in China: The Consequences of Reform*. Colorado: Westview Press, pp. 121–42.

——. 2004, 'The New Crowd of the Dispossessed. The Shift on the Urban Proletariat from Master to Mendicant', in Gries, Peter Hays and Rosen, Stanley (eds), *State and Society in 21st Century China: Crisis, contention and legitimation*. London, New York: Routledge, pp. 50–66.

——. 2008, 'The Political Implications of China's Social Future: Complacency, Scorn, and the Forlorn', in Cheng Li (ed.), *China's Changing Political Landscape: Prospects for Democracy*, Washington, D. C.: Brookings Institution Press, pp. 251–66.

Solow, Robert. 1990, 'Government and Labour Market', in Katharine G. Abraham and Robert B. McKersie (eds), *New Developments in the Labour Market: Toward a new institutional paradigm*, Cambridge, Mass.: MIT Press, pp. 275–88.

Song, Meiyun, 宋美云, 2005, '2004 年商会发展趋势分析' [An Analysis of the Development Trends of Business Associations in 2004], in Huang Mengfu (2005), pp.50–96.

Stark, David and Laszlo Bruszt. 1998, *Postsocialist Pathways: transforming politics and property in Eastern Central Europe*. Cambridge: Cambridge University Press.

Sun, Yongfen. 孙永芬, 2007,《中国社会各阶层政治心态研究》[A Study of the Political Psychology of Social Strata in China], Beijing: 中央编译出版社.

Szelenyi, Ivan. 1988, *Socialist Entrepreneurs*. Madison: University of Wisconsin Press.

Tan, Fei, 谭飞等, 2004, 老区 "富人治村" 现象解读 [An Interpretation of the Phenomenon of the Wealthy Ruling Villages in the Old Districts], 瞭望, 25.

Tan, Qingshan. 2006, *Village Elections in China: Democratizing the Countryside*, Lewiston, NY: Edwin Mellen Press Ltd.

Tang Liang. 唐亮, 2001,《渐进民主》[Gradual Democratization], 八方文化企业公司.

Tao, Qing. 陶庆, 2004, '嬗变、缺位和弥补: 政治安排中私营企业主利益表达: 皖南宣城市实证分析' [Transformation, Absence and Supplementation: the expression of their interests in political arrangements for private business owners: an empirical study in the Xuan City, South Anhui],《社会科学研究》2004 年第 6 期.

——. 2008, '地方政府与民间组织 "正当妥协" 的宪政维度', [The Constitutional Dimension of 'Legitimate Compromise' between Local Government and Civil Organizations'], 当代中国政治研究报告 V [Research Report on the Politics of Contemporary China, volume five]: 185–209.

Thornton, Patricia. 2004, 'Comrades and Collectives in Arms: Tax Resistance, Evasion, and Avoidance Strategies in Post-Mao China', in Peter Hays Gries and Stanley Rosen (eds), *State and Society in 21st-Century China: Crisis, Contention, and Legitimation*. New York and London: Routledge Curzon, pp. 87–104.

Tilly, Charles. 2007, *Democracy*, New York and London: Cambridge University Press.

Tocqueville, Alexis de. 2008, *Ancien Regime and the French Revolution*, translated by Gerald Bevan, Penguin Classics.

Tsai, K. 2004, *Back-Alley Banking: Private Entrepreneurs in China*. Ithaca, NY: Cornell University Press.

——. 2005, 'Capitalists without a Class: Political Diversity among Private Entrepreneurs in China', *Comparative Political Studies*, 9:1130–58.

——. 2007, *Capitalism without Democracy: The private sector in contemporary China*. Ithaca and London: Cornell University Press.

Unger, Jonathan and Anita Chan. 2007, 'Memories and the Moral Economy of a State-Owned Enterprise', in Ching Kwan Lee and Guobin Yang (eds), *Re-envisioning the Chinese Revolution: the politics and poetics of collective memory in reform China*, Stanford, CA: Stanford University Press, pp. 119–40.

Walder, Andrew. 1992, 'Property Rights and Stratification in Socialist Redistributive Economies'. *American Sociological Review* 57(4): 524–39.

——. 1995, 'Local Government as Industrial Firms: An Organizational Analysis of China's Transitional Economy', *American Journal of Sociology*, 101/2: 263–301.

Wan, Huijin. 2007, 万慧进: '"先富能人" 担任村书记的绩效, 存在问题及其对策--以多省市的乡村调查为例' [The Performance of the Wealthy Capable People as Village Party Secretaries: Problems and Resolutions, with cases from multiple provinces],《中州学刊》, 2007 年第 5 期

Wang, Jinwu. 王金鋙, 1985, 中国现代资产阶级民主运动史 [A History of Democratic Movement among the Capitalist Class in Contemporary China], 吉林文史出版社.

Wang, Xiaoyan. 王晓燕, 2007,《私营企业主的政治参与》[The Political Participation of Private Business Owners], 北京, 社会科学文献出版社.

Wang, Zuqiang. 王祖强,《劳资关系与员工权益: 基于浙江私营企业的调查与分析 》, [Labour-Employment Relations and the Rights of Employees: An analysis based on an investigation on private enterprises in Zhejiang], 北京, 中国经济出版社.

Wank, D. 1999, *Commodifying Communism: Business, Trust, and Politics in a Chinese City*. New York and London: Cambridge University Press.

Weber, Max. 1978, *Economy and Society*, Guenther Roth and Claus Wittich (eds), Berkeley, CA: University of California Press.

White, Gordon. 1993, *Riding the Tiger: Politics of Economic Reform in China*, Basingstoke: Palgrave Macmillan.

Whiting, Susan. 2001, *Power and Wealth in Rural China: The Political Economy of Institutional Change*. New York: Cambridge University Press.

Whyte, Martin King. 1999, 'The Changing Role of Workers', in Merle Goldman and Roderick MacFarquhar (eds), *The paradox of China's post-Mao reforms*. Cambridge, Mass.: Harvard University Press, pp. 173–96.

Woodruff, David. 1999, *Money Unmade: Barter and the Fate of Russian Capitalism*, Ithaca, NY: Cornell University Press.

Wright, Tim. 1988, '"The Spiritual Heritage of Chinese Capitalism": Recent trends in the historiography of Chinese enterprise management', *Australian Journal of Chinese Affairs*, 19/20: 185–214.

Xia, Xiaolin. 夏小林, 2004, '私营部]: 劳资关系及协调机制' [The Private Sector: Labour-Capital Relations and Mechanisms of Improvement], 管理世界, No.4.

Xiang, Hui and Zhou, Weifeng. 2001, 项辉, 周威锋: '农村经济精英与村民自治' [The Economic Elites and the Self-Governance by Village Residents],《社会》, 2001 年第12期.

Xin Ming (辛明). 2009, 一名大学生眼中的农村 "贿选" [The Bribed Election Rural Areas in the Eyes of a University Student], 中国青年报 (*China Youth Daily*) 2 November, 2009.

Xiong Wei (熊伟), 2011, '遏制村委会贿选' [Preventing Bribed Elections of Village Committees], 南风窗, 28 April, 2011.

Xiao, and Yue. 肖菁, 岳海智, 2003, '先富群体竞选村官调查报告: 浙江富人治村占 30%' [A Survey Report on the Wealthy Group Competing for Village Heads: the wealthy count 30% among village heads],《都市快报》, 2003 年9 月 20日.

Xu Dixin (许涤新) and Wu Chenming (吴承明), 主编, 1985, 1988, 2003,《中国资本主义发展史》[A History of the Development of Capitalism in China], 北京: 人民出版社。

Xu, Yunpeng. 徐云鹏, 2006, 村官候选人惨遭杀害背后的法律隐痛 [The Legal Pain behind the Murder of Village Head Candidates], http://www.chinaelections. org/NewsInfo.asp?NewsID=91466, 2 July 2006.

Yang, Keming. 2004, 'Institutional Holes and Entrepreneurship in China', *The Sociological Review*, 52(3): 371–89.

———, 2007, *Entrepreneurship in China*. Aldershot: Ashgate.

Yang, Kuisong. 2009, 杨奎松, 中华人民共和国建国史研究 [A Study of the History of the Establishment of the People's Republic of China], 江西人民出版社.

Yang, Mayfair Mei-Hui. 1994, *Gifts, Favours and Banquets: The art of social relationships in China*. Ithaca and London: Cornell University Press.

Young, Susan. 1995, *Private Business and Economic Reform in China*. Armonk, N.Y.: M. E. Sharpe.

Yu, Hui. 余晖, 2008, 我国行业组织管理体制的模式选择 [Which Model to Choose for the Management System of Our Nation's Trade Organizations], in Huang (2008), pp. 111–35.

Yu, Jianxing et al. 郁建兴, 黄红华, 方立明等, 2004,《在政府与企业之间: 以温州商会为研究对象》[Between Government and Enterprises: A study on the business associations in Wenzhou], Hangzhou: 浙江人民出版社.

Yu, Keping. 俞可平, 2003,《政治与政治学》[Politics and Political Science], Beijing: 社会科学文献出版社.

Yusuf, Shahid, Kaoru Nabeshima and Dwight H. Perkins. 2006, *Under New Ownership: Privatizing China's State-Owned Enterprises*, World Bank Publications; illustrated edition.

Zang, Xiaowei. 2008, 'Market Transition, Wealth and Status Claims', in David, S. G. Goodman, ed., *The New Rich in China: Future Ruler, Present Lives*, New York: Routledge, pp. 53–70.

Zhang, Houyi. 张厚义, 1994, '私营企业主阶层在我国社会结构中的地位' [The Position of Private Business Owners in the Social Structure of Our Nation],《中国社会科学》1994 年 6 期.

———. 2006, '私营企业主阶层成长的新阶段' [The New Era of the Growth of the Stratum of Private Business Owners], 中国社会形势分析与预测, Beijing: 社会科学文献出版社.

———. and Ming Lizhi. 1999,《中国私营企业发展报告》[Report on the Development of Private Enterprises in China], Beijing: 社会科学文献出版社.

Zhang, Jianjun. 2008, *Marketization and Democracy in China*, Routledge.

Zhang, Jingpin. 章敬平, 2005,《浙江发生了什么: 转轨时期的民主生活》[What is Happening in Zhejiang: Democratic Life in the Transition Period], Beijing: 东方出版中心.

Zhang, Mingyi. 张明澍, 中国政治人: 中国公民政治素质调查报告 [The Political Man in China: An investigation report on the political qualities of Chinese citizens], Beijing: 中国社会科学出版社.

Zhang Xule. 张徐乐, 2006, '上海私营金融业与" 三反""五反"运动' [The Three-Antis and the Five-Antis Movements in the Financial Industries in Shanghai], in 吴景平, 徐思彦主编《复旦史学专刊》第二辑,《1950年代的中国》, Shanghai: 复旦大学出版社, pp. 55–82.

Zhao, Lijiang. 赵丽江, 2006,《中国私营企业家的政治参与》[The Political Participation of Private Business Owners in China], 北京, 中国经济出版社.

Zheng, Yanfeng and Xie Yang. 2003, 郑燕峰 and 射阳, '10 万元村官" 富干部带领村民致富' [The Wealthy Village Head who Paid One Hundred Yuan for the Position is Leading Fellow Residents to Get Rich], 中国青年报，8 October, 2003.

Zheng, Yongnian. 1994, 'Development and Democracy: Are They Compatible in China?', *Political Science Quarterly*, 109(2): 235–59.

Zhong, Yang. 2006. 'Democratic Values among Chinese Peasantry: An Empirical Study', in Ynag Zhong and Shiping Hua (eds), *Political Civilization and Modernization in China: The Political Context of China's Transformation*, Singapore: World Scientific, pp. 95–120.

Zhu, Guanglei. 朱光磊等, '当代中国私营企业主阶层社会属性问题研究' [A Study of the Social Identity of Private Business Owners in Contemporary China], 《教学与研究》, 1994 年 4 期。

# Index

Printed and bound in the United States of America